Studies in Social Policy

'Studies in Social Policy' is an important series of textbooks intended for students of social administration and social welfare at all levels. The books are directly related to the needs of undergraduate and postgraduate students in universities, polytechnics and similar institutions as well as vocational students preparing for careers in a variety of social and other public services. The series includes the following topics:

the roles of different public and private institutions such as social services departments and building societies in meeting social needs;

introductory guides to new technical and theoretical developments relevant to the analysis of social policy such as political theory and the newly emerging specialism of the economics of social care;

contemporary social policy issues such as the use of charges in the delivery of social welfare or the problem of determining priorities in the health and personal social services.

STUDIES IN SOCIAL POLICY

Editor: Ken Judge
Director, King's Fund Institute

Published

The Building Societies
Martin Boddy

Housing and Social Policy
David Clapham, Peter Kemp and Susan J. Smith

Access to Welfare
Peggy Foster

Health Policy in Britain (second edition)
Christopher Ham

Policy-making in the National Health Service
Christopher Ham

Pricing the Social Services
Ken Judge (ed.)

The Economics of Social Care
Martin Knapp

Choices of Health Care (second edition)
Gavin H. Mooney, Elizabeth M. Russell and Roy D. Weir

Power, Authority and Responsibility in Social Services
Malcolm Payne

Political Theory and Social Policy
Albert Weale

Forthcoming

Introducing Social Policy
Ken Judge and Roger Hampson

The Economics of Poverty
Alan Maynard

Health Care in the European Community
Alan Maynard and Anne Ludbrook

Housing and Social Policy

David Clapham

Peter Kemp

Susan J. Smith

MACMILLAN

First published 1990 by
THE MACMILLAN PRESS LTD
Houndmills, Basingstoke, Hampshire RG21 2XS
and London
Companies and representatives
throughout the world

ISBN 0–333–43551–6 (hardcover)
ISBN 0–333–43552–4 (paperback)

A catalogue record for this book is available
from the British Library

Printed in Hong Kong

Reprinted 1991, 1992

Series Standing Order
If you would like to receive future titles in this series as they are published, you can
make use of our standing order facility. To place a standing order please contact your
bookseller or, in case of difficulty,write to us at the address below with your name
and address and the name of the series. Please state with which title you wish to
begin your standing order. (If you live outside the United Kingdom we may not have
the rights for your area, in which case we will forward your order to the publisher
concerned.)

Customer Services Department, Macmillan Distribution Ltd
Houndmills, Basingstoke, Hampshire RG21 2XS, England

Contents

v

Acknowledgements

Many people have assisted in the preparation of this book. We are grateful for the lively intellectual environment provided by colleagues at the ESRC Centre for Housing Research. Particular thanks are due to Moira Munro and John English for their perceptive comments on various parts of the manuscript. Without the word processing skills and infinite patience of Betty Johnson, Sheena Butler, Tilly Wright and Iona Young, the book would have taken much longer to produce, and without core funding from the ESRC it might not have been written at all.

DAVID CLAPHAM
PETER KEMP
SUSAN J. SMITH

List of Tables

Introduction

This book focuses on two key relationships: that between housing policy and social policy, and that between the provision of housing and the provision of other welfare services such as the health service, the education system, the personal social services and the social security system. Our concern is on the one hand with the role of housing policy as social policy – that is, with the extent to which housing policy is oriented towards meeting social needs; on the other hand we are concerned with the extent to which housing as a welfare service has a bearing on the provision of other social services.

There has always been some debate as to whether housing policy should be considered to be part of social policy; social policy texts often give housing issues only cursory teatment, or exclude them altogether. Likewise, housing studies often neglect the social aspects of housing, or at least fail to place discussions about housing policy or provision in the general context of debates on social policy. This book is an attempt to address both of these areas of scholarship, by exploring trends in the provision of shelter and welfare in modern Britain.

It is true that because of the large element of private provision and consumption in housing, this facet of social welfare does not fit easily into the model of state-provided social services followed by the health and personal social services. Moreover, substantial elements of housing policy seem geared to economic or environmental rather than specifically social policy objectives, and these other concerns frequently dominate political and public debate. This apparent divergence of social policy from housing policy has tended to be reflected in the intellectual division of labour, and this has produced gaps in our understanding of how these fields relate to one another at the levels of teaching, research and practice. The aims of this book are therefore to redress an imbalance in the literature available to students and practitioners, by concentrating on the social elements of housing policy and on the (actual and potential) relationships between the housing system and other social services.

Our starting point is a definition of social policy which clearly includes housing. By social policy we mean those areas of consumption in which the state plays a central role, either by regulating the provision of services, underwriting the cost of their provision, or providing goods and services in kind (see Hill and Bramley, 1986, for a discussion of alternatives). This definition is not uncontroversial, but it does provide a useful starting point for our discussions. In particular, it draws attention to the different mechanisms for state intervention, by including the three divisions of welfare (social, fiscal and occupational) identified by Titmuss (1956), and in consequence by including the state subsidisation of market provision (through, for example, tax relief on mortgage interest payments) as well as the direct provision of state services (through, for example, the provision of council housing). This definition places housing alongside a range of other social services without masking its unique features, but also without denying its status as, partly at least, an arm of the welfare state.

We also require a conceptualisation of housing policy in order to proceed. It could be argued that housing policy as such does not exist – that strategies which affect the quality, quantity, price and location of homes are simply the housing element of economic management. On the other hand, the regulation and manipulation of the housing stock has many aims apart from those of macroeconomic policy. We therefore regard housing policy as any form of intervention in housing production, distribution or consumption that affects the location, character and availability of homes, or the rights associated with housing occupancy – irrespective of the ownership of property, land, or the means of production.

The connections between social policy and housing policy thus defined are complex and difficult to unravel. It is not possible to offer a simple definition of the relationship between the two; rather the following chapters are explorations of this relationship and of the outcomes in terms of policy and different forms of provision which flow from it.

Throughout this book, we shall concentrate on identifying and analysing the social elements of housing provision (those areas of housing and welfare policy impinging on the social objectives of the housing system). This focus necessarily involves consideration of the relationship between housing and other social services, if only because the production, allocation and consumption of housing is affected by, and has consequences for, other areas of social policy. These interactions often involve several agencies, including different central and local government departments as well as voluntary organisations and the private sector. For example, the recent growth in the number of homeless households, which makes increasing demands on bed and breakfast accommodation, has important implications for area health authorities, local authority social services, education, environmental health and housing departments, and for the private and voluntary sectors. Such interactions also reveal important interdependencies between policy measures in that the 'successful' implementation of a given strategy in one policy area may well depend upon the efficacy of changes or adjustments made elsewhere in the system. For example, the implementation of the care in the community policy for mentally ill people has required the co-operation of a range of agencies able to provide accommodation for patients discharged from long-stay residential institutions.

Such interactions between agencies and policies are a major focus of this book. By exploring them, we are able not only to offer insights into the power structure of democratic capitalism, but also to make suggestions as to how housing provision might work towards a more just society in the future. We begin in Chapter 1 by outlining the theoretical and conceptual framework in which our discussions are set. We review a range of competing theoretical interpretations of the place of social policy in modern liberal democracy, and argue that the most plausible of these derives from the notion of 'dual politics' as discussed by Cawson (1986) and Saunders (1986a). A reasoned understanding of what this means for the analysis and implementation of social policy is essential for a full appreciation of the argument which binds the text as a whole. However, practitioners concerned primarily with the 'nuts and bolts' of policy and practice in the areas of housing disadvantage, housing benefits, housing for the homeless, and provision for older people or people with learning difficulties, might be forgiven for reading this selectively, or leaving it until last and proceeding directly to the chapters which interest them.

Chapter 2 moves on to provide an account of the social aims of housing policy. These aims have varied in extent and orientation throughout the present century. To help the reader understand these changes, we introduce two contrasting models of social policy – a market model which suggests social aims are best pursued with a minimum of state intervention in a market economy; and a social democratic model, which argues that state intervention is required to secure a just distribution of the various rights of citizenship.

Treating these models as 'ideal types', we show how different views of housing – as environmental management, as a right of citizenship, and as a marketed commodity – have been variously aligned with one rather than the other at different points in time. Nevertheless, during the 1980s, we note a marked shift in all three areas of housing policy towards the market model. This is partly related to the dwindling power of representative democracy, which Offe (1984) associates with the penetration of corporate bargaining and with the bias which this has towards the interests of capital. The rest of the book considers the implications of these shifts for the implementation and effectiveness of housing and other social services.

Chapter 3 explores the changing role of housing in relation to one of the traditional aims of social policy – the alleviation of disadvantage. After examining some conceptual and definitional problems associated with this notion, we go on to illustrate how disadvantage is both expressed in, and constructed by, housing policies and their implementation. On the one hand, therefore, we show how racism, gender and class inequalities are reproduced by the apportionment of housing of different quality, condition, location and tenure. On the other hand, we argue that, because housing attainment also represents the attainment of location or neighbourhood, access to different kinds of housing also mediates access to that wide range of employment opportunities and social rights (to education, health care and other welfare services) whose quality and availability partly depends on where people live (see Pahl, 1975).

Chapter 3 recognises the extent to which the restructuring of welfare and the restructuring of the economy are spatial as well as economic and political processes. We stress, therefore, that the degree of choice and constraint experienced by individuals in the housing system has important 'knock-on' effects in terms of their wider life chances and opportunities. We use this evidence to argue that housing systems do not merely reflect wider patterns of social inequality, but that they can actively exacerbate such inequality and help structure it in systematic ways. While this seems a pessimistic observation to begin with, it is also an argument that housing is a point at which intervention could, and perhaps should, be directed in any attempt to interrupt the reproduction of social disadvantage. Housing may be a key arena within society's interlocking systems of markets and institutions through which relative deprivation can be tackled.

The remaining chapters consider the extent to which this has occurred, what its achievements and limitations have been, and what this means for the relationships between housing and social policy more generally, now and in the future. Accordingly, Chapters 4 to 7 address some systematic areas of need that are conventionally identified in the analysis of social policy. In housing terms, our argument throughout the book is that the groups we examine can best be served through innovations in mainstream policy, rather than by (or at least in combination with) special initiatives. It may, therefore, seem anachronistic to treat the various grouped needs separately from the outset. We have done so for two reasons. First, we regard this systematic treatment as the most helpful way to organise our material to facilitate teaching and learning. Second, and fundamentally, it reflects the way in which the dominant model of social policy identified in Chapter 2 favours, and therefore enhances, this systematic view of special need. This 'traditional' organisation of the subject matter thus also reflects the drift of policy, capturing too the fact that where welfare professionals are able to exert influence in corporate bargaining procedures, their negotiations have often worked to sustain the status quo associated with 'special' needs provision.

The ordering of Chapters 4 to 7 is important because it exemplifies our more general argument that the market model of social policy leads to patterns of inclusion and exclusion, and to distinctions between the 'more' or 'less' deserving poor, which are stigmatising and divisive rather than integrationist and dignifying.

It is relatively easy to see why this must be the case with means-tested assistance with housing costs and with responses to homelessness. In these areas a large pool of potential beneficiaries must be reduced to a minimum if the overriding object is to minimise public expenditure and free up the market. This is achieved by developing a fine sieve of eligibility rules and by setting a level of means-tested benefits that discourages any notions of actively chosen long-term dependence on this stigmatising form of state subsidy.

By contrast, in political terms, older people and those with learning difficulties are viewed as relatively deserving groups, excluded from the economy by age, frailty or handicap, rather than their supposed disinclination to work. Nevertheless, their treatment can also be stigmatising, in two main ways. The first is exemplified with reference to the experience of housing and community care for older people. Here, policy must cater for a relatively large, and increasing, group of potential beneficiaries. We show that, in order to justify policies which favour older people while bypassing another large group like the unemployed, older individuals have to be defined as 'special' in terms of a set of clearly delimited technical needs. Although this process is invoked to include, rather than exclude, older people from state support, we show that this can nevertheless create demeaning stereotypes, and we speculate as to whether the social 'costs' of this outweigh the benefits of what is often fairly minimal assistance. People with learning difficulties, on the other hand, are a smaller, more readily delimited group whose technical needs are pre-defined (though not uncontroversially) in medical terms. Housing and social policy both aspire to use community care as an integrative device for handicapped individuals. Nevertheless, we present evidence to suggest that even for a group whose special needs seem unequivocal, the main barriers to 'normalisation' relate not to resourcing for special needs, but to the organisation of *mainstream* housing and social policy.

Chapters 4 to 7 provide the empirical core of the book, and it is worth introducing them in some detail. Chapter 4 addresses a vital question for many areas of social policy, concerning the extent and orientation of state intervention to affect the consumer costs of different types of housing. This has ramifications throughout the welfare state, not least because much of the responsibility for means-tested assistance with housing costs now lies in the hands of the Department of Social Security (DSS). To illustrate how this has arisen, we examine the incremental mix of supply-side and demand-side interventions (through price and income subsidies, respectively) that now comprise Britain's housing finance system. We show that, on the whole, the housing subsidies now used tend to favour relatively better-off households, rather than the very poor. This can

be related to efforts to secure the predominance of market provisioning in housing, and it reflects the privileged place of capital interests
in corporate bargaining at the national level. These general points
are illustrated using the example of the housing benefits system.

Assistance with housing costs is important for the welfare and
well-being of a large proportion of housholds in Britain. The
organisation of such assistance makes a significant difference to who
gets what kind of housing. It also impinges on the character and
extent of homelessness, which is the topic of Chapter 5. The chapter
begins with a historical review of homelessness in Britain, illustrating how, for policy purposes, homelessness has gradually been
redefined from being a social work problem to its current status as a
concern of housing policy. In the process, however, Victorian
concepts of the deserving and undeserving poor appear to have been
retained. This is illustrated in a critique of the Housing (Homeless
Persons) Act 1977, which made official the distinction between
people with a right to rehousing (those among the 'unintentionally'
homeless who are in priority need and, usually, have a local
connection), and others (including the hidden homeless, some
immigrant groups and a variety of single people and childless
couples) who do not.

Chapter 5 monitors the steady increase in both official and
unofficial homelessness observed in the last decade. This is creating
an unprecedented burden not only on a diminishing stock of public
housing, but also on other social services. Using the example of DSS
board and lodging payments, we show how the government's
response to homelessness appears to have undermined rather than
enhanced the prospects for homeless people to gain access to
permanent homes. The process of catering to the needs of the poor
and homeless can usefully be contrasted with approaches to housing
older people and people with learning difficulties.

Chapters 6 and 7 are both concerned with the controversial notion
of community care. Chapter 6 provides a general overview of this set
of policies and applies them to the case of people with learning
difficulties. It is evident that the development of community care
gives the housing system generally, and public housing in particular,
a central role in the process of deinstitutionalisation that has
become popular in Britain and other Western nations over the last
fifteen years. However, the account in Chapter 6 identifies a para-
doxical process whereby attempts to move away from special,

institutional provision for people with learning difficulties in social service terms has, because of the way community care is implemented, constructed 'mental handicap' as a special need in housing terms.

Reflecting the pervasiveness of this process, the main body of Chapter 6 assesses the achievements in special housing provision for people with learning difficulties, even though its accommodation still has only one-twentieth of the capacity of long-stay institutions. We provide a critique of the types of provision available, and of its planning, financing and management. We show that this is an example of care in, rather than care by, the community, in that the primary caring services associated with particular schemes are provided by paid professionals. For various reasons, this has allowed housing management to take a marginal role in the whole package of community care. The consequences for people with learning difficulties of the routine application of inflexible, impersonal, standardised procedures draws attention to a more general failure within housing management to cater to individual needs, including the individual needs of tenants with learning difficulties.

Concern about the inflexibility of the housing system in its contribution to community care leads us to conclude with a commentary on the circumstances of people with learning difficulties living outside either institutional care or special housing schemes. Here we are concerned as much with care by the community – provided by family, friends and neighbours – as with care in the community. We expose the family and gender bias in the burden of care, and link the inadequacy of state support for the informal caring role to inequalities in bargaining power between organised professionals and the caring public over the issue of welfare resources.

In exploring care by the community, we identify some organisational problems in linking housing with other service provision. Fundamentally, however, we locate many of the problems facing both people with learning difficulties and their carers in the direction of mainstream policy itself. Such policy is not flexible enough to respond to the more general difficulties of low incomes, the problems of repair and maintenance, and the space requirements that are variously experienced by the people with learning difficulties, but which also beset many other households. As a consequence, there remains an irresoluble tension between the concept of 'normalisation', which seeks proper integration of people with learning difficulties into society at large, and the limited 'special needs' provision which is all the housing system can offer as a means of achieving this.

Some of the same issues arise in Chapter 7, which scrutinises the integration of housing with social policy that arises with the provision of community care for older people. This trend, too, is part of the process of deinstitutionalisation, and it is epitomised in the development of sheltered housing. During the 1970s, this package of housing and social support became the hallmark of community care for older people. Reviewing the implementation, management and effects of this kind of provision, we identify some of its most important achievements. But we also show why this package could not become the panacea for the housing and support needs of older people that was once envisaged. Moreover, the vast majority of older people are not housed in sheltered complexes, and the over-concentration of resources into this sector may be wasteful and ineffective when viewed in the context of the general needs of older individuals throughout the population.

Recognising this, Chapter 7 devotes considerable space to initiatives in housing and special care for older people in other residential contexts. As far as housing is concerned, we examine designated housing in the public sector (amenity housing), care and repair schemes for owner-occupiers, and private retirement homes. As regards the provision of special care, we assess developments in domiciliary care and the increase in community alarm systems. Given the size of the older population and the wealth that many have stored in their homes, we pay particular attention in this chapter to the potential for harnessing the market (as distinct from intervening in it) to achieve social goals.

To summarise, Chapters 4 to 7 examine four areas of housing need, selected for their helpfulness in exemplifying the range of actual, potential and desirable links both between housing and social policy more generally, and between the provision of housing and the delivery of other welfare services. We identify many areas of progress and achievement, and also some important limiting factors. In part, these are rooted in the power structure of society and in the particular set of normative guidelines which now dominate welfare provision. But they are also rooted in a (not unrelated) range of bureaucratic and organisational concerns linked to the pragmatic problems associated with service delivery and planning. This is the theme of Chapter 8.

Chapter 8 explores the role of housing management and considers the potential for service integration. The quest for integration has been a goal of social policy for at least a quarter of a century, and we consider its importance in the context of recent trends in public rented housing. We draw attention to the processes of centralisation of decision-making and fiscal control and (in recent years) of the decentralisation and fragmentation of management. To illustrate the social consequences of these trends, we review in some detail the history of housing management and its links with other social services.

Our review exposes the extent to which public housing is being pushed towards an exclusively welfare role, and so highlights the increasing need for housing management to achieve integration with a range of other social services. We therefore examine the scope for strategic, operational and *ad hoc* case co-ordination along these lines. Where difficulties arise, they relate partly to the differing organisational norms of the various services. We also consider how far such difficulties reflect the problems of meaningful planning at a local level in a political context in which financial decisions are increasingly centralised.

Our final chapter aims to do more than summarise the findings of individual chapters. Rather, we attempt to draw from these the evidence required, first, to re-evaluate the dual politics interpretation of society and, second, to assess the strengths and weaknesses of the models of state intervention introduced in Chapter 2. We pay particular attention to the scope offered by housing provision to create opportunities for residents to participate in key decision-making processes, and so to re-activate the democratic process which is always threatened by the development of a corporate state. We conclude, therefore, by proposing what housing as social policy *could* look like in a society which places as much emphasis on individuals' social, civil and political rights as on their right to participate in the economy and to accumulate wealth.

1

Exploring Social Policy

Any account of housing as social policy must employ some kind of theoretical framework or lens through which to examine the subject matter. If this framework is not made explicit, and drawn upon consciously, it will remain tacit and may cause confusion. Before beginning our analysis, therefore, we examine a range of competing theoretical interpretations of the place of social policy in capitalist society. That is, we look at some different sets of beliefs about the power structure of modern liberal democracies and at the place of social policy within it.

No short review can offer a comprehensive account of the rich variety of interpretations of liberal democracy in the capitalist world. Dunleavy and O'Leary (1987) summarise some of the key approaches, but we focus on just three perspectives which have made a particularly useful and vigorous contribution to the social policy literature (and which are discussed in more detail in standard texts such as those by Mishra, 1977, and Taylor-Gooby and Dale, 1981). These perspectives are: (a) pluralism, which embraces the so-called 'social administration' tradition and also, to an extent, accommodates the neo-libertarian critique of the welfare state; (b) neo-marxism; and (c) corporatism.

These approaches are not entirely discrete bodies of thought, but, grouped in this way, they do differ on a number of fundamental points concerning the scope for, motivation behind, and consequences of, state intervention. None of them can be said to provide a true interpretation of reality (though more than one might appear to claim this for itself). Each must be regarded as open to logical refutation or modification in the light of developments in society and in our understanding of it. Nevertheless, it must also be

1

recognised that these perspectives ask different questions and pursue different issues. They advance distinctive sets of interests, and they carry implicitly differing political prescriptions. To an extent, therefore, to claim that one is more authentic than another will often be as much a statement of political belief as it is a claim to empirical validity.

Fully aware of this, and having scrutinised all three approaches, we go on to adopt a fourth, preferred, perspective – the dual politics thesis – to inform our subsequent discussion. We adopt this framework not because we are convinced that it is unequivocally 'right', but because it combines some strengths and minimises some obvious weaknesses of the other traditions, and because we believe it to offer the most plausible starting point for our own inquiry into the utility of housing as social policy.

Pluralism

Pluralism is founded on the premise that modern liberal democracies 'remain basically if inadequately directed towards the satisfaction of ordinary people's wishes' (Dunleavy and O'Leary, 1987, p. 284). The guarantee that states will pursue this explicit goal, rather than any hidden agenda, is the fragmentation and dispersion of power among a wide range of interest groups. This precludes any marked concentration of power in the hands of a political or economic elite. Society is viewed, in short, as an amalgamation of individuals who further their interests by participating in a range of cross-cutting groups, none of whose demands need go unheard.

Pluralists are not in full agreement concerning the role of the state in policy formulation. Some regard the state as a neutral arbiter, others see it as expressing a balance between competing demands (some of which have more public support than others), while the more sceptical regard the state as a broker, manipulating public interests to conform with the preferences of particular groups or to favour bureaucratic efficiency. All these views, however, regard policy change – the growth or decline of public expenditure, the changing tenure structure of the housing system, and so on – as demand-led developments. Policies are seen as the outcome of open debate through formally established group bargaining procedures: the product may not be optimal, but any deficiencies in policy are more accurately accounted for by a 'muddle through' rather than a conspiracy theory.

This pluralist model of the state is often implicitly linked to some approaches within the traditional field of social administration. Until recently, the assumption of many working in this discipline has been that the purpose of the welfare state is to enhance individual well-being through a gradual process of social reform. The development of housing policy would be seen, for instance, as a stream of progressive legislation aiming to provide an increasing proportion of the population with better housing services. The presuppositions of such an approach include the following.

First, it is assumed that polyarchy (government in which power and authority are dispersed among interest groups) is both the reality of how modern democratic states operate *and* that it is the most desirable form of government. It follows from this that any prescriptions for change or reform will be of a type that can be accommodated within the present set of political and economic arrangements. The emphasis, then, is on incremental social change and on a search for solutions to social problems that are realistic and feasible within the existing power structure of society. This encourages a pragmatic search for immediately viable solutions to pressing social problems, but it also means that analysts may be unable to appreciate the limits of piecemeal reform. The approach implicitly, but firmly, attributes the failures of social policy to 'factors which may in future be brought under control through improved administration and budgetary management' (Offe, 1984, p. 35). This reasoning tends to limit any search for radical or more innovative solutions to social problems.

A second presupposition of the pluralist perspective is that within modern states there is a broad social consensus concerning the aims and objectives for social reform (this assumption is discussed more fully by Mishra, 1977). Within this agreeable climate of opinion, an appeal to empirical 'fact' (the extent of poverty, the location of disadvantage, and so on) is regarded as the basis from which policy decisions flow. This betrays a positivistic assumption that 'reality' is present in appearance (that the forces shaping social life are not hidden or disguised) and an empiricist belief that 'objective' data collection can resolve thorny social and moral debate. The consequence, as Taylor-Gooby and Dale (1981) point out, is that there is now a large literature illuminating the empirical shortcomings of the

welfare state, but little writing from within traditional social administration that offers a critique of the welfare state itself in relation to
the operation of capitalist liberal democracies (though with the
restructuring of welfare provision during the 1980s, this is rapidly
beginning to change).

Finally, pluralist theory portrays actions, values, preferences and
needs as essentially individual, rather than group, characteristics.
While we shall argue later in this book that there is great merit in
recognising the integrity of individuals' identities, this view has
produced some serious analytical shortcomings when adopted in
conjunction with a pluralist theory of the state. Notably, it undermines the authenticity of collective experience, and underestimates
the potential for collective action. This has not only diverted
attention away from class analysis, and away from the structural
roots of social problems, but it has also helped to marginalise the
relevance of patriarchy (a form of gender relations in which male
interests dominate female interests) and racism in the organisation
and implementation of social policy. Social policy, and the housing
service this embraces, is seen basically as a universalising, integrative
and unifying process. From this starting point, the social administration perspective has often found it hard to accommodate the
possibility that such policy could be systematically selective, divisive
and conflict-generating.

To be fair to pluralist theory, and to the practice of social
administration, many of these traditional assumptions are now
being questioned from within. Walker (1984) and Townsend (1984),
for instance, recognise some fundamental structural limits to progressive incremental reform, and Dunleavy and O'Leary (1987)
distinguish conventional pluralism from a neo-pluralism which is
now prepared to accept the overriding political importance of
business and corporate interests (a position most vociferously
advocated by Galbraith, 1969). *Neo-pluralism* operates with an
image of the state that may therefore be regarded as one of
'deformed' polyarchy, in which government is divided between the
economic interests of large corporations and the more diverse range
of needs advanced by interest groups, the electorate and the mass
media. This concession does not, however, imply a belief that
politics and social life are dictated by economic interests. It is only
the business community whose prime concern is to maintain a
capitalist economy by influencing public demand and certain aspects

of economic management. Elsewhere, there is assumed to have been a shift away from class-based politics in favour of a wide variety of power struggles; these are epitomised by the growth of environmentalism, animal rights groups, the growth of nationalism and feminism, and a so-called 'resurgence of ethnicity' in the Western world. Thus neo-pluralism remains committed to the notion of a power-sharing polyarchy and to multi-casual explanations of policy change.

From this neo-pluralist perspective, the fragmentation and dispersion of political power that is taken as the hallmark of a working democracy is expected to be achieved partly through the professionalisation of occupational groups (including, for example, housing managers). The development of codes of practice and a capacity for self-regulation allows the professions to be 'incorporated' into government, where they are given wide discretionary powers over policy development and service delivery (see Dunleavy and O'Leary, 1987, pp. 271–318). This is not only seen as beneficial in spreading political power widely within society, but it is again regarded as a product of public demand. In the modern state the public is thought to place more faith in trained professionals than in politicians to develop the detail of policy in their specialist field.

The problems caused for consumers by the professionalisation of social and housing services tend to be underplayed by neo-pluralism, and in our view this is one of the theory's major shortcomings.

Despite substantially modifying the traditional pluralist assumptions, neo-pluralism retains its faith in democratic decision-making processes, in the altruistic underpinnings of social policy, and in multi-casual explanations of political and social life. Most crucially, while recognising the increasing importance of business interests in determining policy change, it is a perspective which views class relationships as decreasingly relevant to the political process in post-industrial economies. In summary, the pluralist approach sees housing policy as the product of democratic bargaining procedures between different interest groups with power dispersed relatively widely. Therefore, changes in the housing system such as the growth of owner occupation are held to be the result of consumer demand expressed through political channels. Neo-pluralism would also place emphasis on the influence of professionals and other state bureaucrats in policy formulation. Nevertheless, pluralist theories of housing provision have popularised the view that housing policy is a relatively straightforward response to the needs of consumers. Yet as Ball (1983) and others have shown, not all housing policy can be explained in this way. Changes in housing provision, for instance, are driven, even in the public sector, by powerful corporate and business interests. Furthermore, housing policy is determined at least in part by its relationship to the economy as a whole. To gain some insight into these processes it is necessary to look at a second approach to the interpretation of society and social policy, which draws on the classical social theories of Karl Marx.

Neo-marxism

An alternative paradigm, which gained particular prominence from the mid-1970s, is a form of neo-marxism exemplified in the work of Ginsburg (1979), Gough (1979) and Offe (1984). These authors argue that capitalist economies are driven by class inequalities, and that the state is required to protect and sanction 'a set of institutions and social *relationships* necessary for the domination of the capitalist class' (Offe, 1984, p. 120). From this perspective, key questions ask not so much what welfare services do, or how the effectiveness of social welfare can be increased, but focus rather on the role of social policy in the reproduction of class inequality. (For marxism, this in turn helps explain why, despite the many attempts to improve it, the effects of social policy are so limited.)

Since traditional, or orthodox, marxism did not anticipate the development of welfare states, considered marxist critiques of social policy have only emerged in the last few decades. It is worth noting, moreover, that within this framework, social policy has rarely been linked with the structures of racism or patriarchy. Marxism's preoccupation has been with wealth-related inequalities in the process of production and consumption, and other facets of social stratification have tended to be marginalised by analyses of class structure.

Fundamentally, the marxist would argue that social policy is not the product of enlightened altruism: it is, instead, a fundamental prerequisite for the survival of democratic capitalism. It is required to ensure both the reproduction of labour power (i.e. to ensure that a healthy labour force is available) and to secure the legitimacy of the state in the eyes of the working class. Legitimation is an attempt to justify, hide, or seek acceptance for the social inequalities generated by capitalism, and for the forms of social control required to contain mass resistance to such inequalities. Social policy cannot, therefore, be interpreted simply as a demand-led process effected through representative politics as envisaged by the pluralists. Policy direction depends primarily upon the revenues derived from the accumulation process and not upon the voting preferences of the general electorate (Offe, 1984, p. 121). Indeed, from a marxist perspective, the rise of formal democracy, which itself allowed the working classes to claim social policy concessions, is not regarded as the harbinger of a fundamental change in class relations. It is seen, rather, as a way of extending the influence of the well-off by assigning the least powerful to a permanent position of political as well as economic subordination (see Hall, 1984).

Miliband (1977) has identified three reasons why, in capitalist societies, the democratic state – with an electorate dominated by wage-workers – acts in the long-term interests of capital rather than labour. These reasons help explain why, above a particular minimum (i.e. that gauged necessary to sustain the workforce physically and to win its support ideologically) the state under democratic capitalism will always aim to limit rather than expand welfare expenditure. They explain, then, why social policy and housing provision may tend to be residual and divisive rather than universal and integrative. Miliband argues, first, that in market-based democracies the state is structurally bound by the requirements of capital accumulation (i.e. the making of profit) because this process is what provides the tax base from which state expenditures are financed. In housing terms a profitable housing *market* therefore takes priority over a just housing service. Second, he claims that in order to secure the conditions for reproducing this tax-base, there must be a class bias in recruitment to key positions in state administration. This bias in turn ensures that key state institutions operate in ways that sustain the interests of capital, and work to the advantage of the better-off rather than the most needy. Thus, for example, we see that, within the public sector, better-off tenants gain preferential access to the better parts of the stock (Clapham and Kintrea, 1986), and within the private sector, tax advantages benefit higher-income owners more than low-income groups (Ermisch, 1984). Overall, processes favouring capital accumulation and market provisioning tend to take priority over ideals like egalitarianism or the redistribution of wealth, thus securing the conditions for capitalism (and the capitalist state) to thrive. This, in turn, is reflected in the restricted financing and selective targeting of social policy.

This leaves the question of why social policy exists at all if the marxist interpretation is correct. One reason commonly advanced is itself rooted in the observation that in order to retain power, politicians in capitalist democracies must maintain the process of capital accumulation. Because capitalism is basically an exploitative system, as well as securing the conditions for capital accumulation, governments must maintain public order and they must find ways of securing the popular legitimacy of economic policies and (increasingly) of repressive forms of social control. For neo-marxist analysts, social policy is one of these legitimising mechanisms. For example, this reasoning might explain the origins and growth of council housing which was, in the post-war years, helpful to capitalism in aiding the reproduction of labour. That is, by providing subsidised shelter, the state contributed to the health and well-being of wage workers whose labour was required to reconstruct the economy. At a symbolic level, the provision of council housing can also be interpreted as a concession granted by the capitalist class to deflect working-class demands for a more fundamental change in the system of production. Offe (1984, p. 98) therefore regards social policy as a 'strategy for incorporating labour power into the wage-labour relation', while Gough (1979, pp. 44–5) describes the welfare state as 'the use of state power to modify the reproduction of labour power and to maintain the non-working population in capitalist societies'. This leads to the paradox discussed by O'Connor (1973) whereby industrial democracies can afford neither to maintain an adequate level of welfare provision, nor to do without it!

On the other hand, it cannot be denied that workers' own demands provide significant impetus for the development of the welfare services, and in this sense social policy is also important to marxist analysis as an example of concessions won through co-ordinated class action. Paradoxically, therefore, social policy in capitalist societies can be seen both as necessary for the survival of the capitalist class and as an index of the 'success' of class struggle. Social policy must be analysed as both 'an instrument in the hands of the capitalist ruling class' and as 'a little island of socialism created by the working class in the sea of capitalist society' (Hindess, 1987, pp. 100–1). In housing terms, then, we must recognise that the development of council housing was, despite its utility for capitalism, also a real gain for the working classes. Whatever role council housing eventually took on, it was a product of working-class struggle, and its relevance and importance to the working-class public cannot be denied.

This view that social policy does not merely support capitalism, but is also a threat to class inequality and to the class system which generates it, has been developed by a number of authors. Offe (1984), for instance, argues that this threat to capitalism is compounded by the flourishing of welfare states which lead to the growth of administrative and professional employment. The interests of these groups may be advanced less by capital accumulation than by the maintenance of power *within* the welfare sector. In other words, the interest of professionals and administrators is in maintaining a particular form of social policy, to some extent irrespective of the desirability of this from an economic point of view. However, in adapting marxist theory to take account of such interests, it is necessary to move to our third set of interpretations of the power structure of modern liberal democracy – those rooted in the rise of corporate bargaining.

Corporatism

Corporatism is a body of thought which emerged during the mid-1970s as an attempt to account for the political power won (and conceded) by heads of industry and trade union leaders in their direct negotiations with government (see Grant, 1985). The hallmark of corporatism, however, is not unionisation or the organisation of business interests, but rather the circumvention of formal democratic processes with a system that depends increasingly on informal and publicly inaccessible negotiations between the representatives of state and the elites of powerful social interest groups. Corporatist states are therefore characterised by 'para-parliamentary, non-public, informal and poorly legitimised forms of resolving issues' (Offe, 1984, p. 70). They succeed not because they are sensitive to the demands of the electorate, but because they are able to strike bargains with the elite representatives of tightly organised interest groups whose role is important to the process of capital accumulation or state legitimation and who are therefore relatively powerful. Additionally, corporatist states may be seen as successful because, by the very fact of bypassing normal democratic and bureaucratic procedures, they are able to respond quickly (if not necessarily effectively) to rapid economic and technical change.

The label of corporatism is used to describe a variety of power-sharing arrangements, and the place of social policy varies considerably between these. We focus on the two most common forms (and their variants), which may broadly be described as 'liberal' and 'marxist' in orientation.

Liberal corporatism is a further extension of the neo-pluralist position introduced above, and there are points of overlap between writers in the two traditions. Advocates of this approach argue that, side by side with conventional representative government, a system of bargaining has developed in which the state grants certain corporate groups a *de facto* monopoly in representing particular social interests. In one of the most influential contributions to this literature, Schmitter (1974, pp. 93–4) has defined corporatism as a system of interest mediation in which a limited number of monopolistic, functionally differentiated and hierarchically ordered organisations are recognised or licensed by the state as having a representative monopoly over certain groups' interests.

This 'licensing' is granted only in return for assurances that privileged organisations will maintain certain controls over the actions and behaviours of their members. The state is, in this sense, both the arbiter and mediator of decisions made by society's major functional elites (business, labour and agriculture). Having played a key role in deciding who is represented, and under what conditions, the state is expected to have no enduring bias towards the interests of any one of them, although the state *is* regarded as having a power and influence of its own in the bargaining arena. This interpretation differs from that offered by pluralism, according to which any number of interest groups compete for power on the understanding that none has a monopoly on representing their membership, and that none is specially favoured, licensed or subsidised by the state. Under corporatism, the success of corporate groups in securing power depends on the mediating role of the state; under neo-pluralism, success is a function of financing, leadership and membership.

The question of which, and how many, corporate groups gain access to how much power is, according to the liberal version of corporatism, open to empirical assessment. The definitive element is, according to Cawson (1986), not which groups are represented, but the fact that the state plays a part in their negotiations (as well as in setting the 'rules' that admit them to the bargaining arena). With this proviso, any set of functional interests may participate, in theory, providing they have a capacity for self-regulation and hold out the possibility of securing negotiated agreements with which their membership will co-operate. Thus, although much of the literature on corporatism has focused on industrial policy, alighting particularly on the tripartite negotiations between the government, CBI and the TUC over incomes policy (see Middlemas, 1979), Cawson (1982) and others have argued that corporatist bargaining also takes place in the sphere of social policy (see, for example, some of the papers collected by Harrison, 1984). In housing, therefore, we might want to consider both the corporate influence of managers and workers in the housing production industry, and that exerted by housing professionals through, for instance, the Institute of Housing.

The corporate influences with a bearing on social policy are therefore different from those active in industrial bargaining. The most significant are 'the professions (e.g. medicine) and the quasi professions (e.g. social work) as well as the public sector trade unions (e.g. the Confederation of Health Service Employees)' (Cawson, 1982, p. 44). Although the extent of corporatist forms of interest intermediation within social policy has been disputed (compare the interpretations of Cawson, 1982; and Mercer, 1984), there are grounds, from this perspective, for viewing social policy as an area of intervention that is shaped by both business and professional concerns. Nevertheless, consistent with the anti-democratic underpinnings of the corporate bargaining process, the decisions reached may still largely ignore the interests of consumers, for the professional interests which have affected, for instance, the development of the NHS and some areas of housing have been incorporated into the political bargaining process – through informal consultation or formal representation – in ways unavailable to service consumers. An examination of this process has led Cawson (1982) to conclude that, despite the variable influence of professionals between service areas (strong in the health service, weak in housing and the personal social services, and so on), and between different parts of the same service (consider the different influence on public housing provision exerted by local authority housing departments, the Housing Corporation and the National Federation of Housing Associations), overall, social policy operates in the interests of service producers. In this sense social policy is shaped by the advocates of a welfare state whose priority is to sustain itself rather than to address the discrepancies between public experiences of problems and professional constructions of them.

Like pluralism, therefore, liberal corporatism provides a demand-led perspective on the development of social policy. However, these demands are exerted by a corporate elite rather than by a representative democracy. The implications of this for consumers are exacerbated by the fact that some of those 'professionals' closest to them – voluntary sector workers, welfare rights and advice workers, and so on – are least likely to gain admission to corporate negotiations. As they do not have a professional body or a corporate identity based on the possession of credentials, there is no guarantee that individuals will comply with negotiated agreements. Even housing managers (represented by the Institute of Housing) are poorly placed to influence policy when compared, for instance, to doctors or even teachers.

This liberal corporatist interpretation of the organisation of society is only a partial one, however. It accounts for the role of welfare professionals in sustaining the welfare state, but it does not consider the impact on social policy of those corporate interests which determine the role of welfare in sustaining industrial capitalism.

To address this second issue, neo-marxist interpretations of society also increasingly recognise the significance of corporate bargaining power. From this perspective we can begin to discern why interest groups do not compete on even terms, and why the power of welfare professionals is ultimately limited to shaping how social policy works (rather than determing what social policy is). For, during corporate negotiations, the state favours those groups whose co-operation is most obviously required for state intervention to be effective in sustaining the economy (Cawson, 1982, 1986). According to this view, there are systematic differences in the relative bargaining power of corporate groups – differences which derive ultimately from the state's greater dependence on the co-operation of some rather than others in order to implement its broad strategies of economic management and social control.

Taking this into account, Cawson (1986) makes a useful distinction between meso- and macro-corporatism. This enables social policy to be located in a system of bargaining that is susceptible (at a meso level) to the corporate power of welfare professionals, *and* one that is sensitive (at a macro level) to corporate pressure exerted by the representatives of capital and labour. In housing terms, the influence of housing managers, through professional bodies, might be described as meso-corporatist, while the influence of housing producers (through business interests) and of other employees involved in housing provision (through union representation) should be regarded in terms of macro-corporatism.

Meso-corporatism may be understood in terms of bargaining organised around 'sectoral' interests. Here, many of the broad arguments of liberal corporatism apply. Sectoral interests may be organised around the credentials of a variety of occupational groups. These groups include qualified managers (whose bargaining power derives from organised control over the means of administration) and welfare professionals. Both are able to organise around the possession of skill-related credentials rather than around access to the means of production (Cawson, 1986). Thus, if our aim is simply to analyse how social policy, including the social element of housing policy, is organised, implemented and sustained, an assessment of the role of professionals along the lines outlined above will be helpful. However, it may only be by considering the bargaining between class interests – the influence of macro-corporatism – that the place of social policy in advanced democratic capitalist states can fully be appreciated.

Macro-corporatism hinges on the role of the state as mediator in negotiations between capital and labour. Because the state is central to this process, however, such bargaining does have a bearing on social policy. This is best accounted for by Offe (1984), who argues that there is an inherent contradiction between capital and welfare in that the latter aims towards the decommodification of society (removing certain goods and services from the market and assigning responsibility for their production and distribution to the state), while the former is geared to profit accumulation. This contradiction is exacerbated by the fiscal crises which develop when public expectations of benefits and services outstrip the state's ability to supply them at an acceptable level of taxation. These tensions both limit the rational development of social policy and create a situation in which the non-accountable, elite negotiations of corporatism prove vital, not only in securing social consensus over economic management, but also in determining the balance between taxation and welfare. Thus, just as the power of the professionals in meso-corporatism tends to be insensitive to the demands of service consumers, so the bias towards capital at the level of macro-corporatism contributes to the effective disenfranchisement of the working classes. In this sense, whatever perspective it is viewed from, the rise of corporatism at best undermines, and at worst displaces, the direct bargaining power of the electorate.

In the event, neither liberal nor marxist variants of the corporatist thesis have been able, politically or empirically, to sustain the view that incorporation has wholly undermined democratic processes. There are examples where people have been sufficiently organised on the basis of class or locality to exercise power over key decision-making processes (see Duncan and Goodwin, 1982; Bondi, 1985). To take this into account in conceptualising social policy, some of the more structurally oriented corporatist theses have adopted a dual politics interpretation of the modern British political economy. That is, even where the interests of capital are most forcefully advanced through well-developed corporate bargaining procedures, theories of the power structure of society have had to allow scope for pluralist bargaining to operate through representative democracy and pressure group politics. The conditions for the coexistence of corporate and pluralist negotiations are what concerns the dual politics thesis. We examine this below and go on to use it as a basis for our subsequent discussions.

Dual politics

The dual politics thesis is sometimes described as the marxist version of corporatism. While we do not agree that marxism has a mono-poly over this thesis, we do acknowledge that the state in modern liberal democracies typically performs three roles which are drawn from marxist analysis. First, it promotes capital accumulation as a fundamental concern; second, it aims to preserve public order, and so maintain the social conditions conducive to capital accumulation; and third, it seeks legitimation for strategies adopted in connection with both these other projects. A variety of authors suggest that these three roles are variously pursued through different policy arenas, by different tiers of the state (central and local), and in response to different kinds of bargaining procedure (corporatist and pluralist). The dual politics thesis embraces this variety through its interest in the relationships between mode of bargaining on the one hand, and the organisation of state intervention on the other.

Cawson (1986) and Saunders (1986a) have become two of the main advocates of the dual politics thesis, acknowledging a debt to Claus Offe for raising the possibility that 'by modifying marxist theory to respecify the role of the state and the nature of interest organisation, we can explain some of the political processes concerned with production in capitalist society, and that by modifying pluralism and restricting its scope, we can explain those other processes concerned with consumption' (Cawson, 1986, p. 6). From this starting point Cawson argues that there are certain areas of state activity and particular interest categories among which the scope for corporate bargaining is limited, and where more 'competitive' political processes are dominant. The dual politics thesis is therefore an attempt to integrate the concept of corporatism into the analysis of political and economic systems where corporate processes do not dominate political life generally, or the dispensation of social policy in particular. Nevertheless, Cawson (1982) argues that there is an increasing, though uneven, penetration of corporatist forms into social policy.

This argument proposing the uneven and increasing importance of corporate bargaining in social policy follows from Cawson and Saunders' (1983) claim that there is a direct link between the process of centralisation and the exercise of corporate bargaining power. In Cawson's (1986) opinion, centralisation is a necessary (though not sufficient) condition for the penetration of corporatist processes into politics and policy-making. The dual politics thesis, he urges, 'argues for a systematic relationship between state activity, mode of intervention, level of organisation of state, interest representation/intermediation and dominant ideologies' (p. 139). Thus, to the extent that key social welfare decisions are increasingly centralised in late twentieth-century Britain, the increasing penetration of corporatist influences into the development of social policy might be expected.

On the other hand, both Cawson (1986) and Saunders (1986b) make a crucial distinction between essentially centralised policies relating to production and essentially localised processes relating to consumption. This latter, local, sphere is the domain in which the state has traditionally provided and delivered social welfare services. It is in the arena of social policy, therefore, that the tensions between corporatism at the centre and pluralist bargaining at the periphery is, according to this thesis, likely to be most marked. This tension, which is summarised in Table 1.1, is explored in the chapters which follow.

Table 1.1   *Schematic representation of the dual politics thesis*

	Politics of production	Politics of consumption
Power structure	Instrumentalist (class-based)	Pluralist (interest groups)
Ideological preference	Property rights	Citizenship rights
Social base	Class interests	Consumption sector interests
Mode of bargaining	Corporatist	Competitive
Level of intervention	Central	Local

Source: adapted from Saunders (1986b).

If the dual politics thesis is a useful way of conceptualising the power structure of a modern liberal democracy such as Britain, following Saunders (1986b), we would expect the following generalisations to hold when applied to the organisation and effectiveness of social policy. First, where intervention is geared to sustaining the processes of production, the state will act in the long-term interests of capital accumulation – that is, it will conform to the tenets of instrumentalism as advocated by Miliband (1973): the protection of property rights will tend to be secured at the expense of a range of citizenship rights; the wealthy will be favoured at the expense of the poor; corporate interests will tend to dominate policy-making; and state intervention will tend to become more centralised. On the other hand, where intervention is geared to providing for consumption needs, it will tend to be influenced by more democratic forms of bargaining; it will seek to secure the rights of citizenship relating to legal protection, political representation and welfare provision; it will be responsive to the competing demands of a range of socio-economic groups; and it will be more localised.

The dual politics framework seems to us to represent a valuable tool for analysing social policy. It draws together many of the strengths of the traditions already discussed and places them within a coherent framework. Nevertheless, we also acknowledge that, as an account of the power structure of modern liberal democracy, it fails as badly as these other approaches to social policy in its ability or inclination to accommodate inequalities associated with racism, patriarchy or other divisive practices which cannot be reduced to the organisation of production or consumption.

This problematic feature of all the main theories of the power structure of society that are commonly incorporated into social policy has also, until very recently, been reflected in the literature in this field. Texts on social policy, whatever their theoretical starting point, have tended to marginalise or ignore the extent to which social policy is differentially experienced by men and women, or by the black and white communities. Hindess's (1987) approach is all too typical; he observes that 'Feminism gets little mention in most general approaches to social policy, and this book is no exception' (p. 7). The reason is not that authors believe racism and patriarchy to be unimportant, but that there are too few precedents to allow them easily to be incorporated. This neglect is disturbing, since there is no lack of evidence that recent trends in social policy have had disproportionately severe consequences for women and black people (see Edgell and Duke, 1983; Cross, 1982; Williams, 1987).

Thus, although the dual politics thesis has not yet been developed to accommodate those circumstances where the exercise of racism, partriarchy or other axes of discrimination cut across, or displace, consumption sector and class cleavages, this is an omission we wish to confront at the outset. Accordingly, this introductory statement concludes with a comment on why both the practice of racism and the organisation of gender relations seem to be omitted from the dual politics thesis; we also offer a brief note on how these axes of inequality are incorporated into the analyses of subsequent chapters.

The dual politics thesis offers a critique of the power relations which organise the material conditions of life: it is concerned with factors affecting the distribution of goods, services and life chances. It adequately, and properly, focuses on the distinction between state and market provisioning in the context of the ascendancy of corporate interests over both these spheres. It does not, however, take into account the distributional problems that arise when the priority accorded to capital accumulation restricts the availability of resources to the extent that they must be differentially apportioned even within so-called consumption sectors (consumption sectors are usually distinguished according to whether the goods and services consumed are provided by the state, acquired via the market, or fall into the category of self-provisioning). Gender, 'race' and other forms of socially constructed identity (including age, or categories like the deserving and undeserving poor) become important at this point as bureaucratically convenient (though totally unjustifiable) principles employed to guide the inclusion (or exclusion) of individuals in (or from) access to scarce resources.

Additionally, because the dual politics thesis focuses only on the material consequences, and origins, of the struggle for resources, it does not consider the ideological requirements of a political economy in which material inequalities are marked and perceivable. Yet, to persist, such inequalities require not only a material base (in a mode of production and in the social relations of consumption), but also a degree of normative support. At an ideological level, social cleavages which are *not* organised around class or consumption sector cleavages (that is, which cut across the most crucial lines of inequality from an economic point of view) may play an important part in fragmenting any fundamental challenge to the status quo which might be posed by an awakening of class consciousness. From this perspective, the reproduction of racism and patriarchy might be seen as 'functional' to modern capitalist democracy, and this has far-reaching implications for the organisation and potential achievement of social policy. In analysing social policy within the dual politics framework, these considerations are important in at least two respects.

First, it is clear that 'race' and gender are not explanatory variables, but rather forms of social differentiation to be explained. Phenotypic variation associated with appearance, pigmentation or the possession of particular reproductive organs do not give rise to 'natural' social categories. This is why we refer to 'race' in inverted commas and to gender rather than sex. The central question is not what effects – in terms of behaviour or the generation of needs – these ostensibly natural attributes exert. Rather, the issue is that of why biological or phenotypic characteristics have become socially (as well as politically and economically) salient. In short, we must ask: how has social (especially housing) policy contributed to the construction of 'race' and gender, and how has it helped sustain inequalities between the groups so defined? (for a fuller discussion, see Smith, 1989a). This question is given particular attention in Chapter 3, but it is a theme which runs throughout the book, and which may be extended to apply to other forms of social differentiation, particularly those relating to age.

Secondly, explicit attention to 'race' and gender is an important route towards identifying and monitoring the needs and rights to which social policy is addressed. There are some special needs which flow directly from the physiological and demographic characteristics of women and black people (of Asian or Afro-Caribbean origin or descent) respectively. The longer average life span of women than that of men, coupled with their apparently greater susceptibility to rheumatism and arthritis, *may* mean that women require particular forms of care in old age; the legacy of immigration history *may* mean that some Asians require special language classes and other forms of educational service. For the most part, however, the needs we refer to are socially and bureaucratically constructed. The 'needs' of women leaving a violent relationship, for instance, are partly generated by the inflexibility and inadequacy of a housing system which does not always recognise their claim for shelter as legitimate from a welfare perspective, or as potentially profitable from the point of view of the market.

In short, it is clear that the construction of 'race' and gender (and, therefore, the analysis of racism and patriarchy) are, though frequently neglected in major texts on social policy, an integral part of our understanding of the power structure of society when viewed from the dual politics perspective. Of course, the lived reality of women and black people in Britain must have as much to do with the history of imperialism and patriarchy as with the development of modern liberal democracy. In this book, however, our primary concern is with how these enduring facets of social inequality are sustained or reproduced through the processes of capital accumulation and political legitimation that frame the development of social policy in modern Britain.

Conclusion

The use of the dual politics framework as the starting point of the analysis of the links between housing and social policy that are explored in the remainder of this book, means that certain issues arising from this approach will be given prominence. For example, a key task will be to identify areas of corporate and pluralist influence and to assess the relative strengths of each of these spheres in the determination of housing policy. Related to this is an ideological debate between the importance of citizenship rights as against property rights as the touchstone of housing policy. In Chapter 2 the general impact on housing policy of these two contrasting ideologies will be traced, while further chapters give more detailed examples of their influence on specific policy areas and of their relationship to the corporate and pluralist sphere of policy-making. We shall also be concerned with analyses of the levels of state decision-making involved in housing provision and with their relationship to corporate and pluralist policy-making processes. Housing studies provide a means of examining the extent to which social policy decisions are being increasingly made by central government where they are subject to more corporate influence. More generally, the relationship between the level of intervention (i.e. local or central) and the sphere of influence (i.e. corporate or pluralist) will be explored in an attempt to assess whether these two elements do coincide and to what degree.

Finally, the subject matter we have chosen allows the form and relative importance of class and consumption sector cleavages in housing to be assessed, though we are equally concerned to specify the importance of gender, 'race' and age in the provision and consumption of housing (the omission of such considerations being a key shortcoming of the dual politics thesis).

Although we have adopted the dual politics model, we would emphasise, as Saunders (1986a) has done, that this is only a model, and simply a starting point. We have already had to extend the thesis to account for forms of inequality which exist empirically and experientially, but which were excluded conceptually. We use this interpretation of society to guide our own because it offers the most plausible beginning, and not because we regard it as 'true'. As the book develops, in fact, we are forced to qualify and develop this thesis to arrive at a somewhat different interpretation of how power is organised in relation to the development of social policy in late twentieth-century Britain.

2

Housing as Social Policy

In Chapter 1 we examined a number of competing theoretical frameworks for analysing social policy and its relationship with public policy more generally. In the case of housing, it is particularly important to take this wider public policy focus, because housing policy has always had a broader remit than just that of meeting social needs. In this chapter we go on to explore the social aspects of housing policy more generally, in terms of the different roles it has played within the British political economy. Specifically, we consider housing as a tool of environmental management, as a right of citizenship, and as a marketed commodity. In doing so we examine housing policy in relation to the housing system as a whole, rather than concentrating exclusively on the public sector.

This approach follows logically from the working definition of social policy which we set out in the introduction; this portrayed social policy as state intervention which occurs not just through in-kind provision but also via subsidies and regulation of the market. According to this view, social policy is not the domain of any particular institution or legislative arena; rather, it is the outcome of any 'deliberate attempt by government to promote individual and social welfare in certain specific dimensions *using any suitable policy instruments'* (Weale, 1983, our emphasis). In examining the social aspects of housing, therefore, we acknowledge the relevance of Hill's (1983) observation that social policy is not always implemented with welfare objectives in mind, and that legislation apparently formulated outside of the social policy arena may make a significant contribution to welfare and well-being.

In order to understand the development of housing policy and its changing orientation, it is necessary to acknowledge that, threading

21

through the theoretical debate about how society is structured (discussed in Chapter 1) is a practical debate concerning the appropriate aims, scope and organisation of policies orientated towards meeting social need. That is, we need to be aware not only of the social forces that led to particular measures being introduced, but also of the political or moral philosophy that has underpinned the way in which policy has been designed and implemented. In order to help us understand the latter, we set out in the next section two models of intervention which summarise opposing arguments concerning the appropriate normative criteria which should guide the development and implementation of social policy. In Britain, this debate has polarised around the relative merits of market competition and state provision. The virtues of the market model have been vigorously propounded by the new right and, indeed, the Conservative governments since 1979. The social democratic approach, which sees an extensive role for public sector provision, has become less popular in housing in the late twentieth century. Using these models as 'ideal types', we show in the first section of this chapter how the various strands of housing policy have been aligned more or less closely with one rather than the other at various times. We also draw upon these two models in our discussion of housing as social policy in later chapters of the book.

The remaining sections of the chapter examine, in turn, three key strands of housing policy, focusing respectively on housing as environmental management, housing as social welfare, and housing as a marketed commodity. These three sections are broadly chronological, showing that the pursuit of social concerns through housing (a) originated in attempts to secure public health through environmental improvement and the regulation of building standards; (b) expanded as the right to decent housing gradually became embedded in the principles of the welfare state; and (c) survives in an ideological climate which increasingly regards the market as best able to cater for many of the housing needs that in the recent past have been met by the state. These themes are chronological, however, only in terms of the emphasis of policy: the environmental, social welfare and economic aspects of housing policy have coexisted for much of the present century, and it would be erroneous to assume that any one has or is likely to supersede another substantially.

The discussion in these final sections can be read on two levels.

Essentially, it provides a brief descriptive introduction to the development of housing policy, and therefore provides the context for subsequent chapters of the book (readers requiring more detail should consult Holmans, 1987, and Malpass and Murie, 1987). In addition, we use this outline as a vehicle for exploring those key trends in the political management and orientation of social welfare that we now introduce.

The politics of social policy

The dual politics interpretation of British liberal democracy outlined in Chapter 1 allows us to comment on the power structure of society and on the role that social policy plays within this. In setting up such a framework, we are able to discuss the unstated as well as the stated aims of policy, and to go some way towards accounting for its unanticipated, as well as its expected, effects. We are able to probe beyond the ideological and pragmatic debates of politicians devising social policy, and of pressure groups demanding particular measures. By setting our analysis within a broad theory of the power structure of society, we are able to interpret social policy with reference to information, events and forces that are not always immediately available to those involved in the development, organisation and implementation of the welfare services. Nevertheless, ideological debates about the aims and objectives of social policy set within this wider framework are crucially important for the shape of social policy instruments and, therefore, for the quality of life and well-being of many people. Hence in this section we examine a long-running and evolving debate about the normative criteria which should guide (and which have guided) the design and implementation of social policy. Although for the most part this debate has been essentially a pragmatic one, ultimately it is a dispute that is grounded in political philosophy.

It is frequently argued that social policy in Britain developed in the context of a political consensus over the role of the welfare state and that this consensus was only broken following the election of a Conservative government in 1979 (see Gamble, 1987). Yet, as we shall see, such a consensus has rarely been apparent in housing policy, and it is doubtful whether it has characterised other areas of social policy (see Deakin, 1987, 1988). Rather, there is a long history of dispute over the objectives of social policy and over the most appropriate means of achieving them. Nevertheless, while the parameters of this long and frequently bitter debate have changed over time, it does seem that views about social policy have become more polarised over the last decade. By drawing out the nature of these differences, we can provide the practical and political context in which the particular policy issues discussed in this and in subsequent chapters are set. We do this by introducing two 'ideal types' of welfare provision, the market and the social democratic models.

The market model

Since 1979, the view that social services should, where possible, be provided by families, friends or the market, rather than by the state, has become increasingly prevalent. The very term 'welfare state' has come under attack from those who regard the legitimate role of the state as being a minimal one, primarily concerned with upholding private property rights (which are seen as a welcome source of individuals' independence from the state) and with creating conditions that are conducive to the smooth running of the market. This may involve breaking up monopolies to ensure that there are a number of suppliers of a particular commodity, or it may mean intervening to enable individuals to enter the market or to compete more effectively in it (for example, by increasing the effective purchasing power of lower income groups). The consequence is that social services are seen, wherever possible, as the responsibility of the individual and hence of the private sector, so that social policy is relegated to a very marginal role in public policy.

This view infuses that mix of neo-liberal economics and traditional Toryism that is often collectively referred to as the 'new right' (see King, 1987). Despite this appellation, many of the key tenets of this outlook (and many of its best known proponents, such as Hayek) have been around for a long time; indeed, the *laissez-faire* state which this political philosophy propounds was a central characteristic of the British polity in the nineteenth century. What is new about the new right is the much greater currency and legitimacy which that outlook has gained over the last decade.

Neo-liberal economics, a central component of the new right view, has a strong predilection against state intervention in the workings of the market, arguing that the most efficient distribution of resources flows from market competition rather than from state action. The model suggests that the rights of citizenship flow from the right of individuals to accumulate rewards through individual effort. It is geared towards the protection of private property and wealth, and it is predicated on an ideology of inequality. A degree of inequality, it is argued, stimulates initiative and effort; because too much inequality is economically inefficient, market mechanisms will prevent excessive injustice. State intervention, it is argued, reduces efficiency, rarely achieves its aim, and tends to have a wide range of undesirable and unanticipated effects (see, for example, Hayek, 1960). State 'interference' is also thought to erode individuals' liberty (and motivation) to compete in the market and to allow social inequality to become politicised and exploited for electoral gain.

Traditional authoritarian conservatism – a second arm of the new right – also frowns on state intervention in social welfare (though not on intervention to secure social control and the maintenance of public order), favouring instead strategies which strengthen the obligations of kinship and charity by increasing individuals' reliance on the family and on voluntary altruism. It is argued that the family is the centre of civilised life and plays a crucial integrating role in society. Welfare provision is seen as undermining the centrality of the family because it involves the state's taking on responsibilities that lie more properly with the family, so producing a society compromising 'anomic and alienated individuals without secure values' (Barry, 1987).

The new right perspective does recognise that not all people are capable of competing effectively in a market system. It also acknowledges that for those among the elderly, handicapped or destitute who do not receive support from their families or from voluntary charitable organisations, direct state support (albeit of a minimal nature) is necessary. However, it is argued that such assistance should be organised to provide minimum interference with the market and should be of a strictly limited nature. The overriding aim is to minimise public spending in favour of low rates of taxation, which, it is believed, stimulates economic enterprise and initiative. In accord with this imperative (and lending legitimacy to neo-liberal economic strategies) it is argued that state benefits should not be so 'generous' that they reduce work incentives by making people better off in material terms when unemployed than they would be in work.

Likewise, at an ideological level, the pattern of state subsidy should not, in this market-based conception of social policy, be allowed to challenge the principle of economic liberalism.

Consequently, social policy should be organised, wherever possible, to reinforce individual property rights and the principle of market exchange. An example of how this might work is the so-called 'insurance' principle of social security, which dispenses benefits only to those who have contributed adequately to a fund by spending time in paid employment. This condition is seen as reinforcing the work ethic and increasing incentives to participate in the formal workforce.

Two key characteristics of social policy flow from this reasoning. First, because social policy has a marginal role in market-orientated philosophy, and because state intervention directly to achieve social welfare objectives is only used as a last resort, it is inevitable (and, indeed, desirable) that it will be considered inferior to provision by the market. Second, and related to the need to minimise state provision in order to secure the primacy of the market, the boundaries between 'more' and 'less' eligibility for state benefits and provision will be increasingly tightly drawn, echoing an approach that lay explicitly behind the 1834 Poor Law (see Fraser, 1973).

Accordingly, while in its modern guise this model is broadly sympathetic to the special needs of those who are physically (or legally, due to age for example) unable to participate in the labour market, it deals more harshly with the needs of those excluded from the labour market for other reasons (such as redundancy caused by technological restructuring). The model provides for those whose needs can be defined in technical terms (for example, requiring special building adaptations or special forms of care), but not those whose needs hinge on political conflict and which may be less easy to delimit (the unemployed, black people, some groups of women, and so on). This means, first, that some collectively articulated needs are explicitly excluded from state support; and, second, that the receipt of state help is associated with social stigma, and that some groups are more likely to be stigmatised than others.

The degree of stigma tends, in practice, to be related to potential for participation in the labour market. People whose incomes are low because they are physically disabled, mentally ill or physically frail, for example, can be dealt with more sympathetically than can the able-bodied (particularly the young) unemployed. Of course, such differentiated treatment has to be legitimated in some way; distinctions between the 'deserving' and the 'undeserving' poor must not appear arbitrary. As a consequence, for the purposes of receiving (or receiving less, or not receiving) state assistance, individuals must be formally categorised as 'elderly', or 'mentally handicapped', and so on. Despite the more generous treatment that some may achieve as a result, the very process of categorising or labelling people and of designing 'special' programmes for them, can itself be stigmatising (and disabling) and may serve to reinforce their exclusion from the supposed prestige of being able to provide for themselves independently in the market. Because of this, we have chosen to resist such categories and refer instead to 'older people' and to 'people with learning difficulties'.

One further consequence of adopting a market model of welfare on a mass scale is the increasing polarisation of society into those able to provide for themselves through the market system and those reliant on state or voluntary provision, with the latter receiving, or being seen as receiving, an inferior (and hence stigmatised) service. This kind of polarisation can be seen most clearly in housing, but less so in areas such as health care where universal state provision is still the norm. This growing cleavage between those able to buy goods and services through the market and those having to rely on state provision is seen by Saunders (1984, 1986b) as a more salient social divide than class.

This market-oriented model of welfare has provided the normative underpinnings of social policy in Britain for most of the present century. Although the post-war welfare state blunted its force, over the last decade it has gained in significance, and has re-penetrated furthest in housing policy and provision. The traditionally high level of reliance on the private sector for house building (even in public sector housing) and the nature of housing as a commodity means that this 'service' lends itself more readily to market provision than do many other aspects of welfare. Given the close ideological and practical association between the ownership of domestic property and of property rights in general, it would be surprising if this were not so. This market model may, therefore, be said to apply to owner-occupation, despite the substantial state subsidy to owner-occupiers provided through tax relief on mortgage interest payments and through exemption from capital gains tax. This subsidy merely indicates that government eagerness to widen and extend the market can overrule the ultimate 'ideal' of non-intervention in the market itself. Such subsidies are therefore a form of intervention required to sustain the market in conditions where it might not otherwise operate at all or as extensively. Consequently, housing may be regarded as being at the leading edge of the move to privatise responsibility for social welfare. Indeed, this shift towards a market model of housing provision has prompted one of the largest transfers of public assets in British history – a trend described by Forrest and Murie (1988, p. 1) as 'the most important element of the privatisation policy of the Thatcher government'. A major theme of this book is to account for such trends in housing policy and to specify their impact on the structure of social welfare and on the life chances of individuals.

The social democratic model

The traditional alternative to this market-orientated model is grounded in social democratic ideals rather than neo-conservative political philosophy or neo-liberal economics. Advocates of this social democratic alternative are broadly agreed in rejecting the market as necessarily the most efficient and beneficial mode for the delivery of welfare. Thus, as Marquand (1988) has put it, if the project of the neo-liberal right is to subordinate politics to the market, the project of the social democratic left is to subordinate the market to politics.

Central to the social democratic model of welfare are the notion of citizenship and the strategy of equality. We shall deal with each in turn. Citizenship refers to the conditions, or rights, for participation in, and full membership of, the community. Although the virtues of citizenship are propounded from all points on the political spectrum, the right tends to be more concerned with the obligations of citizens within a nation state, whereas the left has always focused more on the social rights of citizens and their ability to exercise them. It is argued from a social democratic perspective that because of the inequalities inherent in and engendered by market society, state intervention is necessary to ensure that the rights of citizenship are fully and equally available. Thus, following Marshall (1950), full membership of society, which is an essential component of citizenship, can only be guaranteed if all of society is able to enjoy not just civil and political rights but also social rights (for example, to employment and welfare).

Building on Marshall's foundations, the social democratic model argues, first, that state intervention is necessary and desirable because of the failure of the market to supply essential welfare services to an adequate standard. In housing, for example, state intervention has been necessary in the provision of housing for rent: local authority housing was introduced because of the failure of private enterprise to provide adequate housing at rents working people could afford (Merrett, 1979; Ball, 1983). Second, it is argued that public welfare provision can be justified on the grounds of economic efficiency. For example, free health care and education, and the subsidisation of decent housing, can be viewed as contributing to labour productivity. The same is true of training, which is often only inadequately provided by the private sector. Likewise, unemployment benefit can act as a counter-cyclical regulator by sustaining demand during recessions (Cawson, 1986). Third, it is argued that the choice which advocates claim is provided by the market is, in many respects, illusory. The market does not offer perfect competition as popularised by the new right, but is frequently characterised by oligopolies or monopolies which can reduce consumer sovereignty and determine prices. Moreover, the provision of welfare is not like that of commodities such as bread, where buyers can shift readily from one supplier to another. Workers cannot easily shift in and out of pension schemes, for example. As we have seen, too, the private housing market is sustained by extensive state subsidies, which act to structure choices in the market. Furthermore, the choices in welfare open to the poor are severely constrained by their low incomes, which are themselves a function of the labour market. Thus, as one author has put it, 'markets structure choice to eliminate or significantly reduce the eligibility of certain types of options' (Harris, D., 1987, p. 330).

Social democratic theorists go on to argue that the negative consequences of a market economy can (and should) be compensated for, and that socially desirable values can be engendered by public welfare provision. Social policy is, in part, to be viewed as compensation to those unfortunate enough to bear the 'diswelfares' caused by change in an industrial society (Titmuss, 1968). To be effective, welfare may therefore have to be seen as a universal right rather than as a selective, means-tested benefit.

Means-tested services and benefits, as advocated by the right, are criticised from the citizenship perspective for being administratively complex, for their low take-up and, in particular, for stigmatising recipients (Deacon and Bradshaw, 1983). They separate out and identify the poor, who have to prove that they can meet the test of eligibility. The tinge of the scrounger, therefore, hangs over even those who qualify for receipt of the benefit, for as Titmuss (1968, p. 134) points out: 'The fundamental objective of all [means] tests is to keep people out; not to let them in'. Moreover, where a service (for example, council housing today) is provided to a minority of the population, there is the very real danger that it will take the form of, or be perceived as, an inferior, second-class service. In contrast to selectively provided welfare, universal services like the NHS are unlikely to stigmatise. They are consumed by the poor and better-off alike, and they therefore enhance rather than diminish the self-respect of those with limited financial means. Moreover, because universal services are used by those who *could* afford to purchase them in the market place, they can gain a level of political support that ensures a relatively higher quality of provision than they might if they were only consumed by the poor.

Closely related to the notion of citizenship, interpreted as the guarantee of full membership of the community, is the so-called 'strategy of equality' which lies at the heart of the welfare state (Le Grand, 1982). Although attitudes to equality vary, as a normative guide to policy it is often taken to mean 'more than equality of opportunity but less than equality of income' (George and Wilding, 1976, p. 65). Such equality is deemed to be necessary in civilised societies for at least four reasons. First, it is regarded as a means of securing some kind of social cohesion in a situation where excessive inequality might otherwise lead to conflict and social breakdown. Second, it is viewed as a means of promoting social efficiency, on the assumptions that excessive inequality reduces social mobility and hinders the creation of a meritocracy, and that market economies misallocate resources by responding only to demand and not to need. Third, in so far as inequality represents a denial to some of their natural rights, equality is viewed as a route to social justice. Finally, equality is regarded as a means of self-realisation, while inequality is thought to prevent many less powerful individuals from realising their full potential. Equality, then, is viewed as a social right *per se,* but it is also portrayed as a means of achieving other social goals such as the extension of freedom and the development of a sense of altruism or social obligation (Titmuss, 1974).

The social democratic model is based on an implicit criticism of the inequalities and inefficiencies that markets inevitably generate and reproduce. Nevertheless, most advocates of this approach accept the context of a capitalist economy in the belief that the detrimental effects of the market can be ameliorated, if not transformed, through state intervention. The ideal driving this model of welfare (whether it is seen as a gesture of state benevolence or as a concession to working-class pressure) is that reforms can be achieved or conceded without altering the fundamental structure of capitalist democracy. Within this constraint, the advocates of the social democratic model have sought to orientate the public provision of welfare to the satisfaction of needs rather than demand, emphasising the broader rights of citizenship over the protection of private property and wealth. The remainder of the chapter shows how this model has vied with the sanctity of the market to introduce a social dimension to housing as environmental, welfare and economic policy.

Housing, health and environmental management

Edwin Chadwick can probably be credited with drawing the earliest links between housing and social policy (in an embryonic sense) in 1842 by mustering some evidence to suggest that, contrary to prevailing wisdom, 'low moral standards' were a consequence rather than a cause of poor housing environments. The legislative response came through public health measures rather than housing policy *per se,* not least because it was in terms of public health that the problem was defined. Hence a major concern of early intervention by the state in the housing market came in the form of basic infrastructure such as drains, sewers, water supplies and refuse collection. The aim here was to prevent the recurrence of the health hazards and epidemics that had been so prevalent earlier in the century; the mechanism was a series of Public Health Acts designed to improve dwelling sanitation and to set minimum standards for construction and amenity provision.

At this time state intervention in housing provision was very limited, and allied closely to the market model; public assistance was regarded as either unnecessary or undesirable. The virtues of thrift, self-help and independence were preached as the best way for the poor to improve their lot, while society's rewards went to those who supposedly put in the most effort, made the greatest sacrifices, or were born with the most talent. This reflects the distribution of state power at this time, which lay primarily in the hands of the middle classes and the wealthy. It was only in 1867 and 1884 that working-class males received the franchise, and even then only if they owned or rented a house over a certain rateable value; it was not until 1918 that women were allowed to vote. Furthermore, for much of the nineteenth century, local government was very fragmented, with numerous *ad hoc* bodies awarded power for particular purposes. For example, the local boards of guardians administered the Poor Law, while sanitary authorities were responsible for public health. More-over, the local state was dominated by the middle classes, who were often opposed to high rates, or to the principle of subsidising the poor (as property owners, or being in other ways associated with the housing market, they were unwilling to act against their own perceived interests). Their influence was great because most housing-related legislation was permissive rather than mandatory, and local authorities were not compelled to implement policies to which they were opposed (Hennock, 1973; Fraser, 1973).

The scope of housing-related measures expanded towards the end of the century. The sanctity of private property was weakened by the Artisans' and Labourers' Dwellings Act 1868, which gave local medical officers of health the power to inspect and report on individual premises which were 'in a condition or state dangerous to health as to be unfit for human habitation'. Local authorities with a population of over 10,000 were empowered by the Act to force the owners of unfit property (in respect of which a report had been made by the Medical Officer of Health) to repair them at their own expense or have the authority demolish them without compensation (Gibson and Langstaff, 1982, p. 21). The Artisans' and Labourers' Dwellings Improvement Act 1875 empowered local authorities to clear areas of unfit housing and to provide replacement housing, and included a provision for the compensation of slum owners whose property was cleared (Yelling, 1986).

Neither the 1868 nor the 1875 Act had much impact. Many medical officers of health were reluctant to use their new powers, while 'the vested interests of landlords, local corruption and political opposition to the financial costs involved played major roles in ensuring inactivity' (Gibson and Langstaff, 1982, p. 21). In fact, as Merrett (1979) notes, much clearance activity was carried out under local Acts of Parliament. This was usually undertaken in commercial operations as part of 'civic improvements', and especially by railway companies constructing city centre termini stations (Kellett, 1969). According to Dyos (cited in Merrett, 1979, p. 12), approximately 76,000 people in London were displaced by railway construction between 1853 and 1901. As with clearance under the 1875 Act, the slum dwellers whose homes were being demolished were simply moved on. Indeed, although some medical officers were critical of this aspect of the clearance process, many others saw it as a positive virtue because it provided a way of demolishing the feared 'rooker-ies' in which were thought to live the criminal and semi-criminal classes. Where replacement housing was built on cleared sites, it was often constructed by philanthropic trusts rather than by the local authorities, while the rents charged for this accommodation were commonly beyond the means of the original inhabitants (Wohl, 1977).

Early responses to poor housing environments were, in short, based firmly on concerns about public health, not least because health epidemics such as cholera were not confined to the poor, while over-crowding, disease and squalor all impaired the produc-tivity of the workforce. It was not until the Housing and Town Planning etc Act 1919 that the state began to exhibit some direct commitment to housing 'as a social policy based upon local initiative and central supervision, compulsion and subsidy' (Fraser, 1973, p. 168), and this, unlike the nineteenth-century sanitary measures, was largely the result of working-class pressure for reform (see Merrett, 1979).

The central belief in manipulating housing environments to improve the quality of life dominated thinking behind the slum clearance efforts of the 1930s and 1950s. Clearance was encouraged by Labour's Housing Act of 1930 (the Greenwood Act), which offered subsidies based on the number of families rehoused and enhanced the powers of local authorities to pursue redevelopment. Similarly, redevelopment was given fresh impetus in the mid 1950s when the Conservative government ended subsidies for the construc-tion of general needs dwellings and restricted them to slum clear-ance, replacement housing and the building of one-bedroom flats for the elderly. Both rounds of demolition and rebuilding were stimu-lated by much the same kind of reasoning as that which underlay the earlier sanitary-oriented legislation. Although never adequately defined by statute, 'slums' were recognised in practice in terms of criteria inherited from the era of sanitary reform. For the purposes of slum clearance, then, social need has always been conceived of in terms of environmental health. The scheduling of houses for demolition has, moreover, always rested heavily on inspecting officers' discretion and, not surprisingly, the threshold for unfitness tended to rise as the overall quality of the stock improved (Gibson and Langstaff, 1982).

The progress of slum clearance is shown in Table 2.1. Between 1930 and 1979, 1.8 million dwellings were demolished or closed, with over five million people being moved out of their homes. In the postwar slum clearance drive, many of the families who were rehoused were given tenancies in what Dunleavy (1981) refers to as 'mass housing' – the large high-rise and flatted estates that were built in the inner city or on the suburban periphery. While initially introduced as a solution to the problem of slum housing, many of these estates have since become policy problems themselves.

Table 2.1   *Slum clearance, 1930 to 1979, in England and Wales*

Years	Houses demolished or closed (000s)	Persons moved* (000s)
1930–44	341	1,340
1945–54	90	309
1955–59	213	669
1960–64	304	834
1965–69	339	896
1970–74	309	704
1975–79	213	378†

*Not necessarily rehoused
†Estimate
Source: Gibson and Langstaff (1982), Table 1, p. 31.

Although the environmental management role of housing has continued to be important in the last two decades, the emphasis has changed. In particular, the 1968 White Paper *Old Houses into New Homes* and the Housing Act 1969 marked a significant shift in state policy towards housing renewal as a policy for older housing. In effect, the White Paper signalled the demise of large-scale slum clearance and increasing priority for rehabilitation of the existing stock. This was confirmed in the 1973 White Paper and 1974 Housing Act, which confirmed that clearance policies were to be replaced by the principle of *in situ* renewal. Although home improvement grants had been available in urban areas since Labour's Housing Act 1949, they were given a new importance and a fresh impetus by the Housing Acts of 1969 and 1974, also passed by Labour.

Although the reasons for this notable shift in policy are complex, it is widely accepted that public expenditure considerations were important. As Merrett (1979) has pointed out, for a given level of resource cost, rehabilitation is cheaper than redevelopment because the latter has generally been entirely publicly funded, whereas the former has involved private sector outlays, at least in part (the private/public distinction is discussed further below). It is noticeable that the White Paper was published the year after the 1967 balance-of-payments crisis and the subsequent, agonised devaluation of the pound, and was preceded by public spending cuts in local authority house-building announced in January 1968 (Merrett, 1979).

But if the shift in policy away from large-scale clearance to rehabilitation was to some extent a pragmatic response to perceived economic constraints, politicians were quick to rationalise it in terms of social concern. A number of community studies (most notably Young and Willmott, 1957) had highlighted the social consequences of slum-clearance policies and their effects on local communities. Although these and other findings were available well before the shift in policy, it was only once the change had taken place that they were in fact highlighted by the government. This allowed politicians to rationalise the move away from slum clearance in terms of social concern. Thus, while not unimportant, local pressure and community action were less significant factors in this change of policy than the needs of capital accumulation, as perceived by the central state.

Other, more technical arguments were also relevant. It was argued on the one hand that the worst areas of slum housing had by then been demolished, thereby undermining the need for large-scale clearance. On the other hand, the house condition survey of England and Wales, carried out in 1967, had shown that despite massive clearance activity, there was an extensive problem of unfitness and disrepair in the remaining stock (Merrett, 1979). It was becoming recognised that the problem of sub-standard housing was not a finite one because of the deterioration of homes which had previously been in acceptable condition. Moreover, although controversial, the use of cost-benefit analysis by economists had suggested that rehabilitation could in certain circumstances be more cost-effective than redevelopment (Needleman, 1965).

Also significant were the ideological consequences of what Merrett (1979) has referred to as the 'partitioning' of housing renewal. That is to say, slum clearance has involved the demolition of private housing and its replacement by public housing, whereas rehabilitation has, for the most part, involved voluntary, private improvement of the private housing stock. Hence redevelopment has involved the substitution of state provision for the market, while rehabilitation has mostly involved the upgrading of private housing and its retention within the market (see Ball, 1978). The shift from the former to the latter is therefore part of a shift away from the social democratic model of provision and towards the market alternative. The significance of this partitioning was becoming more apparent as slum clearance began to involve an increasing number of owner-occupied houses and not just those owned by private sector landlords. Significantly, in 1963 the Conservative government had sponsored feasibility studies to examine the 'private enterprise solution' to slum clearance. Gibson and Langstaff (1982, p. 59) report that 'The verdict of the market on the possibility of private enterprise undertaking large-scale comprehensive redevelopment was an emphatic "no".' Hence, a private enterprise, market solution seemed to imply rehabilitation rather than redevelopment.

As Gibson and Langstaff (1982, p. 64) have noted, the Housing Act 1969 'was the watershed in the transition from comprehensive redevelopment to gradual renewal'. The General Improvement Areas (GIAs) introduced by that Act were aimed at encouraging area improvement. Exchequer subsidies were made available within GIAs for environmental works, but otherwise the designation conferred no special financial benefit on those living within them (grant levels, for instance, were the same as everywhere else). Nevertheless, the designation of such zones was expected to remove uncertainty (perhaps making mortgage finance easier to obtain) and, along with the associated environmental works, help create confidence in the area. In other words, the aim was to foster the market and stimulate private, voluntary improvement activity. Although no social objectives were explicitly built into this Act, the social benefits of the new environmental strategy were very quickly seized upon to legitimise the changes it introduced. For the first time it was recognised that, by emphasising improvement, housing policy had become a technique for retaining the existing stock, which, because it did not blight neighbourhoods or disrupt communities, could also foster residents' confidence in, and commitment to, the future of their locality.

The key problem with this reasoning behind the 1969 Act was the financial inability of many residents to implement the improvements that the designation of GIAs was expected to encourage. Such householders, after all, were living in areas formally acknowledged to contain some of the least desirable parts of the nation's housing stock. It is perhaps hardly surprising that not only was grant take-up patchy (questioning the whole notion of *comprehensive* area-based improvement), but also the majority of grants awarded in the early 1970s improved the better rather than the worst homes, which were occupied by more rather than less affluent households. For instance, over half of the owner-occupiers of grant-aided improved properties in the period 1972–3 to 1973–4 held professional or managerial occupations, while less than one in seven were semi- or unskilled workers (Gibson and Langstaff, 1982, p. 69). Moreover, there was considerable concern and publicity about 'abuses' of the grant system by developers taking advantage of the relatively relaxed conditions attached to improvement grants. A further and related area of concern was the so-called 'gentrification' of certain neighbourhoods in parts of London such as Islington. This involved the displacement of poorer tenants by higher-income owner-occupiers, with the upgrading of an area often aided by the provision of improvement grants (Williams, 1976; Merrett, 1979). Debate about area improvement was thus increasingly focused on the social objectives of policy rather than just physical conditions.

Following a reappraisal of policy in 1973–4, significant changes in environmental management through housing policy were introduced by the Housing Act 1974. This Act introduced Housing Action Areas (HAAs), which were to be designated 'in areas of housing stress where bad physical and social conditions interact and where intense activity will follow declaration' (Department of the Environment, 1975, quoted in Gibson and Langstaff, 1982, p. 110). The significant feature of HAAs was that, for the first time, housing policy was to be directed not only towards improving the stock and securing its effective use and management, but also towards enhancing the well-being of existing residents (though in Scotland, unlike England and Wales, no social criteria were explicitly built into their definition). GIAs were retained but were reserved for areas of mostly owner-occupied, basically sound houses where improvement might be expected on the basis of voluntary action.

It is apparent that HAAs, unlike GIAs, were envisaged as being designated in areas of lower income, privately rented housing where improvement on a voluntary basis was unlikely. The designation of an HAA meant an increase in grant levels (from 50 per cent to 75 and 90 per cent in cases of hardship), the availability of a new grant for basic repairs, an exchequer subsidy of 50 per cent of the cost of modest environmental works, and, significantly, the introduction of new compulsory improvement powers. A preferential rate of improvement grant (60 per cent) was also introduced in GIAs, as were compulsory improvement powers. Priority neighbourhoods (PNs) were also introduced (although their impact was small and they were soon abolished). These zones, which could be declared in areas adjacent to GIAs and HAAs, were designed to prevent housing conditions deteriorating around designated areas. Designation of PNs conferred no special improvement incentives but did give local authorities certain enhanced legal powers (Gibson and Langstaff, 1982).

The Housing Act 1974 was also significant because it introduced the Housing Association Grant (HAG), which has provided a major stimulus to the housing association movement. Since 1974 housing associations have played an important role in the rehabilitation of inner-city housing, often in HAAs. Merrett (1979) has accounted for this by arguing that because of the absence of an investing private landlord class, the Conservatives have had to invent one (albeit one heavily reliant on centralised public funding). The alternative would have to have been municipalisation: the compulsory purchase for improvement of run-down housing that could not be improved by voluntary means.

Area-based housing renewal has never been well integrated with area-based urban policy, which since 1969 (under the auspices of the Urban Programme) has been one of the government's main vehicles for targeting social policy within the inner cities. This lack of integration might have been expected prior to 1977, when the Urban

Programme was managed by the Home Office. For the last decade, however, area-based housing policy and area-based urban policy have both been managed by the Department of the Environment. The failure to integrate the two may well reflect the extent to which economic initiatives are displacing social investment in the Urban Programme (see Keating and Boyle, 1982; Clapham and Smith, 1988) and the speed with which responsibility for urban regeneration through housing renewal has been shifted to the private sector.

We can see these new concerns reflected in the setting up of Housing Action Trusts (HATs) under the Housing Act 1988. Based explicitly on the Urban Development Corporation model, HATs are being established in a limited number of run-down local authority housing estates, and have been made accountable to the Secretary of State for the Environment. HATs take over the ownership of the council houses within the designated area and may also assume certain of the planning and environmental health powers of the local authority if the latter is not sufficiently co-operative. They are also to take on local authorities' duties under the 1976 Race Relations Act to promote equal opportunities and prevent racial discrimination in the housing system. In many ways, though, HATs enable the government to excise the designated areas from local democratic pressures and to place responsibility and accountability for them with central government. The stated aims of HATs are to improve the condition of designated estates, to draw on private finance to fund these developments, to introduce alternative forms of owner-ship and management to that of the local authority, and to stimulate the local economy (Department of the Environment, 1987). Thus the aims of housing policy as environmental management have been extended to include employment generation.

Environmental management in the form of HATs has also been given an explicit role in shifting housing tenure in these areas away from subsidised renting associated with the social democratic model of provision in favour of the subsidised ownership associated with a market or quasi-market model. Previously, since environmental management in housing was concerned almost exclusively with tackling substandard *private* housing, policy involved either a shift to the public sector (as with slum clearance and redevelopment) or retention of provision within the market (as with improvement grants) or quasi-market (as with housing associations) sectors. Now the focus is on sub-standard *public* sector housing and the aim is to use renovation via HATs as a way of eroding the social democratic ideal of a universal entitlement to housing, emphasising instead the rights of private property and the market or quasi-market mode of provision.

This shift towards a more market-oriented approach is also embodied in the new policy on home improvement set out in the 1987 White Paper (DoE, 1987). While some of the details are different, the philosophy underlying the new policy is the same as that of the 1985 Green Paper on home improvement, which argued that 'The cornerstone of policy must be that owners are primarily responsible for the conditions of their houses, though they should be given appropriate help and encouragement in shouldering their responsibility' (DoE, 1985).

Entitlement to home improvement grants will no longer be based on rateable value limits. Instead, in line with new right philosophy, it will be means-tested, so that only those households 'in greatest need' of assistance will receive it. Eligible households living in dwellings below a new fitness standard will qualify for a mandatory grant, while above this standard grant assistance will be at the discretion of local authorities. The present four types of grant are to be replaced by a single form of grant, and GIAs and HAAs are to be replaced by a single type of statutory Renewal Area, within which local authorities will be able to carry out both renovation and selective redevelopment, using powers similar to those already available (DoE, 1987).

Housing as a social service

The First World War marked a crucial turning point in the development of housing policy in Britain. Prior to 1914, the focus of policy, as we have seen, was on environmental management, and state intervention occurred mainly to regulate private provision. Despite the powers granted to local authorities under the Housing of the Working Classes Act 1890 to provide housing directly, few were inclined to promote a sustained role for government intervention. Thus the market model, largely unconstrained by the redistributive influence of the state, dominated housing policy.

After 1914, however, the state began to be more actively involved in housing provision, albeit often reluctantly. The new interventionism not only involved regulation of the privately rented market, but also provided subsidies both to in-kind provision (i.e. council housing) and to private sector house-building. The interwar years saw the emergence of subsidised local authority housing as a major tenure in which the quality of accommodation provided, especially during the 1920s, was significantly better than that provided by the private market prior to 1914. During this period, the notion of housing as a social right entered political debate; as controversy developed over the relative merits of public and private provision of rented housing, shelter became an important element in the construction of the social democratic welfare state.

The fact that state attempts to meet housing needs took the particular form of council housing was not inevitable. In many ways it can be regarded as a fortuitous consequence of war. Before 1918, various experiments with housing provision for the 'working classes' took place, largely in reaction to the failure of the unsubsidised private market to provide decent housing at a price the poor could afford. The most notable of these were the model dwelling companies often set up by wealthy philanthropists, which aimed to show that enlightened private enterprise could provide decent housing at affordable rents and still return a 5 per cent profit (compared to the 8 per cent plus that was common at the time) to the shareholders (Tarn, 1973). However, despite subsidised loans taken out via the Public Works Loan Commissioners and the purchase of land from local authorities (under the 1875 Cross Act) at below market prices, philanthropic capitalism failed to provide a model which the private market was willing or able to emulate on a significant scale (Merrett, 1979).

The First World War was a crucial factor behind the introduction of subsidies for local authority housing. In the face of a severe housing shortage, the collapse of building for private rental, and the threat of social and industrial unrest, political expediency gave birth to state subsidised provision in kind on a hitherto unprecedented scale. Alternatives to council housing (such as the private landlord, central government, and the model dwelling companies) were considered but, for various reasons, were rejected. The advent of the subsidised 'homes fit for heroes' programme can therefore be seen as an essentially pragmatic response of politicians faced with a housing shortage and needing to meet (or buy off) working-class demands for the right to shelter (see Swenarton, 1981; Ball, 1983; Merrett, 1979). After 1920, governments' preferred strategy was to stimulate owner-occupation, and support for council housing for general consumption was both equivocal and short-lived (see Forrest and Murie, 1988, pp. 15–41, for a more extended discussion).

The balance of emphasis between a general needs and a residual role for council housing, while mediated by political ideology, was often primarily the outcome of pragmatic responses to changing circumstances. Thus the Housing and Town Planning etc (Addison) Act of 1919 was passed by a Conservative/Liberal coalition government which then axed the programme in 1921 after the threat of revolution had receded (Swenarton, 1981). Yet despite favouring the market mode of provision, the Conservative government which came to power in November 1922 was forced to re-introduce subsidies in 1923 in the face of a growing housing shortage and the social unrest that this was causing (Kemp, 1984b). Although the Conservatives have always been 'reluctant collectivists' (George and Wilding, 1976), for pragmatic reasons they had to accept the need for council housing, largely because of the failure of the private sector to provide adequate housing to rent. Thus when the Conservatives were returned to power late in 1924, they did not abolish the substantial subsidies for council house-building that Labour had introduced earlier in the year, but rather re-affirmed them in their consolidating Housing Act of 1925 (Bowley, 1945). While the 1923 Housing Act placed most emphasis on subsidies for private house-building, it also provided for Exchequer assistance to local authority construction where it could be shown that such activities would not hinder the work of private firms.

The organisation and management of public housing has always been primarily the domain of local authorities, reflecting their early role in the administration of public health. One consequence of this is that the socialisation of responsibility for shelter was incremental, and housing was never a national service in the same sense as health, education and national insurance (see Kirwan, 1984). This, together with the facts that house-building has always remained the domain of private contractors, and that public housing has developed alongside (rather than provided an alternative to) private owner-ship, means that, even as a social right, housing has never been a fully socialised service. This in itself has limited the scope for even the explicitly welfare-oriented aspects of housing to advance the aims of social policy. On the one hand, governments have had to provide building contractors with attractive alternatives to private speculation, offsetting lower profits with guaranteed contracts and part payment in advance; on the other hand, they have been vulnerable to house-builders acting as a cartel to demand extra profits for public sector construction. Similarly, the altruistic ideals of mass public housing have often been foiled by the inability of the building industry to make effective use of new techniques and technology. With the advent of off-site prefabrication, for instance, 'without adequate training or research and based on an essentially speculative industrial structure, overall unit building costs were much higher than the traditional building' (Duncan, 1986, p. 28). The cost of housing as a social right was thus significantly increased, and only possible on a large scale because of heavy subsidies to local authorities from central government (Dunleavy, 1981).

During the interwar years, political differences over the role of public housing began to cause shifts in housing policy. While the Conservatives' Housing Act 1923 anticipated that subsidised council housing would fill an essentially residual role, Labour's Housing (Financial Provisions) Act 1924 gave council housing a general needs orientation (Merrett, 1979). For Labour, local authority housing was viewed as a redistributive mechanism to provide decent housing for the working classes; it was not only necessary because of the failure of the market, but was also a means of using state subsidies to offset inequalities created by low pay. Until at least the early 1960s, Labour continued to advocate a general needs role for the public sector, even though the requirement that councils should house only 'the working classes' was dropped from legislation in 1949. The view from the right, however, is that the welfare role of housing policy is to alleviate hardship, not to redistribute wealth. Thus in 1933 and again in 1956, subsidies for general needs council house building were abolished by the Conservatives, who held that the primary role of state housing was to accommodate families displaced by slum clearance, while the private sector was to satisfy other housing needs. Though the precise needs deemed eligible for servicing via public housing have changed over the last quarter of a century, the view from the right has increasingly stressed the residual nature of council housing, seeking reliance on the private sector for general needs provision (the consequences of which are examined in the next section).

Nevertheless, during the 1960s and early 1970s council house-building provided generally as well as for special needs such as slum clearance rehousing (though the latter was still important). However, Labour's housing White Paper of 1965 marked a notable change in the way council housing was presented, taking them nearer to the Conservatives' view. Building for owner-occupation was presented as the normal mode of provision, but council housing was relegated to a residual role:

> Once the country has overcome its huge social problem of slumdom and obsolescence and met the need of the great cities for more houses let at moderate rents, the programme of subsidised council housing should decrease. The expansion of the public programme now proposed is to meet exceptional needs: it is born partly of a short term necessity, partly of the conditions inherent in modern urban life.
>
> The expansion of building for owner-occupation on the other hand is normal; it reflects a long-term social advance which should gradually pervade every region. (MHLG, *The Housing Programme 1965 to 1970*, quoted in Merrett, 1979, p. 255)

This apparent move towards a bipartisan political consensus on owner-occupation (as the normal tenure) and council housing (as the residual, specialist mode of provision) became more pronounced in the early 1970s. This is not to deny that there were differences between the two parties, for these were evident over, for example, rent controls in the private sector and rent levels in the public sector. But as the housing market became increasingly polarised between council housing and owner-occupation, so the political differences between Labour and the Conservatives over the respective roles of these two tenures seemed to lessen. The shift was in Labour's outlook rather than in that of the Conservatives.

The convergence in attitudes towards council housing was manifested in a view of its role (now that slum clearance had begun to decline) as providing primarily for 'special needs', in particular for those who were too physically or mentally unstable to use their labour to support themselves financially (see Harloe, 1982). The affirmation by Labour of owner-occupation as the normal tenure signalled acceptance of only a limited role for in-kind provision, and acknowledged the legitimacy of subsidised market provision. Thus during this period Labour afforded a relatively circumscribed role for state provision and assigned mainstream provision to the market. This flew in the face of the social democratic ideals behind council housing. By confirming the new right view of council housing as an inferior tenure to home ownership, Labour has helped to stigmatise tenants in this sector. Instead of integrating council tenants into society, the party has helped to exclude them by identifying them as poor and unable to provide for themselves in the market place. The so called residualisation of council housing – limiting its role, reducing its quality and restricting it to the relatively poor and benefit-dependent – is a process that has been in operation since well before 1979.

The stages in this shift away from using public housing as an element of general social welfare and towards a view which restricts state support to a relatively limited range of special needs – a shift away from the social democratic to the market model of provisioning – is encapsulated in the history of the Scottish Special Housing Association (SSHA). Set up in the 1930s to stimulate employment, the SSHA became a vehicle for experimenting with new building materials in the 1950s, and during the 1960s served the general needs of overspill populations created by comprehensive redevelopment (Al-Qaddo and Rodger, 1987). By the 1970s, its mandate had changed to emphasise urban renewal, while in the 1980s, the SSHA focused increasingly on the special needs of elderly people, the physically disabled and people with learning difficulties. Finally, in 1989 the SSHA (which has a stock of 75,000 dwellings) was merged with the Housing Corporation in Scotland to form a quango called Scottish Homes. Among its functions, this body is to take over some local authority estates with the aim either of carrying out physical improvements itself, or of devolving ownership and renewal to housing associations, co-operatives or private landlords such as the recently formed Quality Street. Scottish Homes is also empowered to provide grants and subsidies to private companies as well as to housing associations, and this testifies to its role in advancing the market model of housing provision. This represents a trend away from what Wilensky and Lebeaux (1965, cited in O'Higgins, 1985) call an institutional model of welfare, in which state provision is the 'norm' for advanced industrial societies, towards a 'residual' model in which welfare services come into play only when the 'normal' channels of provision (the market and the family) break down. However, despite some superficial similarities in the strategies of the left and right, changing views about the possibilities of manipulating the housing system to achieve social ends have spawned some very different sets of views about the future of social rented housing. These views themselves reflect new opinions about social needs, rights, initiative and aspirations.

It is now widely recognised that a crucial factor in orienting housing policy to meet social needs is the extension of choice, flexibility and individual as well as collective responsibility for the management of lives and environments. For the left, the hope is to achieve this new menu of choice and responsibility without sacrificing the merits of social ownership. The aim, then, is to extend choice within the public sector by transforming the way in which housing is provided. The flagship of this strategy is decentralisation of housing management (and, indeed, of other local authority services), but it also encompasses tenant management co-operatives and, for some on the left, community ownership of former council housing (see Clapham, Kemp and Kintrea, 1987).

Reflecting its rather different political philosophy, the right's strategy to achieve this new framework of choice within rented housing is built on deregulation and privatisation – processes which, in practice, have also been accompanied by centralisation. It is the latter perspective that has held sway in the political climate of the 1980s. The advantages of reducing public expenditure and stimulating the market have been canvassed with respect to a wide range of public services and assets (see Le Grand and Robinson, 1984). Given the opportunities available to, and created by, the strong Conservative governments of the 1980s, the remainder of this chapter is concerned with the effects of the current restructuring of housing provision to bring it more closely in line with market principles.

Housing as a market commodity

Whereas debate in the 1960s was dominated not by the question of whether to have a welfare state, but by arguments over the form it should take, by the late 1970s the rationale and achievements of welfare statism were subject to a severe critique from both the left and right. The impact of this on housing policy was always likely to be far-reaching, not least because all governments since the early 1950s have encouraged an extension of owner-occupation and, therefore, implicitly or explicitly questioned the general needs role of the public sector. Indeed, prior to the late 1970s, Labour achieved more than the Conservatives in promoting ownership. In the present decade, however, the social role of housing has been redefined by neo-conservative ideology, and home ownership is increasingly viewed as the major route to securing a redistribution of wealth and to providing working-class families with a means of transcending the lack of autonomy which typifies their lives. Housing has attracted particular interest from the right as an illustration that state provision has promoted inefficiency and undermined individual responsibility; housing policy has become a test case for arguments with neo-liberal (conservative) economics that the competitive market can provide welfare services more effectively than the state.

The policies of the late 1980s, therefore, have succeeded in shifting the locus of debate away from the issue of whether the welfare state has embraced its obligations, and towards concern about whether what *is* tackled is affordable and appropriate for the public sector (see O'Higgins, 1985). From the perspective of the right, the welfare state is a tax burden which contributes to inflation, falling production, rising unemployment, and lack of investment. Any economic recovery predicated on reducing the tax burden was inevitably to include a critical re-evaluation of the merits of public housing. Strategically, housing seemed the most appropriate welfare commodity to lead the privatisation drive, since it is the one welfare service whose benefits are continuously and individually experienced (Whitehead, 1984). Moreover, as an asset and an arena of consumption, privatised housing offers not just shelter, but also the potential for capital accumulation.

The social policy implications of housing in the present decade, therefore, must be assessed in terms of a broader debate concerning the restructuring of the welfare state. Although public expenditure cuts have been used primarily to reduce the Public Sector Borrowing Requirement, and might therefore be seen primarily as part of macroeconomic policy, the withdrawal from state provision in favour of subsidised privatisation has not been devoid of social concern. Government intervention to 'bend' building society lending criteria to extend home ownership down-market, intervention to stabilise building society funds, and the encouragement of easy-start mortgages, are all examples of attempts to spread owner-occupation throughout the social class structure (see Booth and Crook, 1986). Many of these initiatives, like the first major cutbacks in public expenditure, originated during the mid 1970s under a Labour government which viewed the policies as a temporary interruption to capital expenditure to meet pressing economic needs (specifically, the cutbacks were pursued in return for a loan from the International Monetary Fund in 1976). Since 1979, however, public expenditure cuts have become part of the economic and ideological package implemented by a Conservative government whose aim is to stimulate market processes by reducing public spending and using savings to reduce taxation. The aim has been to promote the individual and collective benefits – symbolic as well as financial – of privatisation. It is important to stress that the shift that this entails is as much a product of political ideology as it is a reflection of socio-economic change. As Johnson (1986) shows, it is not arguments against the welfare state that are new in the 1980s, but rather their acceptance and popularisation by the government.

Currently, the government's attempts to reduce public spending are justified by the belief that the market can more effectively meet the many basic needs which, during the 1960s and early 1970s, had tended to be catered for by the state. This epitomises a more general crisis of confidence in social policy following claims that it has failed to reduce inequality or poverty, has been unable to promote social stability or economic efficiency, and rarely affords individuals greater freedom (see Le Grand, 1982). Such reasoning (often inadvertently) added grist to the mill of the new right by apparently substantiating the view that state intervention generally fails to meet its aims and frequently has undesirable, unanticipated effects. Whatever the rationale, it is generally agreed that from a post-war peak in public spending during 1975 (achieved after a steady climb over the last two decades), expenditure declined towards the early 1980s, so that the present decade has marked a period of unprecedented budgetary restraint (at a time, ironically, when increases in unemployment and homelessness are creating equally unprecedented demands on the welfare services). Though this has often been interpreted as a sign of the wholesale dismantling of the welfare state, so far it is primarily in relation to housing that there has been a retreat from direct provision in kind; consequently, it is in examining changes in the housing 'service' that the effects of changing trends in public expenditure might be best appreciated.

In fact, despite political rhetoric to the contrary (from both the left and the right), the period 1979–82 saw an annual increase in public expenditure (rising from 39.5 per cent to 43.5 per cent of GDP, according to Robinson, 1986); since 1982, any overall fall has been slight (see also O'Higgins, 1985). Berthoud (1985) shows that whereas public expenditure on the social services (at 1983 prices) rose from £11.7 billion to £36.9 billion in the two decades up to 1975, the fall between 1975 and 1983 in real terms was less than £2 billion. Notwithstanding the ideological aspirations of the Conservative government, therefore, a number of authors now recognise that the most appropriate focus of interest is not the destruction of the welfare state but its reorientation. Likewise, in the 1980s, it may be important to stress not discontinuity with the past (though in some ways discontinuity is a relevant theme, for example concerning the symbolic consequences of shifting direct subsidy away from local authority housing), but a continuity of processes whose culmination is now being reached (Robinson, 1986; Taylor-Gooby, 1985).

The aggregate figures cited above, however, do disguise some important changes in the balance of the public spending on different areas of social policy, and it is in this reorientation that direct expenditure on housing has diminished. Berthoud (1985, p. 86) thus points out that the cut in the social services budget between 1975 and 1983 (during which time it fell from 14 per cent to 11.7 per cent of GDP) was possible 'almost entirely because government (net) funding of housing programmes has dwindled so rapidly'. Thus, as Table 2.2 shows, total government spending on housing fell in real terms by 57 per cent between 1978–79 and 1986–87. As a consequence, the proportion of all public spending in the UK that was devoted to housing fell from 8.0 to 4.1 per cent over the same period (HMSO, 1988). This fall reflected a transfer rather than net decline in spending, since it does not take into account public spending on housing incorporated, for instance, in the social security programme (notably, rent rebates and allowances); it does not consider the scale

Table 2.2   *Index of public expenditure on housing in real terms (1978–79 = 100)*

	1979–80	*1986–87*
Housing	100	43
Total public expenditure	100	109

Source: *Hansard*, 18 March 1988.

of 'tax expenditures' to owners (primarily tax relief on mortgage interest, and exemption from capital gains tax for those selling their private houses); it does not include the cost of rate rebates; nor does it measure the public sector costs of discounts given on council house sales (see Chapter 4). However, the reduced spending on public housing does represent a real cut in the welfare budget, and so contributes to a wider trend in which social policy is becoming subservient to economic management (Walker, 1982a).

Housing is the one area of the welfare state in which the Conservative governments since 1979 have been able to make substantial cutbacks in the public sector. The reductions in capital spending on housing imposed by the government on local authorities have cut council house-building completions to their lowest peace-time level since the early 1920s. In addition, there has been a significant reduction in the number of dwellings owned by local authorities. The Housing Act 1980 introduced a range of schemes aimed at promoting low-cost home ownership (Booth and Crook, 1986). The most important of these was the 'right to buy' for council tenants, which allows sitting tenants to purchase their home at very substantial discounts. Since 1979, over one million council houses have been sold, two-thirds of them under the right to buy. As a result, the share of the total stock owned by local councils has fallen for the first time since they became firmly established as landlords after the First World War (see Table 2.3).

The sale of council houses is only one of a series of measures implemented in the name of economic efficiency; these also include the determination of national targets for rent increases and a progressive withdrawal of central government subsidy to local authorities (see Whitehead, 1984). The trend towards subsidised privatisation is thus one which has progressively undermined the traditional flexibility and autonomy of local authorities in the management of a significant portion of the total housing stock. The trend towards centralisation, and the bypassing of local democracy, is also occurring within the remaining public sector, most notably through the promotion of the Housing Corporation (whose proportion of net public sector capital spending on housing rose from 15 per cent in 1979–80 to 46 per cent in 1985–86) at the expense of local authorities.

The restructuring of the housing system has gathered new momentum with the re-election of the Conservatives in 1987 for a

Table 2.3 *Local authority housing in England and Wales, 1976–86*

Year	New build	Sales	Total stock 000s	%
1976	112,028	5,313	5,285	29
1977	108,483	13,020	5,398	29
1978	87,799	30,045	5,463	29
1979	69,734	41,740	5,459	29
1980	70,824	81,480	5,477	29
1981	49,407	102,730	5,410	28
1982	30,176	202,050	5,230	27
1983	29,923	141,460	5,108	26
1984	29,185	103,180	5,021	26
1985	23,478	93,145	4,943	25
1986	16,089	89,890	4,867	24

Source: Department of the Environment, *Housing and Construction Statistics 1976–86*, HMSO, 1987.

third term of office. Privatisation of rented housing provision has been placed at the centre of policy and was the focus of the Housing Act 1988. A key objective is to reduce the role of local authorities as landlords and to introduce other forms of provision, including housing associations, private investors and co-operatives.

In the privately rented sector, all future lettings have been decontrolled, whereas previously they were (in theory rather more than in practice) regulated tenancies which gave the tenant strong security of tenure and the right to have a 'fair rent' registered with the Rent Officer service. The Housing Act 1980 had already deregulated newly built properties let by approved landlords, and the Housing and Planning Act 1986 had extended this to include refurbished properties. Yet this had little effect on the supply of privately rented housing, which continued to decline (Kemp, 1988). But the extension of deregulation to include all newly granted lettings represents a significant increase in the scale of decontrol. The revival of private renting is also to be encouraged by the extension of the Business Expansion Scheme to property companies letting assured tenancies, and also by the power given to local authorities by the Local Government Act 1988 to provide financial assistance to private landlords. Thus, encouraging the market provision of rented housing will require considerable state subsidy.

Future lettings by housing associations have also been deregulated and are to be made on the same basis as those granted by private landlords. Previously, housing association lettings had fair rents determined by the Rent Officer. This deregulation of new housing associations lettings has been necessary because of the two other changes that the government wished to make for housing associations, but it also has a symbolic significance for a government committed so strongly to the market model. These two other changes are a significant reduction in Housing Association Grant and the use of private sector finance (as opposed to borrowing via the Housing Corporation) for that part of capital costs not met by HAG (see Chapter 4).

These changes to the way housing associations are financed (including the way that their rents are set) are of the utmost significance for the future role and nature of the housing association sector. They will involve significantly higher rents than those they previously charged. This will mean that, for the first time since 1974 (when HAG was introduced and the movement began to expand), housing associations will have to consider the rent-paying ability of prospective tenants before they decide to whom to grant a tenancy. This ability-to-pay scrutiny will be made all the more necessary by a further, and more significant, consequence of the changed system of housing association finance. For one result of using private finance to fund their development programmes is that it is the associations themselves rather than, as in the past, the government, who will bear the risk. Thus in future any overruns in development costs, or increases in outgoings as a result of, say, higher interest payments, will have to be met by raising rents rather than through higher grant. Housing associations, therefore, will be more subject (to use the government's phrase) to the 'disciplines of the market', and this is bound to influence their orientation and action, however much they may regret the fact. Despite their non-profit status, housing associations who use private finance to fund a significant proportion of their development programme will have to act more like commercial organisations; those who do not will either cease to grow or risk becoming insolvent.

The Housing Act 1988 gave council tenants the right to opt for an alternative (non-council) landlord. This new policy instrument might be more accurately described as the right of prospective landlords to bid for the ownership of council properties. Council tenants who have secure tenancies under the Housing Act 1980 will have the right to opt out of proposed transfers of ownership to another landlord. This new policy is called 'tenant's choice' by the government. Landlords who have been approved by the Housing Corporation have the right to make a bid for council houses, whether tenanted or not, the price of sale being the market value of the properties, subject to tenancy. In order for the transaction not to go ahead, at least 50 per cent of the tenants eligible to vote must vote against the proposal in a ballot. If the transfer is not rejected in this way, those tenants who voted against it remain with the council, but all those who either voted yes or did not vote are transferred to the new landlord. Where transfers go ahead, in the case of flats the freehold of the entire block goes to the new landlord and the flats of tenants who voted 'no' in the ballot are leased back to the council at the market rent for the duration of the occupant's tenancy.

In combination, the setting up of HATs and of Scottish Homes, along with the 'tenant's choice' scheme, could pave the way for a major denudation of the municipal housing stock. The likely scale and pace of change is unknown at present. Although the government would no doubt prefer to see transfers made to the commercial private landlord, the prospects for this do not seem great. Most properties which are transferred will probably go to housing associations, though it seems unlikely that they could swallow up much of the council sector within the next decade: there are currently 4.8 million council dwellings and only 0.5 million housing association dwellings. However, a number of local authorities are in the process of setting up new housing associations to take over their entire stock, or are considering selling it to an alternative landlord, thereby transferring (at least in the case of smaller councils) the properties from one monopoly landlord to another. If there is to be a large-scale demunicipalisation of rented housing, it may be through this route rather than any other.

If tenant's choice transfers take place on a large scale, it is possible that local authorities will be left owning a residual rump of unattractive and unsellable housing in urban areas, accommodating the very disadvantaged and the homeless. Alternatively, few council tenants are likely to opt for an uncertain future with a landlord offering them the prospect of reduced security of tenure and higher rents. At any rate, the government has argued that its new policies will increase competition, reduce local authority monopoly ownership of rented housing, increase choice for tenants, and ensure increased efficiency in the housing market. Even where tenants opt to remain with their council, the very fact that they have the 'choice' to transfer, it is argued, will mean that they should get a better service than would otherwise be provided. This is believed to be necessary because, it is claimed, local authorities are inefficient, insensitive, bureaucratic organisations which have taken control over people's lives and failed to respond to their wishes and aspirations (Patten, 1987; Ridley, 1987). In other words, much of the justification for the radical policies that have now been set in train is presented in terms of the failure of local authorities as housing managers. But the more fundamental basis of the new approach is an explicit critique of the social democratic model and a belief in the virtues of the market.

The advantages to the public of a shift from collective provision in kind to state-subsidised market provision are presented by the government as a boost to consumer choice, as enhanced motivation to maintain properties and residential environments, and as a widening of opportunities for households to use their homes to store wealth. The ideological justification for recent policies is derived from the neo-liberal assumption that individuals (families or households) have equal opportunity to compete in the market, and that an unregulated market will not allow excessive inequality of outcome. The political achievement of the extension of owner-occupation is social stability in the workplace (since secure, regular incomes are a prerequisite of mortgage repayment) and a reduction in politically embarrassing pressure from Labour-controlled local authorities. The validity of this reasoning, the justification for achievements, and the viability of the market model are issues to which we return throughout the book.

Conclusion

This chapter has explored the roles of housing as social policy in the context of its other roles in an advanced capitalist democracy. In doing so we explored some tensions between the market and social democratic models of welfare provision. We first considered the social concerns embedded in the earliest and most traditional role of housing policy as a strategy for environmental improvement, suggesting that although improvements to the stock may be important for public health, policy-makers have not adequately conceptualised (or, *a fortiori,* dealt with) the link they tacitly recognise between the physical environment and the incidence of social malaise.

We then presented an overview of the development of housing as a social right, showing how the notion of public housing for general needs has been increasingly eclipsed by the view that only 'special' needs should require the direct attention of the state. The definition of these special needs is based on the narrow conception of what constitutes housing disadvantage, limiting it to those whose illness or frailty prevents them generating sufficient income to compete in the private market.

Finally, we considered the role of housing in economic management, in the context of a crisis of confidence in the welfare state. We saw that an attempt has been made, most successfully in the case of housing, to reduce public expenditure as a tool of macroeconomic policy. We also stressed that the restructuring of welfare was a political project aimed at reducing state responsibilities in welfare and promoting the private provision of social policy. Although couched in the language of choice and reduced 'dependency' upon the state, fostering private housing provision has involved very substantial subsidies, not all of which (for example, mortgage interest relief) count as public expenditure as it is defined by the Treasury. Private provision can really only be extended in housing (without drastically reducing standards) by underwriting the market with extensive financial assistance. Thus it is not so much 'dependency' that is being reduced, but dependency on *public* provision in kind.

This shift towards a subsidised market approach to housing has involved a marked centralisation in the control and implementation of housing policy. This centralisation has been necessary to encourage and coerce individuals and organisations in the housing system to engage the market model. It has also moved housing policy and provision closer to the corporate sphere of influence. Thus not only has the shift towards the market involved an erosion of citizenship rights and statutory provision; it has also impaired its sensitivity to local democratic pressures and responsibility. As in many other spheres of civil society, the 'free market and the strong state' (Gamble, 1983) have been important features of housing policy in the 1980s.

3
Housing Disadvantage

While most of this book is devoted to a critique of the efficiency of housing policy as a vehicle for achieving some traditional aims of social policy, this chapter centres on perhaps the most contentious of these aims, the alleviation of social disadvantage. We argue that patterns of inequality are much more entrenched than is traditionally allowed for in the market model of provision, and we examine the extent to which housing mediates, sustains or ameliorates some wider aspects of deprivation.

The notion of disadvantage is central to many areas of social science, and it is fundamental to any critique of social policy. The meaning of the term, however, is frequently taken for granted, and it is widely treated as an explanatory device rather than as a condition which itself requires explanation. Partly reflecting this wide and indiscriminate use, there is little consensus concerning what disadvantage refers to. It is rarely distinguished from related terms such as deprivation, poverty and inequality, and a great deal of intellectual energy has been expended on terminological debate (some of which makes little progress in identifying the substance of disadvantage as experienced by the public).

This chapter sets out a working definition of disadvantage, and explains why it is a central concept in social policy. The discussion goes on to show how various forms of disadvantage are mediated by the housing system. We argue that although housing policy and practice can confer disadvantage, the housing system also offers opportunities to intervene to alleviate disadvantage. These opportunities may be exploited both through a greater emphasis on housing as social policy and by more concerted integration between housing and other welfare services.

Disadvantage, deprivation and inequality

A review of the literature identifies two broad definitions of disadvantage, and we suggest that these may be aligned with the market and social democratic models of social policy identified in Chapter 2. The two views are set out below.

Advocates of the market model tend to argue that disadvantage can be measured on an absolute scale. There is, from this perspective, a minimum set of requirements for physical subsistence, health and welfare. Individuals' progress above this minimum is viewed largely as the product of hard work and initiative, while continuing deprivation is depicted as the consequences of individual failure or entrapment in a collective 'culture of poverty'. There is an assumption here that disadvantage is synonymous with poverty, and that it results simply from inability or disinclination to compete vigorously in the economy. The policy 'solution' therefore aims only to raise the most destitute above a supposedly objective poverty line – the level of subsistence – and to increase their incentive to participate in the economy. Inequality is regarded as part of this package of incentives and is therefore seen less as a problem than as an inducement for individuals to work harder to improve their own circumstances.

Despite the popular appeal of this line of reasoning, its definition of the nature and origins of disadvantage are of questionable validity. Absolute need is not a useful concept, since it inevitably diverts attention away from political or economic power-broking, and towards the physical and biological conditions needed for survival. This ignores the extent to which even subsistence conditions are socially defined, and it can fail to acknowledge that minimum needs relate not only to the physical necessities of life, but also to social needs such as the capacity to meet obligations as producers, citizens, members of families, and so on.

An alternative view, while recognising the authenticity of individual and cultural variety in society, rejects both these factors as a route to explaining how disadvantage arises and why it is sustained. This social democratic approach depicts disadvantage as something apart from the social and demographic attributes of those individuals and groups it affects, rooting it instead in the organisation of economic and political processes. From this perspective, disadvantage is a relative rather than absolute condition, defined according to the experience and expectations of particular societies. From this perspective, personal attributes related to income, culture, sex and age cannot themselves be viewed as disadvantageous, even though, as we shall see, disadvantage may be apportioned according to these criteria, shaping social structure along the lines of class, 'race', gender, and so on.

This alternative to the market model, based on a broader conception of what is required for full participation in society, draws on a useful conceptual distinction made by Veit-Wilson (1986). He contrasts deprivation which is related to, or caused by, a lack of control over resources of all kinds, with poverty, which refers more specifically to a lack of financial resources. Similarly, Townsend (1987a, 1987b) recognises that deprivation, or life with inadequate material and social benefits (and, therefore, with an impaired ability to participate fully in society), is different from – if related to – poverty. Poverty here refers to the inability to exchange wealth to gain access to the benefits required to prevent deprivation. This distinction is important for social policy, since it implies that affluence in the market place is not necessarily the key to alleviating deprivation, even though it is undoubtedly helpful; it also suggests that strategies other than income redistribution – whether this is seen as a market or state-induced practice – may be necessary to provide individuals, households and social groups with a fair or adequate share of the opportunities and life chances available in advanced capitalist economies. From this perspective, disadvantage may therefore be conceptualised in terms of the varying combinations of deprivation and poverty that individuals experience. These conditions are related, but are not always reducible one to the other.

This second view of disadvantage, as a process impairing the ability of individuals and groups to exercise their rights as citizens, is used throughout the book. There are, however, some definitional and empirical problems which remain to be acknowledged.

At its narrowest, the multi-faceted nature of disadvantage can and must be tapped with recourse to statistical indicators. While such empirical documentation is important, its predominance has two unfortunate consequences. First, because of demand for efficiency, effectiveness and performance monitoring, the policy-relevant aspects of disadvantage have sometimes (though erroneously) been regarded as inherent in the characteristics of the individuals that most often experience it: black people, lone parents, older people, people with learning difficulties, the physically disabled, and so on.

This is because the characteristics of disadvantaged groups are often easier to measure than are the separate elements of the disadvantage they experience. It is, moreover, easier (and less politically controversial) to target policy towards special groups or areas than to restructure mainstream legislation to deal with the spectrum of processes conferring disadvantage.

Even though the use of statistical measures has to be accepted as a rough guide for policy implementation, at least in the first instance, there is a danger that, in the name of pragmatism or political expediency, measurable indicators will themselves be regarded either as the totality of disadvantage in society or as a balanced indicator of that totality. Certainly, much policy debate has relied on a relatively restricted range of census variables, including the prominence in small geographical areas of unemployment, overcrowding, lone parenthood, lack of housing amenities, population decline, single pensioners, high mortality, and concentration of 'ethnic minorities'. Most analysts acknowledge that these indices of disadvantage combine differently in different areas (see Sim, 1984; McDowell, 1979) and admit that the common practice of collapsing various indicators into a composite measure of disadvantage can conceal the true nature of the problem. Yet, although it is obvious that this mix of variables conflates the incidence and effects of deprivation, failing to distinguish the nature of disadvantage from the identity of those experiencing it, such measures continue to provide the guidelines for much urban social, economic and housing policy.

At the other end of the spectrum, divorced from the constraints imposed by the availability of statistical indicators, disadvantage may be more broadly conceptualised but less easily illustrated. Nevertheless, Townsend (1987b) shows how an overemphasis in the statistical literature on the material aspects of disadvantage neglects some less tangible but equally debilitating components, such as those related to a sense of isolation, fear and discrimination. Goodin (1986) takes this a step further, redefining disadvantage in terms of vulnerability and arguing that individual and collective obligations arise from the wide range of ways in which some sections of society are vulnerable to the actions of others. Because this is a textbook, synthesising existing knowledge rather than developing new methods, we too are often limited to statistical aggregations and surrogate indicators in our analyses of inequality. Nevertheless, we aim, wherever possible, to give a flavour of the lived, as well as measured, reality of disadvantage.

To summarise, in setting out a framework for understanding disadvantage, we have had to take sides in a debate in the literature concerning whether disadvantage should be seen as a condition of 'absolute' material and social need, or defined relative to some common norm or minimum acceptable standard for a given society. We prefer the latter view, which portrays disadvantage as a process rather than a pattern, as politically and economically inspired rather than as a product of individual or group behaviour, and as a consequence of the differential apportionment of a range of citizenship rights rather than as an outcome of individuals' failure to compete in the economy. We now move on to consider this in relation to the operation of the housing system and its links with social policy and welfare provision.

Disadvantage in housing

Within the constraints of available data, patterns of material disadvantage in housing are relatively well documented. There is now a fairly good picture in Britain of who is disadvantaged by the quality and repair of their dwelling, by the property rights associated with their tenure, or by where they live in relation to services, jobs and other resources, including social and leisure time opportunities. Murie's (1983, chapter 4) discussion of variations in housing circumstances, and Kirby's (1979) and Curtis's (1989) outline of the geography of housing in relation to that of other welfare services illustrate well the existence and extent of systematic inequalities in the housing system. Some of these patterns are examined in more detail below. What is most obvious from these accounts is that such inequalities are *structured:* some groups are consistently more likely than others to be in the worst parts of the stock, and in the worst (oldest, most run-down, least convenient and most poorly serviced) locations.

By simply asking who is disadvantaged in housing we are, nevertheless, limited to a descriptive account of the incidence of disadvantage at a particular time. While recognising the importance of collating such information, in order to press our view of disadvantage as part of a process that is also concerned with how relative advantage is apportioned, we must additionally address the question of whether systems of housing provision actively exacerbate, or could be organised to ameliorate, wider patterns of inequality.

In adopting this approach, we acknowledge that disadvantage is sustained widely within advanced capitalist democracies – through the education system, in the labour market, and by a range of social services in addition to housing. Housing is just one of a variety of markets and institutions that mediate social inequality: it is just one of the mechanisms whereby disadvantage is structured, both socially and spatially. Therefore, it is through the operation of a broad range of social, economic and political processes, as well as by households' possession of social, demographic and physical attributes with a more direct bearing on housing availability, that households become disadvantaged in terms of what the housing system provides and how it operates. However, if the distribution of housing quality and amenity cannot be adjusted to accommodate these two facets of social need – relating respectively to the 'structural' and demographic attributes of households and individuals – then the housing system may be implicated in the creation and reinforcement of disadvantage. This may seem obvious, but while it is now common to recognise that housing systems generally, and patterns of residential segregation in particular, reflect the social structure, it is less common to regard housing as a factor actively shaping inequality and structuring disadvantage. Yet the quality and condition of housing is spatially and economically ordered, and housing circumstances express and determine access not only to shelter, but also to a variety of other services such as recreation, education and health care (see Pahl, 1975). Because of this, housing may be a particularly potent element in the structuring of disadvantage.

In illustrating this, we regard measures of disadvantage as one of several normative criteria by which the achievements and shortcomings of housing as social policy can be gauged. Because the static measures of disadvantage on which we rely represent just one point in a dynamic process, our interest is not only in current housing circumstances, but also in housing paths or 'careers'. Our discussion therefore focuses on a range of factors associated with the production, allocation, exchange and consumption of housing – factors which Ball (1983) has referred to as structures of housing provision. In particular, we focus on those which (a) give rise to the qualitative variability of the housing stock, and (b) underlie the differential occupation and use of this stock, structured along the lines of class, gender, 'race' and a range of special needs. Our aim, then, is to examine the extent to which the housing system confers as well as expresses disadvantage, and to draw from this some observations about the significance of housing policy as a point of intervention in the process of disadvantage.

We begin with a discussion of housing production, since the organisation of production is what most fundamentally determines why housing in Britain (by virtue of its quantity, quality, diversity and differential availability) is significant to the analysis of inequality. We then examine patterns of housing consumption, exposing their alignment with three key axes of social inequality, relating to income or wealth, gender and 'race', which recur throughout the thematic chapters which follow.

Housing production and the bases of inequality

While much of the literature correctly identifies housing problems in terms of the public's differential access to properties of varying quality, character and location (that is, as a consumption or distributional issue), it is important to recognise that housing consumption cannot be viewed in isolation from the wider structures of production, finance and exchange within which it is located (Ball, 1978, 1983). Because the determinants of housing supply – the availability of land, labour, materials and incentives – vary in time and space, the production of housing is not a matter of steady replacement and addition to stock in accordance with demographic shifts. It is rather a question of potential profitability which is related to the cyclical booms and slumps of the economy, albeit (especially with respect to public housing) mediated by political concerns. The precise implications of this for the type, quality and quantity of housing available have varied considerably over time, reflecting, among other things, the fact that governments have played a more active role in influencing the production of housing than that of many other consumer goods. Nevertheless, the costs and profitability of production crucially affect all other aspects of housing provision, since, as Duncan (1986, p. 15) observes, 'no amount of enlightened distribution policy can have much effect if the housing is not built'.

A number of authors identify a 'crisis' in housing production in Britain, stemming from at least the early 1970s (see Balchin, 1985; Ball, 1983; Dickens *et al.*, 1985). The house-building industry experienced great instability during the 1960s, and has never really recovered from the effects of a slump in the early 1970s. Between 1972 and 1982, despite increases in the number of households requiring dwellings, total housing starts fell by 45 per cent. Between 1980 and 1984, annual completion rates averaged only 200,000 – 100,000 below the figure which the 1977 housing policy Green Paper estimated would be required to keep pace with the 'baby boom', to replace unfit stock, and to allow adequate scope for residential mobility (DoE, 1977).

Whether or not there really is a crisis in housing production, the way in which the building industry is organised has had various deleterious consequences. First, the majority of householders still rely on stock erected during the house-building booms of the late nineteenth century and the interwar years: almost 30 per cent of the total housing stock dates from before 1919. The problems of modernisation and repairs which this implies do not look set to change in the near future. Malpass (1986b) quotes an estimate that, at the present replacement rate, a house built in 1985 would have to last over 900 years! Moreover, Duncan (1986) shows that modernisation is not keeping pace with ageing. Between 1971 and 1981, the number of dwellings in England in 'serious disrepair' increased by 21 per cent to over 1 million. In the same period, the number of generally 'unsatisfactory dwellings' also increased by as much as 12 per cent to over 18 million homes (DoE, 1982). The 1986 English House Condition Survey showed as much as a quarter of the stock to be defective in some way, and Niner (1989) estimates that there are now 1.5 million homes unfit for habitation or lacking basic amenities. Since housing expenditure increased as a proportion of households' budgets over the same period, this has had severe implications for the effective availability of better quality properties to lower-income groups.

Government strategies have crucially affected the efficiency and effectiveness of the house construction industry, not only through the distribution of supports and subsidies, but also by influencing demand. An interesting example of the effects of subsidies can be seen in the way in which high-rise developments dominated public sector housing production in the 1960s. This was not a consequence of the inherent profitability of flatted estates, nor of local authorities' assessments of the suitability of this kind of building in relation to local housing needs. It was, rather, a trend related to the speed at which high-rise structures could be erected. In an attempt to reduce the housing shortage as quickly as possible, central government subsidies to local authorities favoured high-rise production (Duncan, 1986; Dunleavy, 1981).

The sphere of production is, moreover, a domain in which corporate interests, especially since the mid 1970s, have exerted more influence on government decision-making than have the pluralist bargaining procedures traditionally associated with the democratic ideal. This was most noticeable in the market slump that followed the house-price boom of the early 1970s. This moment of fiscal panic set off a string of takeovers and mergers that was to transform the British house-building industry from an unorganised and technologically backward group of small enterprises to a sector dominated by large firms and corporations (Ball, 1983). By the late 1970s, these large companies were exerting considerable pressure on the government to stimulate demand. The response came in the form of subsidies to building societies to increase mortgage availability and extra allocations to local authorities for new house-building. Crucially, though, this means that state housing policy cannot be seen as a direct response to consumption needs. Rather, changes in housing provision are driven by powerful forces in the private production market.

Consolidation in the building industry had at least two notable effects on the quality and quantity of housing produced. In catering to the public sector, attempts to maximise profits while seeking to undercut local authorities' Direct Labour Organisations led to accusations of 'skimped work, poor safety standards, atrocious working conditions, wage cutting, delays and structural defects in buildings' (Balchin, 1985, p. 48). In catering to the private sector, on the other hand, the large corporations were able to bear the capital outlays required to support the introduction of new technology, such as that promoting timber-framed building. This method of construction accelerates cash flow, cuts down on the need for skilled on-site labour, and allows the construction industry the flexibility to follow and 'create' demand where profitability is greatest. The consequence, which also reflects government restrictions on capital expenditure by local authorities, is a shift in the pattern of housing investment 'away from those areas which rank on General Needs

Indicators as being in housing need, in favour of areas where the ability to generate capital receipts is greater' (Lawless, 1986, p. 72).

In short, with the increasing dominance and power of the large corporations, housing costs to the consumer have increased, while the standard of dwellings is falling in both the public and private sectors. Housing therefore remains a scarce resource of uneven quality which, whether it is apportioned according to need or ability to pay, will confer more direct and indirect benefits to some individuals than to others. While recognising that problems relating to housing production lie at the core of any analysis of housing disadvantage, we now turn to consider how the consumption of the housing stock – its use, distribution, allocation, exchange and maintenance – influences who gets what and where in the housing system.

Housing consumption and the dimensions of disadvantage

Housing consumption refers to the processes by which dwellings are occupied and used. It is, according to Dickens *et al.* (1985, p. 193) 'an essential component in social reproduction and the reproduction of labour power in advanced capitalist countries'. It is the arena in which systematic inequalities in the social structure are mapped on to systematic differences in the housing stock; and it is a medium through which qualitative variations in the housing stock themselves accentuate and sustain different forms of social differentiation. This occurs in a number of ways, relating to the rules and procedures routinely administered by public bureaucracies, to the market-related criteria invoked in the apportionment of housing finance, and to the broad shifts of power, resources and influence between different tenure sectors that are determined by central government, either directly through housing policy or indirectly through broader strategies for managing the economy.

Rather than provide a comprehensive outline of these processes or an exhaustive list of case studies, we shall illustrate the general principles involved using three examples. The ways in which social marginality is expressed in, and conferred by, the structures of housing provision are perhaps most readily appreciated in our first example. This examines the 'residualisation' of the public sector, and illustrates the role of housing in mediating some disadvantages associated with low incomes and little wealth. Equally significant, but, less immediately obvious (because so much housing research concentrates on households rather than on the individuals comprising them) is our second example concerning the extent to which housing may contribute to the reproduction of gender inequalities. Finally, we consider how the differential allocation of housing has helped sustain racism, so contributing to the disadvantage experienced by black people in post-war Britain.

'Privatisation', residualisation and social disadvantage

We have already shown how, throughout the 1980s, a reduction in public expenditure on housing has been justified in explicitly ideological terms. During the present decade, the government in Britain has worked with the assumption that the market can house the majority of the population more adequately and efficiently than the state. In terms of the models introduced in Chapter 2, this represents part of the shift in housing provision away from social democratic concerns about the right to accommodation as shelter and towards a market model which emphasises the right to use property to store and accumulate wealth. In documenting an associated trend towards the extension of owner-occupation as far down-market as possible, housing analysts have begun to draw attention to the social cleavages that derive from differential access to public and private 'modes' of housing consumption (Forrest and Murie, 1986; Saunders, 1984, 1986b). In this example, therefore, we show how broad trends in housing policy give stark expression to wider patterns of social inequality, as tenure differences become increasingly aligned with the differential distribution of wealth, resources and life chances in British society.

Increasingly, the shift of effective public subsidy from council housing provision to tax relief on mortgage interest, and to tax exemption from capital gains on owner-occupied dwellings, is being linked with the physical and socio-economic residualisation of the local authority sector. This is intensifying the social and spatial divide between owners and council tenants in ways formalised by Forrest and Murie (1988, pp. 194–9). Residualisation has been identified as a process whereby public housing 'provides only a "safety net" for those who for reasons of poverty, age or infirmity cannot obtain suitable accommodation in the private sector' (Malpass and Murie, 1982, p. 174). Among other things, this 'involves lowering the status and increasing the stigma attached to public housing' (p. 174). This has occurred alongside an absolute and relative decline in the size of local authorities' housing stocks, caused by a combination of council house sales and low levels of new building. The differential pattern of sales leads Malpass and Murie (1987) to argue that while the extension of home ownership through council house sales has meant that the opportunities for those who can buy have increased, those who must rent are forced to compete for a limited range of inferior and unpopular properties, an increasing proportion of which are flats.

According to Forrest and Murie (1986, 1987), these quantitative, qualitative and socio-economic changes in council housing have produced, in the 1980s, an unprecedented concentration in the public sector of benefit- and service-dependent populations. The tenant population is therefore becoming less mixed in terms of age, income, employment status and social class. This trend is documented by Bentham (1986), who shows that the income distribution of owners and council renters has steadily diverged since the mid 1970s to the extent that, in the period examined (1953 to 1983), renters' median incomes fell from 75 per cent to 45 per cent of those of owners. Table 3.1 illustrates the disproportionate reliance of low-income families on public renting, especially where the head of household is economically inactive. For instance, whereas 29 per

Table 3.1　*Proportion of households in the public rented sector[1]*

Income (£) per week (gross in 1985)	%
Head of household economically active	
less than £100	40
£100, less than £150	29
£150, less than £200	25
over £300	8
Head of household economically inactive	
Less than £50	60
£50, less than £100	48
£100, less than £150	36
£150 and above	24
All households	29

Source: Central Statistical Office (1988). Data for this and subsequent tables in this chapter from government publication are reproduced with the permission of the Controller of Her Majesty's Stationery Office.
1. The table refers to those with local authority or new town, but not Housing Association, tenancies.

cent of the sample as a whole were tenants, this rose to 60 per cent among those whose head of household was economically inactive and where household income was less than £50 per week. The 1985 General Household Survey (GHS) further showed that, in addition to a concentration of the unemployed, there was an over-representation of semi- and unskilled manual workers in the public sector (41 per cent and 48 per cent respectively), and a marked under-representation of non-manual employees.

The implications of the shifting socio-economic composition of the major tenure sectors are far-reaching. It does not simply mean that the poorest, most disadvantaged sections of the population are concentrated within the worst segments of the housing stock. It also means that, as a group, tenants have few financial and, often, political resources to change their circumstances. Forrest and Murie (1983) therefore argue that the 'critical context for discussion of residualisation involves issues of economic, political and social power' (p. 461). To an extent, therefore, the continuing physical 'residualisation' of council housing might partly reflect the power-lessness of tenants to resist reductions in standards. It reflects, too, the impotence of service consumers who are excluded from corporate bargaining procedures, and who have limited scope to exercise that increasingly powerful second alternative to representative democracy – purchasing power. Tenants, then, have so far been unable to resist a process through which the public housing service has come to offer a much more limited range of choice than the owner-occupied sector. They are left, indeed, with a service which sometimes lacks the flexibility even to provide a reasonable response to housing need. It is at this point that we might begin to regard continuing tenancy within the public sector not simply as a passive expression of economic marginality and welfare eligibility, but also as a constraint, actively impairing households' prospects for improving their position in the economy and the status order.

Currently, public tenants may be seen to be disadvantaged because they are public tenants in a polarising housing system in two main, but interlinked ways. The first relates to economic and spatial aspects of the process of 'commodification' itself, and the second relates to the spatial restructuring of the economy and of the welfare state more generally. We consider these in turn.

A number of studies now indicate that better quality council housing has historically been allocated to higher- rather than lower-income renters (see, for example, Clapham and Kintrea, 1986; Twine and Williams, 1983; Williams *et al.,* 1986). In recent years, however, this patterning has meant that those higher-income tenants who were able to buy their better quality homes, often with substantial discounts, have successfully translated their right to shelter into a capital asset through which they are able to store and accumulate personal wealth. By contrast, poorer tenants often live in properties and in areas (flats rather than houses, inner cities or peripheral estates rather than suburbs) where house purchase, even if possible, would represent a poor capital investment.

Large segments of council housing in some areas is of a kind whose use value is diminished by its poor repair, and whose exchange value, should the tenant wish to purchase, would be depressed by its location and design, and by the costs of maintenance and modernisation. As sales of the better properties continue, however, this unsatisfactory stock may increasingly be all that the remaining council tenants in some larger urban areas have available to them; and it means that even those queuing for a transfer within the public sector have a very limited range of options in qualitative terms. Thus the selectivity of sales is sufficient to diminish many continuing tenants' prospects of moving into more pleasant homes and neighbourhoods. This enforced inertia may itself be enlarging the systematic economic and status differences that divide residents in the owner-occupied market from those in the rented segments of the housing system. It may be creating what Saunders (1986) calls a 'consumption sector cleavage' between state-dependent and market-reliant populations, distinguishing between those who can and cannot use their homes to store and accumulate wealth.

The processes we refer to are spatial as well as economic and social. One of the most striking findings of Forrest and Murie's (1988) study is the pattern of increasing tenure polarisation between and, crucially, within, localities. For many households, therefore, a council tenancy represents not only a disadvantage (compared to ownership) in terms of wealth stored in property, but also a much broader constraint on their access to economic opportunities and social welfare. This is the second way in which housing provision may exacerbate social disadvantage.

Because of its spatial selectivity, the process of residualisation has exacerbated a more general tendency within the public sector towards the concentration of disadvantaged households into areas that are poorly serviced and resourced in a variety of other ways. Loss of the better stock in better locations must accentuate the vicious circle identified by Williams *et al.*, (1986, p. 138), 'in which segregationist tendencies within the allocation system further disadvantage the housing chances of low income tenants'. This disadvantage occurs in terms of access to employment opportunities in a spatially restructuring economy, and in terms of access to services during the restructuring of welfare.

Massey (1984) and Massey and Meegan (1982) have shown that the industrial restructuring that has occurred in the last fifteen years, prompted by the internationalisation of the economy and of the labour force, has been spatially selective in its effects, both regionally and within cities. The process of labour shedding has been concentrated in the semi- and unskilled manual segments of the job market, disproportionately affecting male council tenants, while the newer industries have been located in regions and areas where council housing is in short supply. Therefore, the fact of being a council tenant with limited prospects for residential mobility may inhibit households' job prospects in the labour markets of the present decade. The disadvantageous consequences of this are exacerbated by the differential distribution over space of a range of services and resources.

Many large, peripheral council housing schemes contain few, if any, basic shopping facilities, and tenants are often obliged to pay high prices for inferior goods or to travel long distances, often by public transport, to secure general food and consumer goods (this is well illustrated by Hallsworth *et al.*, 1986). Few banks have proved willing to open branches in such areas, and the role of exploitative money-lenders is only gradually beginning to be challenged by the development of credit unions. The same kinds of areas may experience high rates of illness, but are least well catered for by the health service (see Byrne *et al.*, 1986). They also experience some of the highest crime rates, and suffer from the more debilitating consequences of fear of crime (see Smith, 1989b). Yet policing is often aggressive, and neither neighbourhood watch nor victim support schemes have proved successful in many of the large public estates (Smith, 1989c). Finally, tenants suffer from a more general tendency for children from poorer areas to attend schools with below average facilities and less well qualified teachers (Kirby, 1979; Tunley *et al.*, 1979). Since residents of such areas are least likely to

have the economic means to buy privatised welfare, and since the
poorer public estates are least conducive to attracting the investment
required to achieve the mix of public and private services that is
currently politically popular, the restructuring of the welfare state
seems set to exacerbate rather than offset disadvantages associated
with the restructuring of housing tenure and the restructuring of the
economy, with which it has gone hand in hand.

The 'gender relations' of housing consumption

A second illustration of how the different sectors of the housing
system interact to reproduce systematic social inequalities can be
appreciated through the example of gender and housing. Again we
suggest that, while gender differences in housing experiences reflect
similar differences in society as a whole (and especially in the labour
market), the operation of the housing system also has an active role
in sustaining this process and, therefore, in exacerbating gender
inequalities.

Comparisons of men's and women's housing circumstances are
not well documented in modern Britain. This reflects a number of
omissions in housing studies. These include: (a) a tendency to focus
on 'conventional' households, comprising a married man and
woman, with or without children, on the assumption that other
households are either transitional towards this form, or residual
from it; (b) little concern for differences in the housing experience of
men and women even within this 'conventional' family form – a
problem exacerbated by the prevalence of cross-sectional analyses
focusing on household types rather than cohort analyses monitoring
patterns of household formation and dissolution; and (c) the limited
use of gender-differentiated data from surveys that could offer
insight into housing type, quality and condition which are more
refined than the standard measures of amenity deficiency and
structural form. The last of these means that much of what we have
to say must be based on the use of tenure as a proxy for housing
attainment (a measure justified to the extent that public renting is
increasingly a 'residual' form of housing provision, but one which
must be qualified by the increased differentiation of the owner-
occupied stock and the problems faced by low-income owners
within this).

Table 3.2 indicates the tenure differences between male and female

Table 3.2 Tenure of household (%) by marital status of household head

Marital status	Owner-Occupier		Renter			Rented with Job	Rented from Housing Association or Co-op
	Outright	Mortgage	Council/New Town	Private unfurnished	Private furnished		
Married	22	50	20	3	1	3	1
Single man	17	33	20	10	13	4	2
Divorced or sep'd man	12	41	28	10	4	3	3
Widower	43	8	37	8	1	1	3
Single woman	25	19	33	10	9	1	4
Divorced or sep'd woman	11	27	48	6	2	1	4
Widow	42	3	43	8	1	0	3

Source: General Household Survey, 1986; OPCS (1989: 57).

householders in 1985. It is clear that, for every family type other than married couples, women are more dependent than men on renting from the local authority. Even among couples who are married or cohabiting, the most recent sweep of the National Child Development Study indicates that, to achieve owner occupation, women are typically more reliant on the income and job security of a partner than are men (Munro and Smith, 1989). Moreover, while divorce or separation can bring housing problems for both partners, the 1981 Labour Force Survey indicates that slightly more men than women are able to sustain ownership in such circumstances (50 per cent and 44 per cent respectively), and that, among those who live with their children, many more mothers (63 per cent) than fathers (50 per cent) live in council housing. The discrepancies are particularly marked for young people emerging from a relationship breakdown: at age 20–29, as many as 42 per cent of men but only 16 per cent of women attain ownership, whereas between 30 and 44 years the figures are 51 per cent and 37 per cent respectively (overall, in all age groups the two proportions are 45 per cent and 34 per cent). Somewhat more information is available concerning the housing circumstances of single people. Table 3.3 shows that for young or middle-aged singles, ownership rates are consistently higher among men than women. It is only in later years that men and women appear equally likely to own (a generalisation particularly notable among widows and widowers, whose ownership rates, irrespective of age, are around 44–5 per cent). By this time, however, a large proportion of owners are older women, often living in the older parts of the housing stock and often experiencing severe difficulties

Table 3.3 *Rates (%) of owner-occupation among single heads of household in 1981*

Age	Men	Women
20–24	21	11
25–29	45	28
30–34	59	43
35–44	54	50
All	42	41

Source: Central Statistical Office (1985).

with maintenance and repair. The Department of the Environment's English House Condition survey of 1981, for instance, indicated that of people aged sixty and over who are living alone (76 per cent of whom are female, according to the General Household Survey of 1985), 16 per cent live in homes in serious disrepair, 25 per cent live in unfit dwellings, and 29 per cent lack a bath (DoE, 1982).

The housing circumstances of lone-parent families have also received some attention since the Finer Report (1974) drew attention to their poor living conditions, lack of amenities, and poor standards of room occupancy when compared with couples with children. The 1981 General Household Survey suggests not only that these difficulties are being sustained, but also that lone mothers have become an increasing proportion of household heads, and an increasing proportion of lone parents. In 1981, single-parent families were disadvantaged relative to other families with dependent children in terms of type of accommodation (they were underrepresented in detached and semi-detached houses), and the amenities available to them.

There is some indication, then, that women's and men's experience of the housing system differ, both within and between household types. Reflecting the relative disadvantage of women in this process, there is now a growing pool of evidence documenting the difficulties that women face in gaining access to owner-occupation (see Schafer and Ladd, 1981; Watson and Helliwell, 1985) and in negotiating complex public housing rules and obstructive bureaucracies (see Brailey, 1986). A variety of research has also been completed which draws attention to the problems faced by women in different kinds of household types, including lone-parent mothers (Leavitt, 1985), some single women (Austerberry and Watson, 1983), homeless women (Gilbert, 1986; Watson and Austerberry, 1986), black women (Omarshah, no date; Greater London Council, 1984), and so on.

Some gender inequalities in housing are a direct reflection of inequalities in the labour market. Table 3.4 shows that even over the last fifteen years, during which the range of women's employment opportunities is generally felt to have widened, male earnings have consistently exceeded those of women, whether for manual or non-manual work. Although the discrepancies diminished between 1970 and 1981, women's incomes appear to have reached a peak at only two-thirds that of men. This obviously diminishes their purchasing power in the housing market. This means that the trend towards greater privatisation of housing, and an emphasis on the market model of provision, both of which allow ability to pay rather need to determine housing outcomes, will affect women more adversely than men.

Similarly, figures issued by the Department of Employment in 1986 show that economic activity rates are consistently lower for women in the civilian labour force than for men. Almost three-quarters of men are active, but barely half the women. The discrepancy holds for all age groups, but peaks among 25–44 year olds (key child-rearing and house purchasing years), at which age 94 per cent of the male labour force is economically active as compared with just 67 per cent of the female workforce. For single women, moreover, the trend is particularly serious, the proportion in work falling from 72 per cent in 1973 to 59 per cent in 1982.

Table 3.4 *Women's wages as a percentage of men's, 1970, 1981 and 1986 (median gross weekly earnings of full-time employees, £)*

	1970	1981	1986
Manual	50.2	63.5	61.9
Non-manual	51.2	59.7	59.9
All	54.9	66.5	66.7

Source: New Earnings Survey (computed from figures given by Central Statistical Office 1988 p. 85).

Low incomes, insecure employment, or absence from the workforce to care for children or relatives, all help to explain women's greater reliance than men on housing in the public sector. However, there are other factors, within the housing system itself, which exacerbate the problematic effects for women of low income or little wealth. These include factors relating to the slow response of the housing and welfare systems to the demographic and social changes that have occurred in the post-war decades (factors which have also meant that inequalities in income between men and women have not been substantially offset by the development of social policy as the welfare state ideal would expect). Thus, as we suggest below, trends in housing policy and practice can again be regarded not simply as a

reflection of social differences, but as a means actively of constructing them.

This occurs at one level from a failure to adapt to the consequences of demographic differences between the male and female
populations in twentieth-century Britain. The greater longevity of
women, for instance, means that they are disproportionately subject
to the kinds of housing problems facing older people (which are
discussed at some length in Chapter 7). Certainly, much of the
increase in people living alone (rising from 4 per cent of households
in 1961 to 9 per cent in 1983) can be attributed to the greater number
of people surviving to old age as widows and, to a lesser extent,
widowers. Between 1973 and 1983, the proportion of the population
aged 75 or more increased from 24 to 28 per cent for men, but from
48 per cent to 57 per cent for women. Similarly, as Brion and Tinker
(1980) show, women are more susceptible, irrespective of age, to
disabling diseases such as rheumatism and arthritis, so that where
housing is poorly integrated with other forms of care, and without
adequate assistance with repair and maintenance, women may again
be disproportionately vulnerable.

At another, more fundamental, level housing systems have been
slow to respond to the social changes of the post-war years and to
women's changing role and status in society. Thus there are still legal
and administrative iniquities built into the housing system which
directly or indirectly discriminate against women (some of which are
discussed in a collection edited by Birch, 1985, and in practical
guidance to single and married women issued by the London
Housing Aid Centre, SHAC, McNicholas, 1986; Witherspoon,
1986).

These inequalities result, for instance, from the (now diminishing)
tendency to grant tenancies and allocate mortgages to conventional
couples in the man's name (although even as late as 1981 Department of Environment figures on mortgage completions identify
women as the first-named applicant in only 10 per cent of cases).
They also relate to the withholding of mortgages to single women,
not only because of low incomes, but also because of stereotyped
presumptions about their earnings capacity and labour force continuity.

Watson (for example, 1986a, 1986b, 1987) has attempted to
explain why housing systems are implicated in the construction of
gender difference. She argues that the persistence of gender inequali-

ties in both public and private housing testifies to the importance of the housing system not simply in mediating class relations, but also in reproducing patriarchy (a form of gender relations in which men are advantaged at the expense of women). Broadly, her thesis is that in modern Western societies, housing systems are embedded in, and so help sustain, not only the class relations associated with capitalism and the racialised relations that are a legacy of imperialism, but also a patriarchal form of gender relations. This, she contends, has the consequence that some individuals and family types – especially those where women take an 'unconventional' role – are disadvantaged in the housing system irrespective, to some extent, of either need or ability to pay.

Watson (1987) argues that patriarchal familial assumptions are embedded in the process of housing consumption in the main tenure sectors. The conditions of access to owner occupied housing and allocation of public sector housing are all, she suggests, orientated to the needs of 'conventional' families (a married heterosexual couple with one or more children). The reason is that these nuclear families tend, more often than other family types, to be an important arena for the reproduction of patriarchal relations. By this she means that this nuclear family form is most likely to encourage women's dependency on men for income and wealth. This is because childcare (when carried out by a member of the family) is unpaid domestic labour which often limits women's flexibility in and access to the labour market. The nuclear family form may also facilitate men's domination of women in the domestic sphere, assigning women a *de facto* responsibility for housework, food preparation, family health, and so on. This centrality of the conventional family to the housing system is one reason, according to Watson, why other, 'non-family' households are marginalised in a way which has particularly detrimental consequences for lone mothers, who head over 87 per cent of all lone-parent families, and single women, whose labour market position remains much weaker than that of single men.

Watson (1987) shows, for instance, that lone mothers have difficulty entering the owner-occupied market because two wages are increasingly needed to secure a mortgage, and because building societies have traditionally regarded such households as inherently unstable, and therefore as a financial risk. Likewise, in the public sector, where notions of merit or just dessert are tied to assessments of respectability, the prevalence of disingenuous stereotypes may discriminate against lone mothers, who may also be disadvantaged by points systems which give priority to overcrowded or bedroom-deficient households. Similar lines of argument can be invoked to account for the housing position of childless single women. The public sector has always been reluctant to house single people without children so that, given women's still-restricted labour market opportunities, Watson and Austerberry (1986) are able to argue that women often live in inadequate homes and endure dangerous domestic relationships simply because the housing system does not have the flexibility or sensitivity to offer them adequate alternatives.

These kinds of arguments are important, and although the thesis does require some refinement (see Munro and Smith, 1989, Smith 1990), it does suggest how and why housing – the key locus for family life, for the organisation of gender relations and for the reproduction of the labour force – may act to reinforce, rather than simply reflect, the structure of gender inequality in society at large.

Housing, the welfare state and racial inequality

In the same way as the housing system may be examined for its role in mediating class-related and gender-related inequalities, we may also consider the extent to which it is implicated in the reproduction of racism, and therefore in the structuring of 'racial' disadvantage. A range of examples drawing on procedures in the public and private sectors is given in Smith and Mercer (1987) and Smith (1989a), but the theme is perhaps best illustrated by considering the problems black people (of Afro-Caribbean and Asian origin or descent) have encountered in securing council accommodation. The development of housing as a plank of the welfare state coincided with the main period of post-war labour migration from the new Commonwealth to Britain. Migrant labour was largely a replacement labour force, recruited into lower-paid jobs in marginal segments of the economy (see Harris, 1987; Peach, 1968). During the 1950s and 1960s (before it became the residual sector that is described above), public housing should have played an important role for this group, offsetting a range of inequalities stemming from their disadvantageous position in the division of labour.

In terms of access to the public sector, for almost twenty-five years following the war, black Britons, immigrant or otherwise, fared less well than their white counterparts. Despite their greater levels of 'need', reflecting low wages and an overdependence on sub-standard segments of the privately rented sector, and despite their theoretically equal right, as British citizens, to public subsidy, post-war migrants from the West Indies and South Asia were at first virtually excluded from council housing. For reasons amplified in Smith (1987, 1988), even in 1960, after fifteen years of labour migration in the name of post-war reconstruction, only one per cent of black households rented from local authorities. This is doubly problematic, because delayed entry in itself increased the probability that, in the major English cities, black households who eventually qualified as tenants would be offered homes not in the better quality 'suburban' estates, but in the flatted estates of the redeveloped inner cores, and in older inner- and middle-ring properties which had been bought by compulsory purchase but never actually redeveloped.

More than anything else, this initial exclusion of black people from council housing reflected the widespread imposition of lengthy local residence requirements as a prerequisite for admission to the local authority stock. (It was not until 1976 that this indirect discrimination became illegal under the Race Relations Act.) Despite suggestions that some black populations preferred ownership for cultural reasons, once these punitive residence requirements were met by applicants, or removed by local authorities, Afro-Caribbean and Asian households began moving into the public sector in much greater numbers. By 1974 some 36 per cent of Afro-Caribbean and 4 per cent of Asian households were renting from the council (Smith, 1976); by 1982 the corresponding figures were 41 per cent and 19 per cent, as compared with 30 per cent of white households (Brown, 1984). (In order to interpret the significance of Asians' continuing high rates of home ownership, it should be recognised that, unlike white Britons, the relationship between class and tenure does not hold for this population; Asians often own cheap terraced homes in the older parts of the housing stock in the inner rings of Midlands and Northern cities.)

Indirectly discriminatory residence requirements are just one example of the kind of bureaucratic rule that can work to the disadvantage of particular groups within the housing system. Although the ideal which drives the allocation of public housing is that of apportioning a decent standard of accommodation according to need rather than ability to pay, there is now a range of evidence to indicate that the rules and procedures invoked tend to allocate homes according to a range of 'non needs-based' criteria, including income, but also embracing wider patterns of discrimination in British society. One of the best researched examples relates to the role of racism – direct and indirect, overt and institutionalised – in the differential apportionment of the publicly owned housing stock. As the remainder of this discussion shows, most evidence indicates that even where black people have achieved access to council housing, the quality and location of their tenancies give cause for concern.

The Policy Studies Institute survey of 1982, which represents the most comprehensive recent source of information on the black population of England and Wales (a comparable Scottish survey is now underway) indicates that, even controlling for the number of council homes lived in, date of allocation and household characteristics, black tenants live in smaller, more crowded homes than do whites, they tend more often to be allocated flats rather than houses, and their flats tend to be located on the higher floors of multi-storey blocks (Brown, 1984). In short, black people are clustered in the more run-down and difficult-to-let parts of the stock, irrespective of apparent 'need'. Their experience of public housing is, it seems, qualitatively as well as quantitatively inferior to that of white people, in ways that are captured in Table 3.5.

Table 3.5   *Housing conditions of black and white council tenants in England and Wales, 1982[1]*

	Flat	House (det'd + semi)	Pre-1945	Lack amenity[2]	Over crowded[3]
White	27	39	27	3	5
West Indian	54	9	34	3	20
Asian	54	11	35	7	43

1 All entries are row percentages.
2 Lacking exclusive use of bath, hot water or inside WC.
3 Over one person per room.
Source: adapted from Brown (1984, p. 102).

A number of recent studies (CRE, 1984a, 1984b, 1985; Henderson and Karn, 1987; Phillips, 1986) show that black people experience discrimination at each of the four common entry points to public housing: during rehousing following slum clearance, or 'decanting' to allow improvements or modernisation; during rehousing from the waiting lists; when they are unintentionally homeless; and during rehousing from the transfer lists. For the most part, such discrimination is indirect and appears unintentional. Indeed, Phillip's (1986) study was undertaken following the implementation of supposedly anti-racist housing policies in a London borough. To explain how racial disadvantage is (ostensibly) inadvertently structured through the management of public housing, we may turn to the work of Henderson and Karn (1984, 1987). These authors offer an account of how the bureaucratic procedures and discretionary judgements invoked in the interests of efficient management can allow public housing to express and exacerbate racial inequality. They offer, in effect, an insight into how racism becomes institutionalised and so impedes the just allocation of a scarce resource.

Drawing on research completed during the 1970s, Henderson and Karn show that local authorities adopt finely tuned and carefully specified procedures in order to grade applicants according to their need for housing. However, they also show that it is only through an additional informal grading of 'respectability' (which may initially be applied subconsciously by housing officials but may eventually be built even into computerised allocations systems) that an effective mechanism for rationing homes can be sustained. This is because there are wide variations in the quality and condition of council housing, and there are large portions of the stock which prospective tenants may wish to avoid. At times when demand for public housing overall outstrips supply, or where there is a mismatch between areas in demand and the location of vacant properties, this imposes considerable pressures on housing managers to fill homes in difficult-to-let areas. Using a variety of examples, Henderson and Karn show how racial stereotypes (and indeed stereotypes relating to gender and class) can become aligned with scales of distinction and disrepute and so be translated into 'racially' differentiated offers of better or worse tenancies.

The use of stereotypes in this manner need not be deliberate or vindictive. Often it is simply a consequence of the need to devise working criteria by which to meet management imperatives to let homes quickly with the minimum of resistance (especially from the white majority of tenants and applicants). Of course, this does not make the process any more justified or any less illegal. Nevertheless, as a consequence of giving the worst homes in the worst areas to households who fare badly according to a number of subjectively assigned qualitative criteria, racist rather than egalitarian principles can infuse the allocation process.

Other discriminatory practices involved in the allocation of public housing are exposed in a series of studies completed during the 1980s (these are summarised in greater detail in Smith, 1989a, chapter 4). Phillips's (1986) research in Tower Hamlets confirms the continuing potency in some housing departments of discretionary bias on the part of housing officials. Although a commitment to anti-racism removed dubious practices like the grading of housekeeping, Phillips shows that subjective judgements related, for instance, to the perceived nuisance of Asians' cooking smells or to judgements about the likelihood of racist attack, ensure that Asian applicants continue to receive a disproportionate number of tenancies in older proper- ties, homes without gardens, and dwellings without central heating. Similar findings were produced following the Commission for Racial Equality's (1984a) investigation in Hackney, where black households received poorer accommodation than their white coun- terparts, irrespective of their economically determined ability to wait for a better offer. The CRE's (1984b) investigation in Liverpool also confirmed the extent of a continuing bias against black people. This study identifies a further factor influencing the differential ability of black and white households to bargain for better quality council properties. In Liverpool, the best offers were secured by those households who had made representations to the council through advocates such as councillors and social workers. The fact that almost three times as many white applicants as blacks were able to secure such representation immediately gave the former group an advantage in bargaining for better homes.

There is, in short, a wide range of factors conspiring to ensure that the principle of allocating housing according to need is com- promised by the institutionalisation of racism within public housing systems. Although we do not have space to discuss them in detail, racist practices occur in the private as well as the public sector, both in the allocation of finance for owner-occupation and in the organi- sation of private renting (see Karn, 1983, for a succinct review). The inequalities so generated are partly rooted in British history, politics and economy, whose effects are reflected in the housing system; but they derive also from biased procedures that are institutionalised within housing allocation systems, and from the deliberately or uncritically discriminatory actions of individual housing managers. In this sense, discriminatory practices and racist ideologies are not simply reflected in, but are also constructed through, housing policy and its implementation.

Conclusion

This chapter has tackled a central theme of social policy analysis, relating to the nature of poverty, inequality and disadvantage. We have shown how social disadvantage – whether related to income, employment status or other social needs – is expressed in the housing system. This is inevitable where the organisation of housing production creates a variable housing stock of uneven quality, condition and amenity value. It is inconceivable from our knowledge of how markets and bureaucracies work to imagine that the better and worse parts of the housing and residential environment would not be apportioned according to the same hierarchy of economic and social power that structures society more widely.

However, by examining three aspects of the process of housing consumption, we have demonstrated that housing is not simply an outcome, or end point, in the process of disadvantage. As one of several interlocking sets of markets and institutions involved in the allocation of resources and opportunities, the housing system actively shapes social inequality and contributes to the processes by which it is systematically structured. The inflexible procedures adopted by public bureaucracies and the rules invoked by the private sector to promote profitability both incorporate formal and informal (discretionary) bias which perpetuates patterns of discrimination operating in society as a whole. On a number of counts, therefore, the housing system has an important role to play in sustaining the wider range of inequalities associated with life in advanced capitalist democracy.

While this may seem a rather pessimistic conclusion, it is also one which makes a powerful argument for using housing as a point of intervention in combating disadvantage, and, indeed, a range of other problems conventionally addressed through social policy. History testifies to the relevance of this approach, not least in the success which the advent of public housing had in improving average housing conditions during the post-war years. Thus, just as housing may exacerbate economic and gender inequalities and act to reproduce racism, so housing may be one point at which the potency of structured inequality might effectively be challenged. This may occur both at the level of individuals, through special training programmes or disciplinary action for unconscious and overt discrimination respectively, and at the level of institutions, through organisational and managerial changes. Housing interventions might, therefore, be well suited to pursuing the aims of social policy, especially where disadvantage is not reducible to low income or lack of wealth. Our concern about the failure to capitalise on this resource is part of the motivation for this book. Our analysis of what has been, and could be, achieved in this respect is presented on a topic-by-topic basis in the next four chapters.

4

Assistance with Housing Costs

The state has long had an important influence on the amount people pay for their accommodation. Indeed, there are probably very few households in Britain whose housing costs have not been affected in one way or another by state intervention. By intervening in housing provision – whether by means of regulation, provision in kind, or subsidies – the state inevitably has some effect upon the cost of housing to the consumer. In this chapter we examine the way in which help with housing costs is provided in Britain today. We begin with some brief remarks on why the state has become so heavily involved in providing assistance with housing costs. We then describe the various ways in which the state has explicitly attempted to alter the cost of housing to the consumer. Finally, we examine in some detail the housing benefit scheme – a form of help with housing costs that has become of increasing importance since 1979. We use this case study of housing benefit to expose the often neglected interactions between housing and social security, and also to illuminate some important aspects of the political economy of housing in contemporary Britain.

Housing costs and the state

Ever since the state first began actively to intervene in the housing market in the mid nineteenth century, it has affected the cost of housing to the consumer. As the state has become increasingly implicated in housing provision, so it has become increasingly important as a factor affecting the amount people pay to secure their shelter. In some cases this involvement in housing costs has been a by-product or an unintended consequence of intervention aimed at some other aspect of housing. Perhaps the two most obvious examples of this are building regulations and land-use planning. In other cases, the state has deliberately intervened in housing finance, sometimes with the aim of reducing the cost of housing to the consumer, but at other times to increase it, as with the Housing Finance Act 1972 (see Merrett, 1979). In this chapter we concentrate on forms of state intervention that are explicitly aimed at altering the cost of housing to the consumer.

At one level the importance of state intervention in the cost of consuming housing lies in the fact that it is a very expensive commodity to produce. The average price of a house has generally tended to be about two or three times average earnings; hence few households have been able to buy a dwelling outright from their income. Consequently, various different tenure arrangements have been evolved which enable households to pay for their accommodation in ways that they can reasonably afford. Some households take out a loan from a financial institution such as a bank or a building society in order to buy their accommodation over a period of years. Others rent their home from a landlord such as a local authority, housing association, or private investor. (The changing balance between owner-occupation and renting from different types of landlord was discussed in Chapter 2.) But whether housing is being purchased on a mortgage or rented, it still tends to be the largest single item in the budget of most households. As we saw in Chapter 3, housing costs account, on average, for one-sixth of household income in Britain and represent a particularly heavy burden for low-income households.

It is also worth noting that because housing costs are such a large component of household incomes, they can have an influence on the level of wage demands within the economy. Thus the Labour government of Harold Wilson introduced a one-year rent freeze as part of its attempt to restrain wage inflation in 1974 (Merrett, 1979). Therefore housing subsidies and rent controls can at one level be seen as a subsidy to employers, to the extent that they help keep wage levels down.

Help with housing costs: an outline

Help with housing costs in Britain has developed in a disjointed, incremental way and not according to any rational, comprehensive scheme (Berthoud and Ermisch, 1985). The current system of assistance with housing costs consequently comprises a complicated and not particularly coherent structure of regulation, subsidies and tax reliefs. Moreover, the definition of housing subsidies and the calculation of their incidence and impact are the subject of considerable debate (see O'Sullivan, 1984). In this chapter we have space only to provide an outline of help with housing costs. More detail is provided in Bucknall (1984), Goss and Lansley (1984) and the Inquiry into British Housing (1985, 1986).

However, notwithstanding the fact that help with housing costs is provided in a myriad of different and overlapping ways, there are two broad types of assistance. Supply-side interventions act to reduce the price of housing to consumers irrespective of their income, while demand-side instruments increase individual consumers' ability to pay the cost of housing and are often income-related. Supply-side interventions include both subsidies to producers of housing and price controls which regulate the amount they can charge for the accommodation they supply. Supply-side subsidies are sometimes known as 'object' or 'bricks-and-mortar' subsidies. One example of such assistance is the Exchequer subsidy paid each year to certain local authorities to enable them to balance income and expenditure on their housing revenue accounts (see below). Without that subsidy the councils would have to charge a higher rent or find some other means of meeting the deficit on their housing revenue accounts. Demand-side assistance is sometimes known as income supplements or 'subject' subsidies. One example of this kind of assistance is housing benefit, which helps certain low-income households to meet the cost of their rent and rates.

In practice, however, the relationship between these two types of assistance and the amount which consumers pay for housing out of their income is somewhat more complicated than this simple dichotomy might suggest. For example, suppose a government decides to introduce mortgage interest tax relief. By making the cost of housing cheaper, this will increase the demand for owner-occupation. But unless that extra demand is matched by a fully commensurate increase in the supply of homes for owner-occupation, the price of owner-occupied houses will rise. This 'capitalisation' of mortgage interest tax relief (see Kay and King, 1978) into the price of houses will thus make it more difficult for prospective first-time buyers to enter the market, and the beneficiaries of the subsidy will be the existing owners of houses and land.

In Britain, supply-side subsidies have, until recently, been more important than demand-side subsidies. Put differently, governments have tended to put more emphasis on directing subsidies to bricks and mortar than to people. Historically, the main form of price subsidy in Britain has been that provided to council housing, which has been used to lower the rent which council tenants have been charged to a level below that which would otherwise be necessary to meet all the costs of provision. This revenue subsidy to council housing has in the past come from two sources: Exchequer subsidy (known as Housing Support Grant in Scotland) and transfers to the housing revenue account from the general rate fund (that is, from the ratepayers as a whole within an authority). However, as outlined later in the chapter, from April 1990 councils will be prohibited from subsidising their rents by making transfers from the general rate fund.

Since the Housing Act 1935, local authorities have been required to pool the accounts for all of the dwellings built under various Housing Acts into a single housing revenue account for their stock as a whole (Merrett, 1979). Since 1955 they have been urged by central government to pool their subsidy income (payable under the different Housing Acts, each with its own subsidy arrangements) within the housing revenue account rather than allocate specific subsidies to dwellings (Malpass and Murie, 1987). This enables them to pool both the outstanding costs (such as debt charges and management and maintenance expenditure) and the subsidies received. Consequently, the older, less expensive housing owned by an authority in effect cross-subsidises the newer, more expensive housing. Historically, councils have been required to break even on their housing revenue account, but since 1980 they have been allowed to make a surplus.

The relative rents of the individual dwellings managed by a local authority are determined by whatever rent setting scheme it chooses to operate. This is one area in which local authorities still have considerable autonomy. For example, some authorities determine the relative rents of individual dwellings by reference to their rateable value. Others do so on the basis of the attributes of the dwelling, awarding 'points' for each attribute (so many points for a garden, so many points for each bedroom, etc.), with the rent being determined by the total number of points awarded to the dwelling (see Maclennan, 1986).

A further characteristic of local authority rents is that, other things being equal, authorities with an older stock need to charge a lower rent than those with a newer stock because the outstanding debt will be smaller. Combined with the differences in rent-setting regimes, this means that tenants of dwellings of similar types receiving a similar amount and quality of management and maintenance services will almost certainly be charged a different rent in each local authority.

Since the Housing Act 1974, housing associations registered with the Housing Corporation have been able to receive a capital grant (Housing Association Grant or HAG) which enables them to charge rents well below the cost of provision. The cost of completing each newly built or rehabilitated property is met by a combination of a mortgage and HAG. Under the system set up by the 1974 Act, the proportion of the scheme costs paid out of the mortgage was determined by the size of the loan that could be serviced by the rent after management and maintenance costs were taken into account. The rent for each dwelling was determined independently of the housing association by the rent officer, who set a 'fair rent' as defined by the Rent Act. The capital costs not covered by the mortgage were met by the grant. Thus HAG was a residual, the size of which was determined by the fair rent. Under this system, HAG (which was paid as a lump sum) accounted on average for about 85 to 90 per cent of the total scheme cost (Hills, 1987). Where an association's rental income was still insufficient to meet its outgoings, Revenue Deficit Grant could be paid in certain circumstances to meet the shortfall (see Bucknall, 1984).

Under the Housing Act 1988, a new system of housing association finance is being developed. Under this new regime, the relationship between rent level and HAG on new schemes is inverted. Instead of the rent being set by the rent officer and thus determining the level of grant, HAG will be set in advance as a predetermined amount, and the rent level will be adjusted to cover the remainder of the costs which have to be met by the mortgage. As well as deregulating housing association rents in this way, the amount of HAG is required by the government to average 75 per cent rather than the previous outturn average of 85 to 90 per cent. Consequently, rents will be significantly higher than fair rent levels. At the same time, housing associations are being encouraged to secure loans from the private sector, rather than the public sector as they mostly did under the previous system (Hills, 1987). Revenue Deficit Grant is to be phased out (except in the case of hostels) because under a deregulated rent regime associations will be able to adjust rents levels to avoid any shortfalls on their operating costs.

Another price intervention is rent control or regulation in the private sector. First introduced in 1915, rent controls have been in operation in Britain in varying forms and with differing degrees of jurisdiction ever since. Under rent control, rents are kept below the market level. In this way, tenants' housing costs are subsidised not by the state but by the private landlords who own rent-controlled properties (Robinson, 1979). The Housing Act 1988 decontrolled the rents of newly granted lettings but retained control for sitting tenants.

Improvement grants, which (as we saw in Chapter 2) local authorities have been able to award since 1949, are a capital subsidy. They can reduce the cost to the owner of carrying out essential repair and improvement or conversion works. Likewise, the substantial discounts at which council tenants are able to purchase their home also represent a price subsidy, since they reduce considerably the cost of entry into the owner-occupied sector. Table 4.1 shows that, in 1985, the average discount from the market value of houses sold to council tenants under the right to buy was 46 per cent. In cash terms this amounted to £11,281 per dwelling. Between 1980 and 1985 the total value of the discounts was £5.6 billion, or an average of £0.9 billion per annum.

Demand-side subsidies in Britain come in four main forms. First, owner-occupiers on income support receive a 'housing addition' to their income support benefit which is equivalent to 100 per cent of their eligible mortgage interest payments; it does not cover the capital element of the loan repayments. During the first sixteen weeks of an income support claim by owners under 60, however, only 50 per cent of mortgage interest payments is paid as a housing addition. The latter provision was introduced in 1986 because, the government argued, paying 100 per cent of interest costs from the beginning of a claim was 'too generous' and there had been a rapid

Table 4.1 *Value of discounts on local authority house sales, England and Wales, 1977 to 1985*

	No. of houses	Total capital value of discount (£000)	Average discounts %	£ per dwelling
1977	13,020	17,848	16	1,371
1978	30,045	15,576	18	1,814
1979	41,665	146,651	27	3,520
1980	81,485	471,323	38	5,784
1981	102,825	689,147	41	6,702
1982	201,880	1,464,791	43	7,256
1983	141,615	1,012,987	41	7,153
1984	97,560	944,821	44	9,685
1985	86,495	975,711	46	11,281

Source: DoE, *Housing and Construction Statistics* (1986).

increase in benefit expenditure (SSAC, 1987). The contrast between the treatment of unemployed home owners and that of better-off, employed owners (see below) is stark, for the same arguments could have been applied with equal force to mortgage interest tax relief, which has not been cut back.

Second, low-income ratepayers (including owner-occupiers) and households who rent their home are eligible for housing benefit. This is a means-tested form of tied income supplement administered by local authorities and largely financed by the Department of Social Security (DSS). Under the housing benefit scheme, help with rent for council tenants is called rent rebates, but for housing association and private tenants it is called rent allowances; help with rates is known as rate rebates irrespective of the tenure of the recipient. The amount of benefit received is determined by three main variables: the level of rent and rates that applicants have to pay, the household's composition, and their assessed income. For those receiving income support or with a comparable level of income, the benefit received is equal to 100 per cent of eligible rent and 80 per cent of eligible rates. Above the income support threshold, the amount of benefit received declines from these maxima to nil, along a sliding scale (or 'taper') related to income (Kemp, 1987).

Third, some households on income support whose housing costs include an amount for meals are eligible for a board and lodging allowance payable by the DSS. This now only applies to claimants living in residential homes for elderly or disabled people. Board and lodging allowances have played an important part in the care-in-the-community policy discussed in Chapters 6 and 7. Many of the residents who have been moved out of long-stay residential institutions and into the community have been placed in accommodation providing board and special care services which are paid for by board and lodging allowances under the income support scheme. The provision of these allowances has also been an important factor in the rapid expansion of private residential homes since 1979.

Finally, home owners receive a number of tax reliefs which act to reduce the cost of housing to them. These are mortgage interest tax relief and exemption from taxation on both imputed rental income (the notional income they receive by letting their property to themselves rather than to an actual tenant) and capital gains. Economists argue that which of these three 'tax expenditures' can be regarded as a subsidy depends upon whether owner-occupied housing is treated as a consumption or an investment good. If it is viewed as a consumption good, then mortgage interest tax relief (but not exemption from imputed rental income) is indeed a subsidy, for it reduces the cost of acquisition and is not available on other consumption goods such as cars. On the other hand, it is argued that if owner-occupied housing is regarded as an investment, then mortgage interest relief is not a subsidy because it is a cost incurred in acquiring an asset and should, therefore, be deducted from rental income in assessing tax liability; in this case, it is the absence of taxation on imputed rental income and the exemption from capital gains tax that comprises the subsidy.

The problem here is that owner-occupied housing is both an investment and a consumption good. Capital gains can be made out of home ownership, and this is an important fact behind the consumption sector cleavage between owners and tenants which Saunders (1984) has identified. But people also buy a house in order to secure shelter. On pragmatic rather than theoretically pure grounds, therefore, we have chosen to focus our discussion here on mortgage interest relief. In the first place, at a common-sense level, people seem to find it easier to accept that mortgage interest relief is a subsidy than they do the absence of taxation on imputed rental income. They can see that they are paying their building society or bank a lower rate of interest than they would do in the absence of the relief, but they find it difficult to accept that they are being excused a tax on an income that they do not physically receive from owning their home. Second, owner-occupation by definition involves consumption of the dwelling by its owner – that is, it is of necessity a consumption good – whereas capital gains are a contingent phenomenon, the existence of which cannot be guaranteed. Indeed, although house prices have tended to rise in line with earnings in Britain, there have been periods (such as the decade from the early 1920s) when prices have fallen in nominal terms.

Mortgage interest relief is in effect a subsidy on the interest home buyers pay on their mortgage. Currently, the subsidy is available only on the first £30,000 of a loan. At present, this subsidy is available at two different rates, each of which is administered in a different way. First, for non-taxpayers and those who pay tax at the standard rate (currently 25p in the £), the subsidy is equivalent to 25 per cent of their mortgage interest payments. For example, if the nominal or gross rate of mortgage interest is 10 per cent, the net rate of interest that they pay to the lender is only 7.5 per cent. The Inland Revenue then reimburses the remaining 2.5 per cent to the lender. This is known as mortgage interest relief at source (MIRAS). Second, those whose marginal (highest) rate of tax is at the higher, 40 per cent level, receive a subsidy on their mortgage interest payments that is equal to 40 per cent. Thus the effective rate of interest they pay on a 10 per cent loan would be 6 per cent. In these cases, however, the buyer pays the gross rate to the lender and receives the subsidy in the form of a higher tax code. Basic-rate taxpayers whose mortgage is in excess of £30,000 can opt out of MIRAS and receive the relief in their tax code instead.

Other things being equal, therefore, higher-rate taxpayers receive more subsidy than lower-rate taxpayers. We can demonstrate this point using an example. Under MIRAS the monthly cost of a repayment mortgage of £25,000 taken out at 10.25 per cent interest over 25 years is £190.19 for house buyers who are non-taxpayers or who pay tax at the standard rate of 25 per cent. But for those who pay tax at 40 per cent, the monthly cost of the same mortgage is only

£158.16. In this example, therefore, the higher rate (and hence better-off) taxpayer gets £32 a month more subsidy than do other house buyers.

A survey by Le Grand (1982) of the evidence on who benefits most from subsidies found that tax reliefs to home owners are strongly pro-rich; that is, they benefit the better-off more than they do the less well-off. Moreover, although subsidies can be defined and measured in different ways (see O'Sullivan, 1984) much of the evidence suggests that, on average, home owners receive more in subsidy per household than do council tenants. Le Grand also found that general subsidy (Exchequer grant and rate fund contributions) received by council tenants are pro-poor – that is, they benefit the less well-off more than they do the better-off. Although much of the evidence surveyed by Le Grand is now a little dated, the overall pattern today is probably the same. While general subsidies to council tenants (as we show below) have declined considerably during the 1980s, they have been replaced by housing benefit which, being income-related, is targeted on the poor. Again, all of the recent data on mortgage interest relief show that it is still strongly pro-rich. Thus Table 4.2 shows that the average amount of relief received in 1988/89 was inversely related to income. For example, tax units (single persons and married couples) whose total income was less than £5,000 received £400 of relief, but those with a total income of £30,000 or more received, on average, £810.

Table 4.2   *Distribution of mortgage interest relief, 1988–9*

Income	Taxpayers receiving relief (%)	Total cost of relief (%)	Average relief per mortgagor (%)
Over £30,000	5	7	810
£25,000–£29,999	9	15	1,020
£20,000–£24,999	11	12	650
£15,000–£19,999	19	19	590
£10,000–£14,999	28	26	560
£5,000–£9,999	20	17	510
Under £5,000	8	5	400
Total	9.1m	£5,500m	600

Source: calculated from *Housing Associations Weekly*, 3 February 1989, p. 4.

The ideology of assistance with housing costs

The way in which the state intervenes to alter the cost of housing to consumers in Britain has been extensively criticised on the grounds of efficiency and equality (see Berthoud, 1989; Ermisch, 1984; Maclennan and O'Sullivan, 1987). Orthodox economists have argued about the relative merits of price versus income subsidies or in kind provision versus cash benefits (see Inquiry into British Housing, 1986). Yet the instruments with which the state intervenes in housing are not only technical issues. They are not selected merely on the grounds of which type of subsidy makes the most economically efficient use of scarce resources. This is because the way in which assistance is provided has at least three important sets of political implications.

First, different types of intervention will have different distributional consequences. Once a particular policy measure such as rent control or mortgage interest relief is introduced, a group of beneficiaries will be created who may see themselves as having an interest in its retention. Withdrawing that measure will create losers which may make it politically difficult to carry through reform without transitional arrangements, or even at all.

Second, supply- and demand-side interventions can have different implications for modes of provision in housing. To some extent state intervention on the supply side has tended to subvert the market, whereas demand-side subsidies have helped to underwrite it. For example, rent controls have been used to keep private sector rents below market levels. This has reduced landlords' rates of return and has been one factor behind the decline of the privately rented sector in Britain. Similarly, in-kind provision of houses at subsidised rents by local authorities and housing associations has made it more difficult for the private sector to compete in the market for rented housing. Partly because supply subsidies have tended to be associated in Britain with in-kind or socialised provision, new right critics have preferred the alternative of income-related cash assistance.

It is, indeed, no coincidence that the recent trend towards the reprivatisation of rented housing in Britain (see Chapter 2) has been accompanied by a shift away from general supply subsidies or interventions to individualised demand assistance with housing costs. In Britain and elsewhere, governments have tended to emphasise income-related assistance such as housing benefit at times when they are attempting to increase rent levels (as in the early 1970s and the 1980s). Unless rents are at market levels, private provision is unlikely to be a viable alternative to public housing.

However, recent experience has indicated that private provision is scarcely viable even at market rents underwritten by housing benefit. Market rents are not necessarily economic rents. That is to say, current market rents in Britain appear not to be high enough to cover the long-run marginal cost of housing or the opportunity costs of investing in other assets. There seem to be two main reasons for this. One is that many of the households who rent their home are not able to afford the economic cost of decent housing because their incomes are too low. The other is that most households who could afford to pay an economic rent choose to become owner-occupiers, not least because of the tax concessions available to that mode of consumption. Indeed, as the Milner-Holland Committee (1964) pointed out, and as the House of Commons Environment Committee (1982) affirmed more recently, it is cheaper to buy a home with mortgage interest tax relief than it is to rent an equivalent dwelling from a private landlord.

Third, the way in which assistance with housing costs is delivered has important social and ideological connotations. Supply-side and non-means-tested forms of assistance tend to be universal in the sense that they are available to all who fall into the specified category (home owners, tenants of a local authority, and so on) irrespective of their income. And they are usually available in an anonymous way without the need for an application or test of eligibility. In contrast, demand-side subsidies are often income-related and, therefore, means-tested; they have to be applied for, thus identifying recipients – 'claimants' – as poor and distinguishing them from other households. Thus demand-side subsidies that are income-related stigmatise those who receive them; they are exclusionary rather than integratory. Although mortgage interest tax relief can be regarded as a demand subsidy, it is not means-tested but is instead provided on a universal basis to mortgagors. Thus demand-side subsidies are not necessarily stigmatising. It is the consequence of a political decision to means-test one kind of housing subsidy (rent rebates and allowances) rather than another (mortgage interest relief) in order to support an ideologically favoured form of housing consumption.

Another characteristic of most means-tested welfare benefits, to which housing benefits are no exception, is that many eligible households do not apply for them (Deacon and Bradshaw, 1983). Take-up can be measured in terms of the number of claimants who fail to apply or the value of benefit not awarded. In Table 4.3 both these aspects of take-up are shown for housing benefit in 1984 (the latest year for which data are available). The table shows that 1.9 million eligible households were *not* receiving housing benefit in 1984, and the take-up rate was 77 per cent. The total amount of unclaimed benefit was £500 million, and the average amount per eligible non-recipient was £4 a week or £208 a year.

Table 4.3   *Take-up of housing benefit, 1984*

Unclaimed benefit – annual amount	£500 million
– average weekly amount	£4.00
Eligible non-recipients	1,910,000
Caseload take-up	77%

Source: DHSS, *Social Security Statistics 1986*, Table 15.17.

Trends in housing subsidy since 1979

Since 1979 there has been much change in the provision of housing subsidies. Within the local authority sector, there has been a marked reduction in Exchequer subsidy, as a result of which rents have risen considerably. In 1987/88 prices, Exchequer subsidy to local authority housing revenue accounts in England and Wales was reduced from £2,237 million in 1979/80 to £473 million in 1987/88. This was a cut of 79 per cent in eight years. Partly as a result, local authority rents increased substantially. Table 4.4 shows that between April 1979 and April 1987, while the retail price index increased by 87 per cent, the average weekly council rent increased by 168 per cent.

Much of the impetus for this change in subsidy and rent levels came from the new system of Exchequer subsidy for housing revenue accounts introduced by the 1980 Housing Act. This new system gave central government considerable leverage, at least initially, over council sector rent increases (Malpass and Murie, 1987). It involved the introduction of a notional housing revenue account (HRA) for each local authority, which provided the basis for determining the amount of Exchequer subsidy each would

Table 4.4   *Local authority average rent in England, 1979 to 1987*

April	Average weekly unrebated rent		Retail price index (UK)
	£	Index	
1979	6.41	100	100
1987	17.20	268	187

Source: *Hansard*, 21 April 1988, cols 561–2.

receive. In brief, the amount of subsidy received by a local authority in any year under the new system was the previous year's subsidy, *plus* an assumed increase in reckonable costs, *minus* an assumed increase in reckonable income (principally rents). This calculation can be expressed as follows:

$$\text{Subsidy} = BA + HCD - LCD$$

where BA = Base Amount, or previous year's subsidy;
    HCD = Housing Costs Differential, or increase in reckonable expenditure, mainly loan charges plus management and maintenance;
    LCD = Local Contribution Differential, or increase in reckonable income, mainly from rents. (Source: Maclennan, 1982; Malpass and Murie, 1987)

By assuming that rents increased faster than costs, the government was able (as we have seen) substantially to reduce Exchequer subsidy to local authority housing revenue accounts. However, it is important to note that some councils put up their rents by significantly more than the government's guideline increases, while others put them up by less than that amount (making up the difference through a larger contribution from the rate fund). Some local autonomy, therefore, has in practice remained.

The fall in subsidy combined with the rise in rents has had a profound impact on the income side of the housing revenue account. On average, the contribution of Exchequer support to the account fell from 36 per cent in 1979/80 to only 8 per cent in 1985/86, as Table 4.5 shows. Over the same period, gross rents (that is, including housing benefit) increased from 45 to 64 per cent of housing revenue

Table 4.5 Local authority housing revenue account income: England and Wales, 1979/80 and 1985/86

	Rate fund contributions (%)	Exchequer subsidy (%)	Gross* rents (%)	Other (%)†	Total
1979/80	12	36	45	7	100
1985/86	8	8	64	19	100

*Includes housing benefit payments. Net rents (i.e. excluding housing benefit) were 37 per cent in 1979/80 and 31 per cent in 1985/86.

†Includes rent on property other than dwellings and (particularly for 1985/86) interest on capital receipts.

Source: DoE, *Housing and Construction Statistics 1976–1986*, 1987, Table 10.25.

account income. Also significant is income under the heading 'other', the marked rise in which is the product of interest received on invested receipts from the sale of council houses.

The combined and related effect of reduced subsidy and increased rents was that by 1986/87 only 25 per cent of local authorities in England and Wales were in receipt of subsidy from the Exchequer. Indeed, some 29 per cent of councils were transferring money out of the HRA and into the general rate fund; instead of ratepayers as a whole subsidising council tenants, council tenants were subsidising the ratepayers (Malpass and Murie, 1987).

For central government these changes have had several significant consequences. First, because the number of local authorities receiving Exchequer subsidy on their housing revenue accounts has fallen significantly, central government leverage over rent levels in the council sector has been reduced. Second, the process of raising rents and shifting subsidy to an income-related basis through the housing benefit scheme has now reached the point where

> any further increase in rents means, on the one hand, an increase in the housing benefit budget of the DHSS, and, on the other hand, an increase in HRA surpluses in large numbers of authorities. It clearly makes little sense to continue raising rents if the effect is ultimately to produce rates reductions for the population as a whole, funded by the DHSS. (Malpass and Murie, 1987, p. 199)

It seems likely that this situation has been an important consideration behind the introduction from April 1990 of a new financial regime for local authority housing revenue accounts. The government outlined this 'more businesslike' regime in a recent consultation paper (DoE, 1988a). It is proposed that housing revenue accounts be 'ring fenced' so that councils will no longer be able to subsidise their rents by making contributions from the general rate fund. It is also proposed to merge into a single 'housing revenue account subsidy' Exchequer support to the account and rent rebate 'subsidy' (that is, the reimbursement of the rent rebates that local authorities pay to council tenants under the housing benefit scheme on behalf of the Department of Social Security). This aggregation of 'housing subsidy' is a way of giving central government leverage over the rent levels of the 75 per cent of local authorities who do not receive Exchequer subsidy to their housing revenue account. In calculating the amount of reimbursement that they should receive in respect of their expenditure on housing benefit payments to council tenants, central government can assume that have made a certain level of increase in their rents.

It is further proposed that councils will not be permitted to transfer surpluses from the housing revenue account to the general rate fund unless they have repaid the rent rebate 'subsidy' they receive from the Exchequer. Because of rising rents and the decline in new building, an increasing number of councils are making transfers to their general rate fund. This new proposal is a way of creaming off those surpluses to pay for the cost of the housing benefit scheme. The effect of this will be to transfer part of the cost of housing benefit from the taxpayer to those council tenants not receiving a rebate on their rent.

Although proposed transitional arrangements over a three-year period will cushion the impact, the prohibition of rate fund contributions to the housing revenue account will almost certainly result in significant rent increases in those local authorities presently making such transfers. Part of the motivation for this proposal would appear to be revealed in the assertion made in the consultation paper that it will enable council tenants to:

> take better informed decisions about the alternatives the Government's housing policy is placing before them, and to decide whether to exercise the options the Government is giving them through the Right to Buy and Tenant's Choice. (DoE, 1988a, p. 7).

Thus council rents are to be increased, partly in order to reduce the relative price advantage of council housing and thereby persuade tenants to opt out of the sector, either by buying their home or agreeing to be transferred to an alternative landlord.

Partly because of the real increase in local authority rents, the rise in unemployment and the spread of low pay, there has been a significant increase in the proportion of council tenants receiving housing benefit and also, therefore, in the cost of the scheme (Kemp, 1987). The proportion of council tenants receiving housing benefit increased from 41 per cent in 1979 to 67 per cent in 1984. Thus there has been a switch from a general price subsidy to income-related support through the housing benefit scheme. It was argued by the government that Exchequer subsidy was too indiscriminate – that it was received by all council tenants irrespective of their financial circumstances. Housing benefit, it was argued, would protect the poorest tenants from the effect of rising rents as a result of the withdrawal of general subsidy.

Ironically, however, the government's response to the increase in housing benefit expenditure has been to introduce a series of cuts in that benefit. For any given rent level, these cuts have reduced both the number of beneficiaries and the amount of benefit received by those claimants still getting housing benefit, and have mostly affected those not in receipt of income support. The main way in which this has been done has been to increase greatly the rate (known as the 'taper') at which the benefit level falls as income increases above the income support level. The justification used by the government in support of these cuts has been that housing benefit goes too far up the income scale (see Kemp, 1987).

Nevertheless, increasing the rate of withdrawal of housing benefit as income rises has had the effect of exacerbating the 'poverty trap'. Housing benefit recipients have faced a significantly increased marginal tax rate since 1979. For every pound by which take-home pay increases (that is, after tax and national insurance) recipients now lose 65 pence in rent rebate and 15 pence in community charge rebate. In effect, they have become trapped on a low disposable income with little ability to improve it by working harder.

Paradoxically, this unfortunate result can best be explained in terms of the government's general ideological assault on the welfare state, which supposedly aims to break this cycle of hopelessness. The government has referred to benefit recipients as being imbued with a 'culture of dependency' resulting from 'excessive' public expenditure and 'high' benefit levels, from which claimants must be weaned. Thus, instead of unemployment and low pay being something for which the poor should be compensated, it is something for which they are to be blamed. The poor, then, are to be made poorer in order to encourage them to work harder and to make them more self-reliant. In contrast, the rich are to be made better off by tax cuts and tax concessions in order to encourage an 'enterprise culture'. This dual approach was made explicit in the spring of 1988 when the top tax rate was reduced from 60 to 40 per cent (and the standard rate from 27 to 25 per cent) while cuts in housing benefit (which increased the combined marginal tax and benefit withdrawal rate of working households in receipt of rent and rent rebate to a minimum of 90 per cent) and in income support were introduced for the poor. At the same time, the poor were required to contribute at least 20 per cent of their rates out of their income (thus reducing the maximum rent rebate from 100 to 80 per cent). This is to be followed by the replacement of domestic rates by the 'community charge' or poll tax, which will involve a flat tax on almost all adult individuals within a local authority irrespective of their income.

While housing benefit has been cut in order to reduce the 'culture of dependency' and because it goes 'too far' up the income scale, mortgage interest tax relief has been maintained. Indeed, because of the growth in owner-occupation and the increase in house prices, the cost of this tax expenditure has increased from £1.2 billion in 1979/80 to £4.75 billion in 1986/87. It is received by around one in three households – a similar number to those receiving housing benefit. The government has declined to cut back on mortgage interest relief because it fears the electoral consequences of doing so and also because it is perceived to encourage the ideologically favoured tenure of owner-occupation (see DoE, 1987).

One significant consequence of the shift from Exchequer HRA subsidy to housing benefit has been the transfer of the cost of subsidising council rents from the Department of the Environment to the Department of Social Security (DSS). This appears to have led to some conflicts between these two central government departments over local authority rent increases and the level and cost of housing benefit. The inter-departmental conflict of objectives has manifested itself even more clearly over the deregulation of new lettings in the private sector as provided by the Housing Act 1988. An increase in private sector rents by deregulation of new lettings is seen by the Department of the Environment as central to its key objective of reviving the private provision of rented housing. But since a third of all unfurnished and a quarter of all furnished tenants are in receipt of housing benefit, higher private-sector rents mean higher housing benefit expenditure (Kemp, 1988). The DSS, however, has been reported as being unwilling to have its budget increased substantially to pay for a revival of private renting.

104 *Housing and Social Policy*

Housing benefit

There is some ambiguity about whether rent rebates and allowances are to be regarded as an instrument of housing policy or of social security (Advisory Committee on Rent Rebates and Rent Allowances, 1976). However, it is clear that rent rebates and allowances are a form of *transfer payment*. That is, they involve the transfer of spending power from one group (taxpayers) to another (housing benefit recipients, some of whom pay tax, of course). Unlike, say, local authority capital expenditure on house building, rent rebates and allowances are not a *resource expenditure* used to provide goods and services (see Gough, 1979). How, then, do transfer payments fit into the dual politics thesis that was outlined in Chapter 1?

Initially, in assigning production and consumption functions to higher and lower tiers of the state, the thesis did not distinguish between transfer payments (that is, provision of the means of consumption) and provision in kind (consumption services and goods). However, both Dunleavy (1984) and Sharpe (1984) have pointed out that whereas consumption goods and services tend to be located at the local level, social security payments are centralised. Sharpe argues that monetary payments are easily centralised because of the scale and low levels of discretion required to administer them. In contrast, services (such as council housing or home helps) are less easily centralised because they require high levels of discretion as a result of variations between different local authorities.

These criticisms have been accepted by Cawson (1986) and Saunders (1986a), who have modified their views of the thesis to take into account this distinction between monetary payments and in-kind provision. However, it is clear from their discussions of this issue that they had in mind social security payments such as the then supplementary benefit scheme, which was administered through local offices of the DHSS (now the DSS). Cawson (1982) had earlier pointed out that social security is delivered through state organisations (the local offices of the DHSS) which conform most closely to the Weberian ideal type of bureaucracy. Policy decisions, he noted, were strongly centralised and there was relatively little discretion available. Benefit decisions were governed by case law, and DHSS officers worked according to a detailed guidance manual. Cawson also pointed out that there were no welfare professionals involved in the administration of the supplementary benefit scheme. However, there are some significant differences between the income support scheme which replaced SB and the housing benefit scheme. Research has indicated considerable variations in the way in which local authorities interpret the rules governing the payment of rent rebates and allowances (Kemp, 1984a; Means and Hill, 1982) which can affect the amount of benefit that claimants receive. Furthermore, unlike income support (but not the social fund) there is a degree of administrative discretion actually built into the scheme, though this was significantly reduced in April 1988. Local authorities thus have a limited, but at the margin important, degree of policy choice which welfare professionals (housing managers, local authority welfare rights workers and voluntary sector advice workers) have not been slow to exploit to the benefit of claimants.

Contrary to what the dual politics thesis would suggest, the administration of housing benefit is currently a local rather than a central government function, although the central department responsible for policy and the budget is now the DSS. Furthermore, the administration of the scheme has recently been decentralised. Prior to 1982/83, when 'housing benefit' as such was established, there were two separate schemes, one administered by the local offices of the DHSS and the other by local authorities. When the administration of these schemes was brought together in 1982/83 to produce housing benefit, the centrally adminstered scheme was handed over to local government. This was an important development, not least because it brought local authorities back into the mainstream of income maintenance for the first time since 1948, when social security was centralised. This development was also interesting from a theoretical point of view, however, because the dual politics thesis would have suggested that housing benefit would be centralised rather than decentralised. It is instructive to examine why and in what way the two schemes were brought together and their administration handed over to local authorities.

The scheme administered by the DHSS was the housing component of the then supplementary benefit scheme. In addition to the SB that beneficiaries received for their day-to-day living expenses (heat, lighting, food, etc.), they received a 'housing addition' to help them meet their housing costs (rent or mortgage interest and rates). Because housing costs vary so much between different areas, the housing addition was based on a claimant's actual rent and rates rather than a notional sum. In order to qualify for SB, claimants had to meet certain qualifying conditions, the main ones being (as they still are for its replacement, the income support scheme) that they are not in full-time work, do not have capital in excess of a certain limit, and have an income (net of tax, national insurance contributions and certain other disregards) less than a given threshold.

The scheme administered by local authorities was for low-income households not on SB. This provided rent rebates for council tenants, rent allowances for private tenants and rent rebates for those in all tenures. Although local authorities have had permissive powers to operate rent rebate schemes since the Housing Act 1930, rebates were put on to a mandatory basis by the Housing Finance Act 1972. The scheme was intended to protect low-income tenants from the rent increases envisaged under that Act. The scheme was designed on a different basis from SB, the amount of benefit received being determined by three variables: household composition, assessed income, and rent and rates bills.

Given that the dual politics thesis would 'predict' that, under a reallocation of functions, the DHSS local offices would take over the administration of the rebate scheme, why did the opposite in fact occur? The reasons for this reform have been discussed at length elsewhere (Kemp, 1987) and only a brief summary can be attempted here. But three main factors seem to have been particularly important.

First and perhaps of most significance, much of the pressure for changing the way means-tested help with housing costs was provided stemmed from the need to reform the SB scheme (Kemp, 1984; Malpass, 1984). When the present system of social assistance was set up in 1948, it was intended to have a residual, safety-net function. The National Insurance scheme, based on contributions whilst in work, was intended to provide against the contingencies of unemployment, sickness and old age. National Assistance (SB from 1966) was to provide a safety-net for the few who had not been able to insure adequately against these contingencies. But as Beveridge (1942) made clear in his report, a national insurance system based largely on contributions made in work assumed the maintenance of full employment. With the growth of unemployment during the 1970s, however, an increasing number of unemployed people received SB rather than unemployment benefit under the National Insurance system. Consequently, the SB scheme came under growing strain as it increasingly took on a mass role rather than the residual function originally envisaged for it (DHSS, 1978).

By 1978 one in ten of the population was reliant on SB (Malpass, 1984). At the same time as the SB caseload was growing, its composition also changed. In proportionate terms, pensioner recipients declined, while those who were lone parents or unemployed increased. The circumstances, and hence the benefit entitlement, of the latter two groups changed with much greater frequency than was the case with pensioners. This increased volatility of the SB caseload added further strain on the system (Deacon and Bradshaw, 1983).

In the late 1970s, a review of SB was carried out under the Labour government of Harold Wilson, the main goal of which was to achieve a simplification of the system. According to the consultation document *Social Assistance,* 'In our view the most realistic aim is to fit the scheme to its mass role of coping with millions of claimants' (DHSS, 1978, p. 5). One way in which this simplification was achieved was to reduce the degree of administrative discretion built into the scheme. Another was to hand over the administration of the housing component of SB to local authorities. Because the housing component had to be based on actual rent and rates rather than a notional, uniform amount, they had to be verified, calculated separately and adjusted every time rent or rates altered. It was estimated that about 10 per cent of DHSS staff was taken up simply with adjusting SB payments as a result of changes in housing costs. According to *Social Assistance,* the housing part of SB was 'a major source of complexity, high staff costs and duplication of effort with local authorities' (DHSS, 1978, p. 58). As the chairman of the then Supplementary Benefits Commission (SBC) later recalled,

> as we looked more deeply into the supplementary benefit scheme which was now being reviewed from top to bottom, it became increasingly clear that we could only achieve a radical simplification of our own system if we first got housing payments out of it. (Donnison, 1982, p. 189)

A second factor was that the Conservative government of 1979 was very keen to reduce the number of civil servants as part of its strategy of pushing back the boundaries of the welfare state. It was estimated that 2,900 DHSS jobs could be 'saved' by transferring the housing component of SB to local authorities, though the latter would need to take on extra staff to deal with the additional workload it would mean for them (DHSS, 1978).

Third, local authorities were not unwilling to take on this extra work because it involved 'rent direct' for council tenants on SB. That is, instead of council tenants receiving their help with housing costs as part of their SB, the administration of the housing component by local councils meant that the benefit could be paid directly into the tenant's rent account, thus ensuring that it was actually used for the purposes for which it was intended. As the Association of Metropolitan Authorities noted in a memorandum to the House of Commons Social Services Committee in June 1984, 'Local authorities were asked to adminster the scheme and could see some advantages in having rent paid direct' (quoted in Kemp, 1987, p. 175). Under the old scheme, the SBC had discretionary powers to deduct rent from a claimant's SB and pay it directly to the landlord. Faced with a rising tide of rent arrears in the late 1970s (rising from £34.8m or 3 per cent of the total rent collectable in 1975/76 to £138.7m or 4.4 per cent in 1981/82 – Duncan and Kirby, 1983), local authorities were pressing for a more general use of this power. The SBC had been reluctant to use it except in cases of persistent default, because 'direct payment procedures may in fact weaken the claimant's ability to manage his own budget' (Supplementary Benefits Commission, 1978, p. 57). Although the number of SB recipients on rent direct was increasing, by 1981 only 154,000 tenants (or 7 per cent of the total) were on it. But with local authorities administering the housing component of SB, rent direct would be automatic. Hence a reform of housing benefit offered local authorities the prospect of containing rent arrears and of making savings in their collection costs.

To sum up, the administrative relocation within the state of means-tested assistance with housing costs did not occur – as the dual politics thesis would suggest – in order to insulate it from local democratic pressures. Rather it occurred because it offered the prospect of attaining goals (simplifying SB, reducing the number of civil servants, and introducing mandatory rent direct for council tenants) that were largely external to it. If nothing else, this serves to remind us of the dangers of attempting to explain everything in terms of a single principle or theory (Hindess, 1987). Reality is fortunately more complex than that.

The new housing benefit that was established in 1982/83 still comprised what were essentially the previous two schemes (albeit with some modification – see Kemp, 1984a), but largely unified their administration by handing over the housing component of SB to local authorities. DHSS local offices still had a role to play, however, in that they had to authorise the payment of housing benefit by the authorities to SB recipients. Moreover, the DHSS in central government was made solely responsible for the budget and for the rules governing the administration of the scheme.

Although it was essentially only an administrative reform, the introduction of housing benefit resulted not in a more efficient delivery of assistance with housing costs, but in widespread administrative chaos. *The Times,* not known for overstatement on these matters, called it the biggest administrative fiasco in the history of the welfare state (*The Times,* 20 January 1984). That administrative chaos is now well documented, and the reasons for it have been discussed in some detail elsewhere (see Kemp, 1984a; Walker, 1985, 1986). These widespread implementation problems continued well into 1984 and beyond. Thus a survey of local authorities carried out in the spring of 1984 found that the majority were still experiencing problems (Kemp, 1984a). Surveys by Walker (1985) in May and December 1984 found broadly similar results, though there was some improvement between the two dates.

Much of the initial difficulties that local authorities experienced were the result of the hurried implementation of the scheme, which was itself the result of the desire of the DHSS to make civil service staff savings in the 1982/83 financial year. The more enduring problems of administering the schemes were the product of two main factors. First, the continued dual structure of assistance with housing costs (one for those on SB, a second for other claimants) meant that the scheme was very complex to administer. Second, the scheme was predicated upon effective inter-agency liaison between local authorities and DHSS local offices (this is discussed in some detail in Walker, 1986), which proved very difficult to achieve in practice.

Following a review of the housing benefit scheme by an independent team in 1984 (along with reviews of several other parts of the social security system) a new housing benefit scheme was introduced in April 1988. This involved the unification of the previous dual structure of assistance into a single benefit applicable to all low-income households, whether or not they are on income support (Kemp, 1987). The administrative involvement of DSS local offices has been minimised. However, the discretion which authorities previously had to operate 'local schemes' in order to enhance benefit for groups of claimants whom they deemed to be deserving of additional assistance, was greatly reduced and restricted to war pensioners and individual cases of hardship. This reduction in discretion is consistent with the dual politics thesis because it reduces the openness of housing benefit expenditure to local democratic pressures.

Conclusion

In this chapter we have seen that state intervention has a very important influence upon the amount that people pay for their housing, whether it is in the public or the private sector. Broadly speaking, such intervention acts either to reduce the price of housing relative to other goods, or it increases people's ability to pay the cost of housing. However such assistance is provided, it has important political and ideological implications. Indeed, the changes that have taken place in housing subsidies since 1979 reflect both the economic and the ideological premises of the new right perspective on government policy-making. There has been a shift away from forms of assistance developed in the social democratic tradition (such as Exchequer subsidy and rate fund contributions to council housing) and towards subsidies and tax reliefs (such as MIRAS and housing benefit) which favour and reinforce market-orientated forms of provision. This shift in assistance has both reflected and facilitated the privatisation of housing provision that has been at the heart of Conservative housing policy since 1979.

Privatisation has also been encouraged by government policy on rents within both the public and the private sectors. In the private sector, rents have been deregulated (and security of tenure weakened) in order to make investment in this part of the housing market more profitable. Similarly, housing association rents have been deregulated so as to facilitate a reduced level of capital subsidy and to attract private sector finance. Local authority rent increases have been induced by the reduction of Exchequer subsidy, thus making the alternative of purchase (with a discount) under the right to buy more attractive to council tenants, and making the acquisition of tenanted council estates more viable for investors under the 'tenant's choice' scheme.

Finally, we looked in detail at housing benefit, setting the recent decentralisation of the scheme's administration within a dual politics perspective. We again showed that the thesis is over-generalised, but we were nevertheless able to use it to illuminate some key concerns about the shifting emphasis of housing subsidy in the 1980s. We saw, for instance, that while the administration of housing benefit has been decentralised, control over the rules governing eligibility and benefit levels have remained with central government, and local authority discretionary powers have been reduced. This suggests that central government concern about the cost of welfare has prevailed over professional and consumer concerns about benefit delivery and responsiveness to individual claimant needs. Much of the centralisation of policy and the increasing conflicts in central–local relations since 1979 have resulted from attempts by central government to restrain local government expenditure and to shift its orientation to favour the market (see Loughlin *et al.*, 1985). From this point of view, leaving local authorities with responsibility for administering housing benefit in a context where benefit levels are being reduced, has the advantage for central government that its responsibility for the cuts is not necessarily obvious to claimants, so that blame can partly be deflected on to the administrative agency which has to implement them.

5
Homelessness

We saw in Chapter 3 that housing is an important component of social well-being and that disadvantage is mediated through housing provision in important respects. Gaining access to housing is crucial, therefore, because it can affect people's life chances in many important ways. At its most basic, securing accommodation provides essential shelter against the elements and a locus for social reproduction. For those households who have been unable to obtain a home for themselves, access to other social services such as health care or education can become difficult. Homelessness, therefore, is an important concern for social policy as a whole, not only because it represents the ultimate in housing disadvantage but also because it challenges the inflexibility of service provision in those areas of welfare whose delivery requires a fixed personal address.

Access to housing

In considering homelessness it is important to relate it to the wider issue of access to housing. The ways in which households gain access to housing were touched upon in Chapter 3 (see also Clapham and Kintrea, 1986; Henderson and Karn, 1984, 1987). Here it is necessary only to stress that access channels into housing differ significantly between the private and the public housing sectors. In the private sector, access is mainly determined by ability to pay, albeit mediated by the actions and decisions of 'gatekeepers' (Pahl, 1975; Foster, 1983) such as estate agents, building society managers and private landlords. For low-income households, therefore, access into the owner-occupied housing market can be difficult. This is not only because of the need for a sufficiently large and stable income to repay a mortgage, but also because a deposit is often necessary before a lender will agree to grant a loan. The practice of building societies refusing to lend on certain types of property in certain kinds of areas has had particularly severe consequences for low-income owner-occupation among Asians (Commission for Racial Equality, 1985), and stereotypical judgements about what sorts of people and what kinds of occupation provide a sound investment has led to discrimination against both black people and women in terms of access to the housing market (Karn, 1983; Watson, 1987).

For low-income households, as well as for migrants, the privately rented sector has traditionally provided a gateway into the housing market. This sector has always been difficult to regulate with respect to racial discrimination, physical conditions and harassment. Nevertheless, it has at least provided relatively easy-access accommodation, which is especially important to those who are too poor to buy but are unable to fulfil the bureaucratic requirements of entry to the public sector. However, the privately rented sector now only accounts for about 8 per cent of the total stock, and recent years have witnessed (as we show later in the chapter) the emergence of an 'access crisis' in the housing market.

In the public housing sector, access is supposed to be determined by 'need' rather than by ability to pay. It is important to note here that 'need' is a social construct. That is to say, rather than being objectively determined and self-evident, need is defined by professionals such as housing managers (Foster, 1983, provides a useful critique of the notion of need in access to welfare). It is important to recognise, therefore, that where demand for accommodation is greater than its supply, definitions of need become a bureaucratic rationing device. A particular definition of need can be used to determine which households are to be given priority for accommodation. Those deemed to be in 'greatest need' can then be allowed to join the waiting list or go to the top of the queue.

As Chapter 2 showed, local authorities have been the predominant providers of public rented housing since 1919. In 1986 they still accounted for 90 per cent of all public housing in England and Wales (DoE, 1987). Local authorities have considerable discretion in determining how and to whom they should let their accommodation. Originally, they were only empowered to provide housing for the 'working classes', but that ambiguous phrase was dropped in

1949. The Housing Act of 1957 stated that, in the selection of their tenants, local authorities should give 'reasonable preference' to certain groups of household (such as those being displaced by slum clearance schemes) in allocating accommodation. But beyond these general guidelines, authorities were able to determine their own priorities as to whom they should house and in what order. It was not until 1977 that they were given a statutory duty to rehouse the homeless, and even then this only applied to those in certain 'priority need' groups who met certain specified conditions (discussed below). Indeed, the attitude of many councils to the homeless has often been ambiguous and, at times, distinctly punitive.

The social construction of homelessness

Homelessness can be defined in a variety of ways, so the number of people who are regarded as homeless in Britain today varies from thousands to millions. Even given a particular definition of the term, the homeless are not always easy to count. A particular concern of some pressure groups, for example, has been the so-called 'hidden homeless', such as women living in unsatisfactory relationships which they want to leave but for economic reasons feel they cannot (Watson with Austerberry, 1986). Yet unless these people express their homelessness in some recognisable way (for example, by moving into a women's refuge) there is little way of knowing that they are not adequately housed. Likewise, although there are large numbers of people living on the streets or in night shelters, the exact total is difficult to ascertain. As Greve, Page and Greve (1971, p. 55) pointed out in their well-known study of homelessness in London, 'nobody knows, or has ever known, how many homeless persons there are, and there is no agreement about what in fact homelessness is.'

Watson argues that homelessness lies at one end of a continuum that ranges from absolute rooflessness to outright (unmortgaged) home ownership (Watson with Austerberry, 1986). Instead of specifying a particular point at which a household can be regarded as homeless rather than just badly housed, she argues that homelessness is a relative concept that is socially constructed within a particular political economy. It follows from this that definitions of the concept can be expected to change over time, to be a matter of debate, and to be produced through social discourse and political struggle. Echoing the debate over how poverty should be defined (discussed in Chapter 3), we would expect those who adhere to a pure market model of welfare to favour an absolute definition that tends towards rooflessness, and those in the social democratic tradition to extend the concept further along the continuum to embrace a more relative definition in which homelessness begins once the social rights associated with shelter are infringed upon.

In the remainder of this chapter we examine how the state has defined and dealt with the issue of homelessness. In doing so, we show that despite the important advance made by the Housing (Homeless Persons) Act 1977, the legislative response both before and after that date has been imbued with an overriding concern to protect individuals' rights to private property, sometimes at the expense of the broader social rights conferred on all individuals by virtue of residence and citizenship.

Homelessness before 1977

Homelessness is not unique to advanced capitalist societies; nor is legislation to deal with it a recent event. State action in respect of those who were both destitute and homeless goes back to medieval times, though it was not necessarily benevolent either in intent or in outcome. Prior to 1948, the Poor Law authorities were responsible for dealing with the indigent homeless. Those who were not recognised as citizens of the parish could be ejected under the Vagrancy Acts and the laws of settlement. Even those who did have local ties were provided with only meagre assistance in the workhouses or casual wards run by the Poor Law authorities (Donnison and Ungerson, 1982).

The number of people housed in the casual wards was not small. In 1911, for example, 5 per cent of all single women and 25 per cent of all single men aged 65 or over in England and Wales were living in workhouses (Donnison and Ungerson, 1982). That so many people were relying on the workhouse at the time is not surprising. Social security provision for older people, the unemployed, the sick and the disabled was very limited (see Fraser, 1973), while the labour market was subject to marked seasonal and cyclical fluctuations (Beveridge, 1908). Rented housing before the First World War was almost

116   *Housing and Social Policy*

entirely provided by private landlords; only those who could afford
to pay the market rent were housed by the private sector, and
eviction for the non-payment of rent was very common (Wohl,
1977).

Thus, at a time when public housing scarcely existed, a primitive
and punitive form of state shelter was provided by the workhouse
for those without the means of subsistence. In accordance with the
principle of 'less eligibility', conditions within these workhouses
were deliberately harsh and unattractive in order to deter would-be
applicants for relief. As we shall see below, the two principles of
requiring a local connection and of less eligibility have been carried
over in part into current policy towards the homeless.

The National Assistance Act 1948 marked a significant development in state provision for the homeless. This Act abolished the
Poor Law and closed most of the remaining casual wards. The
National Assistance Board maintained a number of the old casual
wards as short-stay reception centres in order to meet its obligation,
under the 1948 Act, to provide shelter for those without 'a settled
way of living' (Donnison and Ungerson, 1982). The DSS still
maintains 22 of these reception centres, but it has a long-term policy
to close them down. The 1948 Act also obliged local authorities to
improve permanent residential care for the people 'who by reason of
age, infirmity or any other circumstances are in need of care and
attention which is not otherwise available to them.'

Section 21 of the National Assistance Act also required local
authority welfare departments to provide 'temporary accommodation for persons who are in urgent need thereof, being need arising in
circumstances which could not reasonably have been foreseen or in
other such circumstances as the authority may in any case determine' (quoted in Watchman and Robson, 1983).

Several points are worth making about this new duty that was
placed upon local authorities. First, it is significant that the responsibility was placed upon welfare rather than housing departments.
This reflected the view that homelessness was not a housing but a
welfare problem. As Watchman and Robson (1983, p. 23) have
pointed out, this conception 'had the consequence ... of emphasising a traditional pathological social work approach to homelessness,
that is to say, the use of counselling, the case-work method and other
social work skills'. Second, the need for assistance had to be
'unforeseen', a criterion that was later carried over into the Housing

(Homeless Persons) Act 1977. Already, then, the concept of need was being qualified with the notion of intentionality. By implication, those who foresaw and did not avert their plight would be among those deemed to be undeserving of assistance. Third, the assistance to be provided was to be only temporary. This seems to have reflected the view that 'legitimate' homelessness was a product of either an emergency (such as fire or flood) or of some crisis that could be solved by social work skills. In either case, all that was required or deserved was interim accommodation to help the family get back on its feet.

Fourth, the Act gave local authorities a great deal of discretion in interpreting the legislation. The three key requirements, stressed in the extract from section 21 quoted above, were that the authority's duty was to provide 'temporary' help for those in 'urgent need' which was 'reasonably unforeseeable'. Yet in each case the Act gave no guidance as to how local authorities should interpret these phrases in carrying out their new statutory duty. Not surprisingly, there were considerable variations between councils in the way that they met their obligation to the homeless (Watchman and Robson, 1983).

Many councils appear to have taken a punitive approach to those for whom they provided temporary accommodation. For example, the Morris Committee (1975) found that many councils in Scotland used former workhouses to provide temporary accommodation, while others used bed and breakfast establishments, rather than normal housing. Watchman and Robson (1983, pp. 26–7) noted that many authorities interpreted urgent need to apply exclusively to 'homeless families, or more exactly the mother and children of homeless families, rather than to homeless persons.' Homeless families were often split up (as had often been the case in the Poor Law workhouses) through the practice of excluding fathers from the temporary accommodation that was provided (Glastonbury, 1971).

The number of households admitted to local authority temporary accommodation fell during most of the 1950s, though it began to rise again by the end of the decade. Donnison and Ungerson (1982) point to the onset of full employment, the substantially enhanced income maintenance system, and the new National Health Service, as factors which may have helped to reduce the number of families unable to secure a roof over their heads. The high levels of local authority housebuilding for general family needs at this time may also have played a part in reducing the need for families to apply for temporary accommodation.

In the 1960s homelessness emerged as a 'social problem' for the first time since the establishment of the welfare state; it was part of the 'rediscovery' of poverty by politicians and by academics such as Abel-Smith and Townsend. In 1961 the London County Council set up an inquiry into homelessness in London, which was published in 1964 (Greve, 1964). However, it was the screening in 1966 of the television drama 'Cathy Come Home' that helped turn homelessness into a media issue. Several pressure groups, including Shelter, were subsequently set up to campaign for the homeless. The Greater London Council (which had superceded the LCC) set up a new inquiry into homelessness in London, which reported in 1971 (Greve, Page & Greve, 1971). During the 1970s there was a marked growth in the number of households provided with temporary accommodation by local authorities in England and Wales.

Homelessness gained further recognition as a policy problem with the publication during the late 1960s and early 1970s of several official reports on various aspects of housing and the social services. These included those by the Seebohm Committee (1968) on local authority and allied social services, the Cullingworth Committee (1969) on council housing, the Finer Committee (1974) on lone-parent families, and the Morris Committee (1975) on the relationship between housing and social work in Scotland. Each of these reports emphasised that homelessness was essentially a housing, not a welfare, problem. Accordingly, they recommended that statutory responsibility for the homeless should be transferred from social services to housing departments, while recognising that effective liaison between them was essential.

The Seebohm Committee also recommended that a further responsibility should be placed upon housing departments to give whatever help may be needed to provide permanent accommodation. The Committee stressed that this help need not involve the allocation of council housing, but it

> should ensure that families do not break up and children do not become separated from their parents *just* because they cannot secure a home together. We believe the community should accept this as a basic principle upon which policies for the homeless should be firmly based. (Seebohm Committee, 1968, p. 127)

The Committee added that it was 'particularly important for the preservation of families' that they should not be split up on reception into temporary accommodation: 'domestic friction is an important factor in precipitating homelessness; we should not by public policy help to make this a permanent separation of husband and wife' (Seebohm Committee, 1968, p. 127). Leaving aside this apparent elision between relationship breakdown as a cause of homelessness and as a consequence of it, Seebohm's concern in calling for a new statutory responsibility for homelessness seems to have been the preservation of the family and the prevention of children being taken into care.

In what was supposed to be a 'tidying up' provision of the 1972 Local Government Act, the mandatory duty of local authorities to provide temporary assistance for homeless families under the 1948 Act was replaced by a discretionary power only. This was, however, subject to powers of direction by the Secretary of State for Social Services, who could make it mandatory. According to Raynsford (1986), this change helped to galvanise a number of voluntary organisations in their campaign for the homeless.

During 1974 the Labour government responded to these reports and the voluntary group pressure by issuing a directive which made local authorities' duty under the 1948 Act mandatory instead of permissive, by announcing a review of homelessness duties, and by issuing a joint DoE/DHSS circular (18/74) on the subject. The consultation paper which resulted from the review argued that it was unrealistic (because of their limited resources) to place a duty on housing departments to provide either permanent or temporary council housing for the homeless (DoE, 1975). This led to renewed lobbying and pressure from the voluntary organisations representing the homeless to introduce new legislation and to keep the issue on the political agenda (Richards, 1981; Raynsford, 1986). The joint DoE/DHSS circular of 1974, however, did advise local authorities to transfer primary responsibility for providing temporary accommodation from social services to housing departments. But it stressed that social services departments should continue to use their resources to help prevent homelessness and to continue providing residential care for the elderly and the infirm. Significantly, the circular also identified certain 'priority groups' for assistance – namely, families, pregnant women, the elderly and those who were vulnerable.

The Housing (Homeless Persons) Act 1977

The Housing (Homeless Persons) Act of 1977 marked a significant turning point in the legislative response to homelessness. Specifically, it represented an important advance towards securing citizenship rights in an area of social welfare in which the rights of private property are paramount. For the first time, certain groups of homeless people (identified below) were given a statutory right to be rehoused by their local authority.

This Act shows that significant concessions can be won for the poor and the powerless, even in a society increasingly dominated by corporate groups. Homeless people are a fragmented and relatively powerless group who have to rely on pluralistic bargaining and democratic pressure to further their interests. Accordingly, much of the literature on the introduction of this Act focuses on the role which a number of pressure groups and certain key individuals (such as civil servants and a few MPs) played in getting this private member's bill (which was drafted by the DoE but was introduced by a Liberal MP) through parliament at the time of the 'Lib/Lab pact' (Richards, 1981; Donnison and Ungerson, 1982; Raynsford, 1986).

Although it is instructive to focus on the pressure group influence behind the 1977 Act, it is also important to grasp the broader political context within which it was passed, for it was enacted at a time when a new complacency emerged about housing policy and a redefinition of the 'housing problem' took place (Ball, 1983; Malpass, 1986b). This new approach was laid bare in the Housing Policy Review green paper which was published in the same year as the Homeless Persons Act was passed (DoE, 1977). As defined in this document, the housing problem was no longer a national shortage of dwellings, but rather a localised and essentially residual problem that affected some areas and a limited number of disadvantaged groups (see Cullingworth, 1979). From this perspective it was possible to acknowledge the need to provide immediate accommodation for a small number of 'deserving' homeless families without recognising or taking responsibility for a wider problem of housing market or policy failure. Homelessness was portrayed and responded to as an isolated problem faced by a few unfortunate individuals.

Also relevant to our understanding of the genesis of the 1977 Act is the increasing polarisation between owner-occupation and local authority provision that occurred as private renting continued to decline through the 1970s. Previously, the privately rented sector had provided a relatively easy access route into the housing market. The main rented alternative, council housing, usually required a lengthy period on the housing waiting list. With the decline of privately rented housing, the supply of immediate-access housing was drying up, particularly for low-income households wanting unfurnished accommodation. To an extent, then, the Homeless Persons Act provided an alternative to private renting for those who, for whatever reason, needed immediate access to housing but were unable to secure it for themselves.

Homelessness under the 1977 Act

The duty of local authorities to rehouse people under the Housing (Homeless Persons) Act 1977 (now Part III of the Housing Act 1985) is actually rather limited. As Watchman and Robson (1981) have pointed out, homeless people have successfully to traverse a series of obstacles before they will be accepted for rehousing; and eligibility to enter the race is strictly limited. Councils' duty to provide housing is restricted to 'deserving' groups in three main ways.

First, local authorities have only to rehouse those groups who are defined as being in 'priority need'. These are:

1. households with dependent children or in which a woman is pregnant;
2. people who are vulnerable in some way (for instance, due to their age, or physical or mental disability);
3. people made homeless by an emergency (such as a fire or flood).

With respect to the first category, we have already noted the concern expressed by the Seebohm Committee (1968) and others to ensure that children are not taken into care because of homelessness (this principle is particularly important to the new right's ideology of the family in the 1980s). Since individuals subsumed in the second category have, for the most part, no direct relationship with the labour market, they can be defined as deserving of assistance, in that the provision of state help would not be expected to inhibit the qualities of initiative and self-reliance which the undeserving homeless (those who could, theoretically, compete in the labour market and provide for themselves) are deemed to lack. The third category of households falls into the 'unforeseen homelessness' situation discussed above in relation to the 1948 Act.

Second, only those households who are deemed to be unintentionally homeless have a right to permanent rehousing by the local authority. Those in priority need but who are deemed to be intentionally homeless have a right only to be provided with temporary accommodation (but this does not mean that an authority will automatically refuse to rehouse them).

The intentionality clause of the Act can and is being interpreted in ways that cause particular problems for the families of those who have emigrated to Britain and become British citizens. One London borough (Tower Hamlets), which has a large Bengali community, has argued that those who return to Bangladesh to bring back their wives and children to Britain and who find themselves homeless on their return, have become so intentionally. The authority has maintained that these families have given up a home that was available to them in Bangladesh, even though many of the fathers concerned are British citizens and have lived in Britain for over a decade. The authority's decision has been upheld by the House of Lords. This problem for immigrant British citizens from the Indian sub-continent has been made worse by the Immigration Act 1988, which removes from Commonwealth citizens who settled in Britain before 1973 their right to bring wives and children to Britain unless they can show they can support themselves without recourse to public funds.

Third, councils have a duty only to rehouse those unintentionally homeless households in priority need who have a 'local connection' with the area. If they do not have a local connection, councils can refer them on to an authority with whom they do have such a connection. In 1986, 755 households in England were referred on in this way to another local authority by the one to whom they had applied for assistance (DoE, 1988b). This clause has been used by one London borough (Camden) to repatriate Irish migrants who had moved to London to seek employment. Instead of providing them with housing, the borough gave them travel warrants back to Ireland, and argued that, in principle, the same strategy might be applied to migrants from the Indian sub-continent.

To summarise, local authorities have a statutory duty to provide permanent accommodation for those households who apply to them under Part III of the Housing Act 1985 who meet three criteria: that is, they are in priority need, they are unintentionally homeless, and they have a local connection. These households have a legal right to be provided with accommodation. This is an important exception to the general rule that there is no statutory 'right' to housing in Britain. With this exception, and unlike health care and education – and contrary to the implicit claim of Cawson and Saunders (1983), as set out in Chapter 1 – the rights of private property rather than of citizenship have been predominant in housing provision. Even so, these three criteria act as a sieve to limit eligibility for assistance under the Act, and they are constructed to avoid challenging the rights of private property or undermining the market model of welfare provision. As we shall see below, the way in which the Act has been implemented has also been infused with these concerns and has employed notions about the deserving and the undeserving and about 'less eligibility' in the provision of shelter for homeless people.

Working the Act

The implementation of the Homeless Persons Act has been a subject of much controversy and considerable litigation. The Act is only a general statute and is supported by a code of guidance (Watchman and Robson, 1983) which indicates how councils should interpret the legislation and discharge their duties. According to Widdowson (1987, p. 220), the Code of Guidance was 'designed by the government to provide uniformity of interpretation and to soften the effects of amendments such as the intentionality provision'. But in 1980 the Court of Appeal undermined the apparent authority of the Code by holding that it was advisory only. However, section 71 of the Housing Act 1985 made it clear that authorities are required to 'have regard' to its guidance. The 1980 ruling has allowed local authorities greater discretion in interpreting their duties under the Act and has led to more legal challenges to their decisions (Widdowson, 1987). Consequently, a great deal of case law has developed on homelessness under the Act. In 1986 the House of Lords remarked in an appeal case that too many local authority decisions were being challenged and that this should, in future, be reduced.

Under the Act, when people apply to the local authority for assistance or accommodation, and the authority has 'reason to believe' that they may be homeless or threatened by homelessness, housing departments are obliged to carry out enquiries into the applicant's personal circumstances and into the circumstances leading up to the application. The authority's subsequent duty under the Act will depend upon the findings of these enquiries and varies from providing advice to providing permanent accommodation. They will have to provide one of the following:

1. advice and appropriate assistance;
2. reasonable steps to secure that accommodation does not cease to be available;
3. temporary accommodation;
4. permanent accommodation.

At all levels in the process there is scope for differing interpretations between councils as to their duties in each case. This even applies to the crucial first gatepost of determining what is an application. For example, a survey of the implementation of the Act by six London boroughs (Goss, 1983) found that there was wide variation in what was regarded as an application. Table 5.1 shows the action taken by local authorities in England in 1986 in respect of those who were regarded as having made an application under the Act. As can be seen, over one quarter (28 per cent) of applicants were considered not to be homeless.

Table 5.1   *Action by local authorities in England in 1986 under the homelessness provisions of the Housing Act 1985*

	No. of households	%
Total enquiries completed	219,300	100
of which:		
Accepted for rehousing	102,980	47
Advice and assistance	54,780	25
Found not to be homeless	61,540	28

Source: DoE (1988b).

Where a homeless applicant is found either not to be in priority need or is deemed to be intentionally homeless, the authority's duty is limited to providing only 'advice and appropriate assistance'. This rather limited duty includes action such as giving financial advice, informing applicants of the possibility of registering on the housing waiting list, or providing a list of accommodation agencies or bed and breakfast establishments. As Table 5.1 shows, one-quarter of applicants were provided with this type of help under the Act.

Where applicants are in priority need and threatened with homelessness, the Act requires authorities to take 'reasonable steps' to ensure that their accommodation does not cease to be available for occupation. Watchman and Robson (1983) have suggested that this might include such action as making discretionary payments towards rent arrears under section 1 of the Child Care Act 1980 (section 12 of the Social Work [Scotland] Act 1968) in order to prevent an eviction taking place, or providing advice on the legal rights which attach to the occupancy of accommodation under the common law, or under statute in a case of relationship breakdown. This example emphasises the need for close co-operation and good co-ordination at the individual case level between housing and social services departments (an issue that we explore in more detail in Chapter 8).

Local authorities are required to provide temporary accommodation in two circumstances. First, they should provide such accommodation pending the completion of their enquiries under the Act. This duty prevents them from leaving a homeless applicant in priority need on the streets while they make their enquiries (Watchman and Robson, 1983). Second, temporary accommodation must be provided where a household is in priority need but is deemed to be intentionally homeless. Temporary help of this sort is intended to give them a reasonable opportunity to secure accommodation for their own occupation. It appears that there is a considerable variation between authorities in the use of the intentionality provision. For example, a survey by Shelter carried out in 1980 found that the average rate at which applicants were deemed to be intentionally homeless in England and Wales was 8.4 per cent, but the range was from less than 5 per cent in some authorities to more than 50 per cent in others (Widdowson, 1987). In 1986, according to the DoE quarterly homelessness returns, 3,070 households were found to be in priority need but were treated as intentionally homeless (DoE, 1988b).

The *duty* on councils to provide permanent housing extends only to those who are in priority need and unintentionally homeless. In fact, however, a significant minority of households deemed to be intentionally homeless and placed in temporary accommodation are eventually given permanent housing by the authority. For example, about one-third of the priority need, intentionally homeless households whose period in temporary accommodation came to an end during 1987 moved to permanent housing secured by the local authority. A further third found alternative accommodation for themselves, while the remaining third were required to leave the temporary accommodation with which the council had provided them, presumably without any other accommodation to go to. It is in situations like this that the non-statutory, voluntary agencies often have an important role. Some of these households may end up having a further period in bed and breakfast accommodation, but not under the homelessness provisions of the Housing Act.

Table 5.2 shows that 92 per cent of those homeless households accepted for permanent rehousing were in a priority need group. Of these, 80 per cent had dependent children to support or a member of the household who was pregnant. Some 18 per cent were accepted because of some degree of vulnerability, and 2 per cent because they had been made homeless as a result of an emergency.

Table 5.2 *Priority need of homeless households accepted for rehousing by local authorities, England, 1986*

	% of all households in priority need	% of all households rehoused
In priority need:		
dependent children	66	
pregnancy	14	
vulnerable	18	
—old age	(8)	
—physical handicap	(3)	
—mental illness	(2)	
—other	(5)	
emergency	2	
Total in priority need	100	92
Not in priority need		8
Total		100
Number of households		102,980

Source: DoE (1988b).

Again, however, there appear to be variations between authorities in the ratio of applications to acceptances for rehousing under the

Act. Widdowson (1987) points out that, for the final quarter of 1985, 40 per cent of applicants were accepted for rehousing under the Act in England. But in some localities, for example Cleveland (24 per cent) and Shropshire (27 per cent) only about one-quarter were accepted, while at the other end of the scale the London Borough of Southwark accepted 70 per cent of applications and Bristol accepted 88 per cent. While these differences to some extent reflect the variation that exists between local authorities in their practice of deciding what constitutes an application for assistance under the Act, it seems also to reflect differences in interpretation of the legislation.

For example, local authorities vary in their interpretation of what situations constitute homelessness. A recent DoE survey of local authorities asked whether applicants living in specified types of accommodation were usually accepted as homeless (Evans and Duncan, 1988). It was found that while 78 per cent of metropolitan authorities usually accepted people living in squats as being home-less, this was true of only 33 per cent of district councils. Again, while 76 per cent of metropolitan authorities accepted people living in hostels as homeless, this was the case with only 32 per cent of London boroughs. Overall, as Table 5.3 shows, the main accommo-dation type for which authorities in England and Wales accepted people as homeless was women's refuges (78 per cent of authorities), followed by statutorily unfit accommodation (53 per cent).

As well as in accommodation types, there were variations in the other circumstances in which local authorities accepted applicants as

Table 5.3 *Accommodation types from which applicants are usually accepted as homeless by local authorities in England and Wales*

Accommodation type	% of LAs
Mobile home/caravan	11
Statutorily overcrowded accommodation	32
Squat	39
Bed and breakfast	38
Hostel	42
Statutorily unfit accommodation	53
Women's refuge	78
Base (no. of LAs)	(358)

Source: Evans and Duncan (1988).

homeless under the 1985 Housing Act. Thus while all metropolitan authorities usually considered childless battered women to be homeless, this was true of 76 per cent of London boroughs and 80 per cent of district councils. Again, while 88 per cent of metropolitan authorities usually considered applicants who were children leaving care to be homeless, only 37 per cent of London boroughs did so (Evans and Duncan, 1988). Table 5.4 shows the results for England and Wales as a whole and reveals significant differences in how people leaving different categories of institution are regarded under the Act.

An important but contentious issue has been the type of accommodation with which homeless people have been provided by councils rehousing them. Although the wording of the Act effectively prevents the pre-1977 practice of splitting up families, it does not provide detailed guidance as to the nature, standard, or location of the accommodation which authorities should offer homeless people. The code of guidance states that homeless persons should be given permanent housing as soon as possible and that they should not be obliged to spend a period in interim accommodation as a matter of policy. In fact, considerable numbers of homeless households accepted for rehousing do spend some time in temporary accommodation prior to being given permanent housing by the authority. At 30 June 1987 some 23,050 households in England were in temporary accommodation during enquiries or pending permanent rehousing under the Act (DoE, 1988b). Of these, as Table 5.5

Table 5.4   *Circumstances in which applicants are usually considered as homeless by local authorities in England and Wales**

Circumstances	% of LAs
Childless battered women	84
Applicants leaving long-stay hospitals	87
Young single people (on basis of age only)	17
Children leaving care	57
Applicants leaving hostels	57
Applicants leaving prison	47
Base (no. of LAs)	(358)

*Includes LAs who automatically define these cases as priority need and those who do not.
Source: Evans and Duncan (1988).

Table 5.5 *Households in temporary accommodation during enquiries or pending permanent provision in England as at 30 June 1987*

Type of temporary accommodation	Households No.	%
Bed and breakfast	10,870	47
Hostel*	5,020	22
Short-life dwelling, etc.	7,160	31
Total	23,050	100

*including women's refuges
Source: DoE (1988b).

shows, almost one-half were in bed and breakfast, a form of accommodation that has been criticised as unsuitable and expensive (Conway and Kemp, 1985; Audit Commission, 1986a). About one-fifth were in hostels (including women's refuges) and the remainder were in short-life housing – that is, housing awaiting demolition or substantial improvement. Moreover, 'temporary' can mean periods of more than a year. For example, a sample survey of households placed in bed and breakfast by Brent found that about one in eight had been there for twelve months or more (Bonnerjea and Lawton, 1986).

Further, it seems that, contrary to the code of guidance, some councils do place some homeless households in temporary accommodation as a matter of policy. In her survey of six London boroughs, Goss (1983) found that all of them attempted to rehouse the older people directly into permanent housing. Most also mentioned that direct rehousing was a possibility in the case of private sector evictions where adequate advance warning was given. Families with children, however, could expect to spend a period in temporary accommodation. Thus some households were treated as more deserving than others. Furthermore, those households that were 'co-operative' (by remaining with friends or relatives until a permanent tenancy was made available to them) were often rewarded for their 'good' behaviour.

It appears from the limited evidence available that some councils use temporary accommodation such as bed and breakfast as a punitive measure and as a deterrent to those who might attempt to 'jump the queue' of the housing waiting list. While some authorities point to the scarcity of housing as a reason for using temporary accommodation, it has been suggested that the underlying reason for its use has more to do with making the homeless wait their turn or to 'test the authenticity of homeless applicants' (Grosskurth and Stearn, 1986, p. 13).

Councils are advised in the Code of Guidance to treat homeless people in the same way as other applicants in their council house allocation policies; they should not discriminate against them in the number of offers they are allowed to refuse or in the types of dwelling or area for which they are made offers. Although the evidence is not comprehensive, it seems to indicate that some councils do in fact discriminate against the homeless compared with those whom they rehouse through the 'normal channel' of the housing waiting list. For example, a GLC survey found that 19 out of 33 (58 per cent) London authorities made fewer offers to the homeless than to other types of applicant (GLC, 1985). Indeed, many councils in the GLC survey appeared to operate a one-offer-only policy, while others tended to offer homeless people housing that other applicants had refused, such as flats on deck-access estates (see also Goss, 1983). Likewise, the DoE survey found that 75 per cent of local authorities in England and Wales had a policy of making just one offer to homeless people accepted for permanent rehousing (Evans and Duncan, 1988).

Homeless people are in any case in a poorer bargaining position than other types of applicant because they tend to have less scope for holding out for something better, a fact of which councils are naturally aware (Clapham and Kintrea, 1986). Households in bed and breakfast are often made aware by the council that their stay there will be longer the more 'choosey' they are about the offer they accept. While these measures seem unfair and even draconian in the 1980s, we should emphasise that they are, to a large extent, a by-product of political pressures on management to let the housing stock quickly and efficiently, to keep waiting lists short, and to re-let empty properties. This necessarily involves the development of informal and bureaucratic rules to persuade some applicants to live in difficult-to-let houses and areas. This matching of the less popular dwellings with those in the weakest bargaining positions is, in a sense, not so much intentional vindictiveness on the part of housing managers as the uncritical application of procedures developed to 'make life easy', or more tolerable, for them.

The growth in 'official' homelessness

Since the 1977 Act was passed, the number of households accepted for rehousing by local authorities has increased each year. As Table 5.6 shows, in England the numbers accepted more than doubled between 1978 and 1987, rising from 53,110 to 112,730. That is an average annual increase of 12.5 per cent. Data on the number of households who applied for assistance have only been available since 1981. Between that date and 1987 the number of applications for assistance under the Act increased from 157,600 to 228,020, a rise of 45 per cent in six years.

Table 5.6 *Homeless households accepted for rehousing by local authorities in England, 1978–87*

Year	No. of households
1978	53,110
1979	57,200
1980	69,920
1981	70,010
1982	74,800
1983	78,240
1984	83,190
1985	93,980
1986	102,980
1987	112,730

Source: DoE *Quarterly Homelessness Returns*, 1979–88.

The reasons for this sharp rise in official homelessness are a matter of debate. The DoE's statistics record only the main reason for rehousing. These are shown in Table 5.7 for the years 1978 and 1986. It must be stressed that these can only be regarded as proximate reasons for homelessness. Often the actual moment of becoming homeless under the Act is the latest stage in a chain of events that may be far from straightforward. This is particularly likely to be the case with the main proximate reason, that of being asked to leave by friends or relatives. With that important caveat in mind, we can see from Table 5.7 the changes that have taken place in the relative importance of different proximate reasons for homelessness.

Being asked to leave has become more important and now

Table 5.7   *Proximate reasons for homelessness of households rehoused by
local authorities in England, 1978 and 1986*

Main reason for loss of home	1978 (%)	1986 (%)
Evicted from friends/relatives, etc.	36	40
Relationship breakdown	15	19
Rent arrears	6	4
Mortgage arrears	6	10
Loss of privately rented home*	14	10
Loss of service tenancy	6	5
Other reason	23	12
All reasons	100	100

*reasons other than rent arrears.
Source: Widdowson (1987); DoE (1988b).

accounts for about two out of every five households accepted under
the Act. Most of the other significant changes do not seem surprising. Relationship breakdown has become more important as a cause
of homelessness, reflecting the growing incidence of this phenomenon in British society (see Logan, 1987). Mortgage default also
increased over the period and now accounts for about one in ten
acceptances under the Act. Again, this reflects the rise in mortgage
arrears and repossessions that has taken place since 1979 (Doling,
Karn and Stafford, 1986; Stafford *et al.,* 1988). According to the
Building Societies Association, there have been two main reasons
why arrears and repossessions have increased since 1979: the rise in
unemployment and the growth in relationship breakdown (so clearly
these proximate reasons for homelessness are not water-tight categories).

The growth in official homelessness has had an important effect
on access to local authority housing. An increasing proportion of all
new council tenancies is accounted for by the rehousing of homeless
households. Thus for England as a whole, the proportion of all new
secure tenancies accounted for by the rehousing of the homeless rose
from one in eight in 1978/79 to one in four in 1986/87. The
homelessness route into council housing has become especially
important in London. Over the same eight-year period to 1986/87, it
increased from one-quarter to one-half of all new secure tenancies
granted (see Table 5.8).

Table 5.8 *Homeless households housed as secure tenants by local authorities as a percentage of all new secure tenancies*

	Greater London	England
1978/79	25	14
1986/87	52	24

Source: Hansard, 18 November 1985, and DoE, *Housing and Construction Statistics* 1977–87.

With the growth in official homelessness there has also been an increase in the use of interim, temporary accommodation (such as bed and breakfast) by local authorities. Indeed, as Table 5.9 shows, the use of bed and breakfast by local authorities has increased at an even faster rate than has the number of households accepted under the Act. At 30 June 1978, 1,230 households were placed in bed and breakfast under the Act by local authorities in England; by 30 June 1987 the total was 10,920. Most of this increase occurred over the last two years of the period.

Lengthy stays in bed and breakfast can cause significant problems for homeless families in gaining access to health care and education for their children. One reason for this, which is particularly import-ant in London, is that the location of bed and breakfast establish-

Table 5.9 *Homeless households placed in bed and breakfast accommodation by local authorities in England, 1978–87*

30 June	No. of households
1978	1,230
1979	1,800
1980	2,050
1981	1,620
1982	2,030
1983	2,460
1984	3,020
1985	3,850
1986	6,950
1987	10,920

Source: DoE Quarterly Homelessness Returns, 1979–88.

ments is uneven spatially. Consequently, families may be moved some considerable distance from their previous home. The DoE survey found that 38 per cent of all local authorities in England and Wales made use of temporary accommodation in other local authority areas, while in London the proportion of boroughs doing so was 70 per cent (Evans and Duncan, 1988). This can make it difficult for children to get to school, thus disrupting their education and possibly resulting in learning difficulties. Likewise, being moved some distance into bed and breakfast can make it difficult and expensive for families to visit the doctor with whom they are registered or for them to be visited by their usual social worker or health visitor. Moreover, in areas of particularly high concentrations of bed and breakfast hotels used by local authorities, such as the Bayswater area of London, which takes in homeless families from many London boroughs, health visitors have found it very difficult even to keep track of who their clients are, still less to cope with the workload facing them. Thus homeless families can find themselves excluded from the normal support services that others can take for granted and to which they have a right. The DoE survey found that only a minority of councils who placed homeless households in temporary accommodation in other local authority areas contacted the relevant agencies there (see Table 5.10).

Furthermore, life in a bed and breakfast establishment can be very difficult and may itself create problems which have to be dealt with by welfare agencies and services other than the housing department. Despite outside appearances, the condition inside many of these hotels is often very poor (see Conway and Kemp, 1985). They may be damp, dirty and in a poor state of repair. The facilities provided

Table 5.10 *Proportion of local authorities having contacts with agencies when using temporary accommodation in other local authority areas*

Agency	% of LAs
LA housing department	24
LA environmental health department	7
Education authority	6
Health authority	11
LA social services department	26
DHSS	50

Source: Evans and Duncan (1988).

are commonly inadequate for lengthy stays. One survey of homeless families that had been rehoused by local authorities in London found that, of those that had been placed in bed and breakfast, 89 per cent had just one room for their exclusive use, 94 per cent shared a bathroom, and 95 per cent shared a toilet (Randall *et al.,* 1982). Fire precautions in these establishments have frequently been found to be inadequate and fire regulations are difficult to enforce. In areas where there are high concentrations of 'hotels' for the homeless, local authority environmental health departments are usually unable to police and enforce regulations on standards of management, overcrowding or physical conditions, because of the workload involved.

In some of these 'hotels' hot water is only available for a few hours each day, and facilities for the washing of clothes are usually unavailable. These problems cause particular difficulties for people with babies, who may have nappies to wash and feeding bottles to sterilise. Likewise, cooking facilities are often lacking or inadequate and, if available, may be located several floors away, which makes cooking difficult to do for parents on their own with small children. Consequently, many residents chose not to use a kitchen where one is provided. Instead, they eat in cafés, or buy take-away food, or cook in their rooms on temporary hot rings – the latter often located on the floor in the narrow space between bed and wall and, therefore, within reach of babies and small children, with consequent risks of burns and fire. In these circumstances it is difficult for families to maintain a proper diet; stomach disorders are common and, in Bayswater, health visitors have reported cases of malnutrition (Conway and Kemp, 1985; Conway, 1988).

Thus while homelessness can be regarded as extreme housing disadvantage, being placed in bed and breakfast can create all sorts of other problems to do with physical and emotional health and may make gaining access to other welfare services difficult. These problems, in turn, can mean that homeless families require greater help from a range of other services (health visitors, social workers, educational psychologists and so on) than they would have if they had been rehoused directly into permanent accommodation. Moreover, it has been shown that the revenue cost to the public purse of keeping families in bed and breakfast is substantially greater than that of building additional council houses or of acquiring and renovating private sector dwellings for letting by the local authority

(Conway and Kemp, 1985; Walker, 1987). But (as we saw in Chapter 2) because of the Conservative government's antipathy to local authority housing provision and its commitment to the market model, it has very substantially cut back council house building.

Homelessness under review

The Department of the Environment is currently carrying out a review of the homelessness legislation. Press reports suggest that in response to the rising tide of homelessness, the 1977 legislation may be repealed and replaced by a new statutory code which 'redefines' homelessness as, literally, rooflessness. It is further suggested that instead of having to provide permanent housing for those accepted as homeless, local authorities would have a duty only to provide temporary shelter. This, then, would represent a retreat to the situation which prevailed prior to the 1977 Act. Whether or not such changes will be introduced remains to be seen. It certainly seems that the right of homeless people to be rehoused offends the sensibilities of those who hold dear to the market model of welfare.

However, irrespective of this internal DoE review of the homelessness legislation, the de-municipalisation of rented housing, which is a major objective of government policy, will in any case reduce the ability of local authorities to tackle homelessness. For whereas councils have at present a statutory duty to rehouse the homeless, the bodies that are likely to replace them as landlords do not. Further, in order for a local authority to get the DoE's permission to transfer its stock to an alternative landlord, the authority must have no nomination rights to the transferred stock (DoE, 1988c). It is not clear, consequently, how a local authority will be able adequately to meet its present statutory obligations towards the homeless if it transfers its stock in this way. Thus the de-municipalisation of rented housing is likely to represent a weakening of the rights of citizenship in housing provision.

'Unofficial' homelessness and the 'access crisis'

So far we have focused mainly upon the 'official' homeless, by whom we mean those accepted for rehousing under the Housing Act 1985.

But in fact there are a great many people who are not rehoused in this way, mainly because they do not fall into one of the priority need groups we outlined above. Homeless single (non-elderly) people and childless couples are not usually provided with accommodation under the homelessness provisions of the Housing Act 1985; these 'able-bodied' households are expected to be able to fend for themselves in the market-place.

Although, as we have seen, there are considerable grounds for debate about what constitutes homelessness, it does appear that there has been a sharp increase in the number of non-priority group households having difficulty in gaining access to the formal housing market, particularly in London (Conway and Kemp, 1985; Kleinman and Whitehead, 1988). This is reflected in the growing use of 'non-tenured' forms of accommodation such as bed and breakfast, hostels, short-life housing, and squats. Advice agencies and charities have also reported an increase in the incidence of sleeping rough, and a new word has come into use – 'skippering' – which refers to the use of derelict property and building sites for sleeping in overnight (CLSSAF, 1987).

The precise number of households affected by this so-called 'access crisis' (Kleinman and Whitehead, 1988) is not known. However, another study of homelessness sponsored by the GLC and undertaken by Greve and co-workers (Greve *et al.,* 1986) estimated that in London there were around 30,000 people living in squats and about 10,000 living in direct access hostels and night shelters. In addition, it has been estimated that there are around 30,000 people (other than those placed there by local authorities) living in short-life housing, and possibly 2,000 people sleeping rough in central London every night (London Housing Forum, 1988). What we do know for certain is that the number of supplementary benefit claimants living in what the DHSS called 'ordinary board and lodging' accommodation (bed and breakfast accommodation, hostels and common lodging houses) has increased greatly. In 1979 there were 49,000 recipients living in such accommodation, but by 1986 the total had risen to 166,000 – an increase of over 200 per cent in seven years (DHSS, 1987).

DHSS figures for 1982 showed that almost all of these people (97%) were single, while the remainder were childless couples. For the most part, single people, especially the young, have a very low priority among public housing landlords. A survey of local authorities in England by Venn (1985) found that some councils did not even allow single people who were not pensioners or who were below a certain age to register on the housing waiting list. It has been claimed that this growth since 1979 in the use of bed and breakfast by young, single people was the result of the rise in youth unemployment and the decreasing supply of privately rented housing (Conway and Kemp, 1985).

For unemployed single people, competing successfully in the market for the dwindling supply of privately rented housing is particularly difficult. Many private landlords in London refuse to let to the unemployed. Moreover, even those that will let to this group often demand a substantial deposit and a month's rent in advance, while accommodation agencies also require the equivalent of several weeks' rent to be paid in return for their services. All this can mean that several hundred pounds are required to gain access to a privately rented home, which is well above the means of the unemployed. Prior to April 1988, it was possible under the supplementary benefits scheme to obtain single payments for rent in advance and deposits, even if it sometimes took some while for them to be paid by the DHSS. But with the introduction of income support, single payments were abolished and replaced by discretionary loans from the Social Fund, which have to be repaid out of a claimant's weekly benefit. It is because of the difficulty of securing shelter in the formal housing market that unemployed single people in recent years have had to resort to non-tenured forms of accommodation such as bed and breakfast establishments. Claimants living in this type of accommodation used to receive a board and lodging allowance but now get housing benefit (see Chapter 4).

This increase in the occupation of bed and breakfast accommodation by single people living on supplementary benefit, led to a corresponding increase in public expenditure on DHSS 'ordinary' board and lodging allowances. This rose from £52 million in 1979 to £380 million in 1984 – a six-fold increase in only five years (DHSS, 1984). The government's response was to introduce restrictions on board and lodging payments. First, local limits on the payments were replaced by only two, centrally determined, ceilings above which benefit would not be paid. Second, these ceilings were frozen at their 1985 level (the date at which the changes were introduced) and remained at that level until 1989, thus eroding their value in real terms. Third, time limits were introduced for the first time on these payments for claimants under 26 who did not fall into a number of exempt categories (pregnant, vulnerable, etc.) These time limits ranged from two to eight weeks, depending upon the area concerned. Once the time period was up, claimants lost eligibility for a board and lodging allowance and were paid only a (much lower) 'no fixed abode' allowance unless they moved on to another local area to make a fresh claim.

In seeking to restrict eligibility in this way, the DHSS was only a step away from re-introducing the parish test of the Elizabethan and Victorian Poor Laws (see Fraser, 1973). Indeed, the initial proposal, set out in a consultation paper in 1984, was that boarders would only be allowed to claim in their 'normal local office area', a term that was not defined (DHSS, 1984). The introduction of these restrictions had been preceded by a media campaign about young unemployed adults 'lured by high benefits' to live it up on the 'costa del dole' of seaside resorts on the south coast and in London (Middleton, 1984). The consultation paper itself used this theme as a justification for the cuts in benefit for boarders, suggesting that young people with boarder status were enjoying a lifestyle 'not normally available to them' (DHSS, 1984). This suggests a concern that the implicit principle of less eligibility was being breached. Thus the DHSS response to the problem of homelessness among young, unemployed adults was to punish the victims by restricting their benefit entitlement. For the DHSS, the problem was not a housing one – that was the DoE's concern – but one of excessive demands on public funds.

In commenting on the restrictions proposed in the original consultation paper, the Social Security Advisory Committee warned that the result could be the creation of a class of rootless unemployed adults, disenfranchised and disillusioned, and unable to find work or permanent accommodation. Certainly, as we noted above, advice agencies and charities noticed a growing incidence of unemployed young people sleeping rough after these restrictions were introduced. Because they do not have a fixed abode, they are less likely to be able to register on the electoral roll, and indeed will have an incentive not to do so when the poll tax is introduced.

Moreover, it appears that some GPs are reluctant or even refuse to allow homeless single people to register with them for health care (SHIL Health Sub-group, 1987). For those who are mentally ill there can be particular problems. Under the policy of care in the community, many single people have been discharged from long-stay psychiatric hospitals without adequate back-up care and support. Some end up on the streets, while others may be placed in hostels or bed and breakfast accommodation with only minimal access to psychiatric services and support. Indeed, it has been claimed that in some instances hospitals have refused to admit them for treatment (Medical Campaign Project, 1987).

Problems of inadequate provision of either accommodation or social work and other support have also accompanied the discharge of young adults from care and ex-offenders from prison. While many unemployed young people are having increasing difficulty in finding or keeping a home, those leaving care may be especially vulnerable. This is not because they are necessarily a 'problem' group, for ex-offenders and those with behavioural difficulties are in a minority according to a study by Lupton (1985). Rather, their greater vulnerability stems from their experience of care itself.

Lupton found that whilst in care many youngsters were given little opportunity to exercise self-determination or personal responsibility, and few were allowed to have a say in the running of the home. The care leavers that she interviewed (see also Carey and Stein, 1986) had received little well-planned advice from staff on practical matters such as money management, household maintenance, or personal health care. Yet despite this lack both of the opportunity to develop as adults and of adequate preparation for leaving care, the young care leavers are expected to attain independance at a relatively early age. When they reach 16, many feel they have to leave and, in fact, some feel pressure from staff to do so. While some youngsters are only too keen to go, others find the experience of leaving care traumatic (Lupton, 1985). Once young people have left care, however, social services departments often feel that their role is over and that it is the housing department's responsibility to provide accommodation. Housing departments, on the other hand, are sometimes reluctant to provide accommodation for young people under 18, whom they regard as still the responsibility of social services. While there are a number of instances of effective collaboration between the two departments, for example in the provision of half-way house schemes which provide a stepping stone to full independence, they appear to be an exception rather than the rule.

Conclusion

In this chapter we have examined the way in which the state has defined and responded to homelessness. The Housing (Homeless Persons) Act 1977 represented an important step forward in policy towards homeless people. It has provided a significant extension of the rights of citizenship in housing, thereby safeguarding the welfare of eligible households who have been unable to secure accommodation for themselves. Although the homeless legislation is currently under review, to date the provisions of the 1977 Act remain intact after a decade of Conservative housing policy under Mrs Thatcher's government.

Nevertheless, it is clear that, in many respects, the punitive and stigmatising treatment of the homeless which characterised the old Poor Law are still present, if in a less severe and less explicit form, in policy and practice towards the homeless in Britain today. In particular, the themes of local connection/local office area, less eligibility, and the distinction between the deserving and the undeserving are embodied in the homeless persons legislation, the Code of Guidance, and in social security board and lodging regulations. Moreover, perhaps because the definition of who is deserving of accommodation under the Act is so tightly drawn, the taint of the 'scrounger' touches even those who successfully pass the enquiries that are made into their circumstances and those leading up to their becoming homeless. They are still deemed somehow to have jumped the queue (though many families accepted under the Act are already on the waiting list) and therefore deserving only of offers of the least desirable accommodation. This is probably an inevitable result of the fact that housing policy and provision in Britain secures the rights of private property before safeguarding the broader rights of citizenship, thus implying that better homes should be available to those who have successfully competed for them in the market-place. Access to housing is seen as something that should be bought, or at least 'earned' by serving time on the housing waiting list – that Fabian equivalent of purchasing power.

Queueing for accommodation is inevitable under administered housing allocation systems where demand is greater than supply. But the way in which such systems have been operated in British public housing has meant that the welfare state has not easily coped with the need of homeless people for immediate access to housing. While market allocation might in theory meet need more promptly, it can only achieve this among groups whose needs can be translated into effective demand. The homeless, however, tend to be among the unemployed or the low-paid – groups who are least able to compete in the market-place. Unless the overriding concern with the rights of property is replaced by more broadly based notions of citizenship entitlement, the punitive and discriminatory treatment of those who are without a permanent home is almost inevitable.

6

Housing and Community Care for People with Learning Difficulties

During the last fifteen years, use of the term community care has become commonplace throughout social policy, reflecting widespread disillusionment with traditional forms of institutional care. It only needs a superficial acquaintance with the use of the term in various contexts, however, to realise that it means different things to many people. Walker (1982b) has drawn a useful distinction between care *by* the community and care *in* the community. Care *by* the community implies that family, friends, neighbours or volunteers have a primary role in caring for people with learning difficulties (a term we use in preference to the more commonly known, but frequently stigmatising, label 'mentally handicapped'). This may reflect the ideological view, outlined in Chapter 2, that the state should only intervene as a last resort and that family or friends should bear the primary responsibility for care. Alternatively it may reflect a view that the state should bear the primary responsibility for ensuring the well-being of people with learning difficulties, but that it should discharge this responsibility through family and friends by ensuring that they have the means to provide care without undue burden. By contrast, care *in* the community implies that it is the geographical location of care that is important rather than who does the caring. The emphasis here is on providing care which meets the 'special' needs of people with learning difficulties by providing 'special' forms of provision in a way which aims to minimise the geographical and social distance between people with learning difficulties and the local community.

Walker argues that, in practice, the development of community care policies has been concerned with the provision of care by paid social workers *in* the community rather than with care by the community. This is undoubtedly true of care for people with learning difficulties because policy has been almost exclusively concerned with providing non-institutionalised forms of 'special' residential provision with support from paid professionals, whether employed by statutory or voluntary agencies. This area of overlap between housing and other social services is, therefore, central to the concerns of this chapter.

Despite this emphasis on 'special' forms of housing and social support, often for those who are already in long-stay institutions, many people with learning difficulties live in ordinary houses and receive varying degrees of support from their family, friends, or voluntary or statutory agencies. For example, it is estimated that 40 per cent of adults classified as 'severely mentally handicapped' live at home with their families (DHSS, 1971b). In considering the achievements and limitations of community care, therefore, it is also necessary to look at the implications of mainstream housing policy and practice for people with learning difficulties and their carers. This is particularly important in the light of recent calls for more emphasis on general housing policies and for a widening range of support services to be linked to them (Purkis and Hodson, 1982). This is a second area of overlap between housing and social policy which merits attention.

The analysis that follows is divided into three sections. First, there is a discussion of the meaning of community care in general, which pays particular attention to the specific form it has taken for people with learning difficulties. Second, 'special' forms of housing provision are described and the processes of planning, financing and managing these projects are considered. Third, the impact of general housing policies on people with learning difficulties living in ordinary housing is analysed, and the problems such people experience are described.

The meaning and practice of community care for people with learning difficulties

Tyne (1982, p. 150) argues that 'community care has always suffered by being only negatively defined – it was to be all that "institutional" care in the past was not'. Henwood (1986, p. 148) argues that 'the earliest policy aspirations emerged out of a disenchantment with institutional provision, but with little consideration paid to the development of community-based alternatives'. This applies particularly to care for people with learning difficulties, where much of the pressure for community care has arisen as a reaction to conditions in large mental institutions. A series of critiques, exposés and investigations of these institutions was made during the 1960s and 1970s (DHSS, 1969, 1971a, 1974, 1977). These pointed to bad physical conditions, a shortage and lack of training of staff, and to the dehumanising regimes often imposed on residents.

The response of successive governments was to make plans to move patients from institutions through an active discharge policy whilst preventing inappropriate admissions. The assumption of policy was that many existing residents – half of the 60,000 existing residents of institutions, according to the White Paper *Better Services for the Mentally Handicapped* (DHSS, 1971b) – could and should move into 'community care'. Hospital provision was still to exist, but in the form of small units of 100–200 beds, preferably associated with general hospitals.

If the move towards community care was based essentially on the desire to avoid the worst features of existing institutional care, it did have a more positive aspect, associated with the objective of 'normalisation'. This idea has been actively put forward by pressure groups such as the Campaign for Mentally Handicapped People, and has often informed policy-making even if it has never received whole-hearted endorsement from policy-makers. A specific example concerning people with learning difficulties is the large influence this concept had on the principles inherent in the model of care adopted by the Jay Committee in their enquiry into mental handicap nursing and care, and which formed the basis of their recommendations (Jay Report, 1979). Tyne identifies the aims of normalisation as:

first, helping handicapped people to gain skills and characteristics, and to experience a lifestyle which is valued in our society and to have opportunities for using skills and expressing individuality in choice; secondly, regardless of people's handicaps, providing services in settings and in ways which are valued in our society and supporting people to participate genuinely in the mainstream of life. (Tyne, 1982, p. 151)

The idea of normalisation not only reinforced the move away from institutional care, but also gave a set of guidelines for the form that community care should take. It placed emphasis on individual development, on independence, on fostering a sense of worth, on avoiding stigma, and on enabling people with learning difficulties to enjoy as 'normal' a lifestyle as possible.

One aspect of this is the desire for care *in* the community – the prevention of ghettoisation by breaking down barriers between people with learning difficulties and the outside world and bringing about their integration into the 'community'. The belief is that this not only opens up opportunities for people with learning difficulties but also reduces stigma, and in that sense it marks a shift away from the divisive notion of special needs towards a more universal model of individual care. Normalisation also places emphasis on the accommodation of people with learning difficulties. It should be designed to improve individual autonomy, privacy and independence, be flexible enough to meet individual needs, and provide the appropriate environment for social support. In addition, it should aid integration into the community by emphasising, in design, location and management, the objective of allowing people with learning difficulties to enjoy a 'normal' lifestyle (Purkis and Hodson, 1982).

Types of accommodation meeting these requirements may vary from small hospital units to ordinary mainstream housing:

> If, however, one conceives of a range of accommodation from large institutions at one end to ordinary houses at the other, too many people are at the special end of the range for want of adequate services in more normal settings. (Purkis and Hodson, 1982, p. 3)

Hunter and Wistow (1987) argue that, in practice, the philosophy of normalisation has had two particularly important consequences for community care:

> first, it has focused attention on the values and principles which underpin community care policies and underlined the need for them to be made explicit and consistent; second, it has led to an increasing appreciation of the role and importance of 'ordinary' housing, as opposed to traditional residential services, being

located at the core of community care programmes. (Hunter and Wistow, 1987, pp. 89–90)

This, they argue, has been at least partially responsible for the growing, albeit modest, involvement of housing agencies in community care.

Trends in housing policy, outlined in Chapter 2, are also creating the situation in which housing organisations are showing an increasing interest in groups such as people with learning difficulties. Recent government policy towards public housing has been dominated by a view of the sector as a last resort reserved for vulnerable people, or 'social cases' as they have been labelled by some. Councils and housing associations are being encouraged by the government to concentrate their attentions on 'special needs' groups. The well-documented residualisation of public housing (Clapham and English, 1987) means that public sector tenants or those demanding housing in the sector are increasingly being drawn from these groups.

Housing authorities are therefore being encouraged to become more involved in community care provision for people with learning difficulties. However, it is evident that the implementation of community care and the involvement of housing organisations has lagged far behind official statements of policy or the hopes of those urging the 'normalisation' of services. For these and related reasons, criticism of the practice of community care was being made even as the recording of the inadequacies of institutions was reaching a peak and the concept of community care was becoming the cornerstone of government policy.

For example, Titmuss commented in 1968 that 'Beyond a few brave ventures, scattered up and down the country ... one cannot find much evidence of attempts to hammer out the practice, as distinct from the theory, of community care' (Titmuss, 1968, p. 105). Although examples of 'brave ventures' are now more common, community care has not developed into a dominant form of care in practice. Its slow growth, coinciding as it has with restrictions on government expenditure, has led to a growing disenchantment with the idea itself, which 'threatens to become devalued or even discredited' (Purkis and Hodson, 1982, p. 2). It is sometimes seen as 'little more than a smokescreen for cutting services and increasing burdens on unaided families' (Purkis and Hodson, p. 2). Griffiths (1988, p. iv) concludes that 'At the centre, community care has been talked of for thirty years, and in few areas can the gap between political rhetoric and policy on the one hand, or between policy and reality in the field on the other hand have been so great.'

The reality of community care in general is reflected in the field of services for people with learning difficulties. The need to act in the short term to improve conditions in mental handicap hospitals, highlighted by the numerous enquiries, has placed governments in a difficult position in a period of severe restrictions on resources. There has often been resistance to the closure of existing institutions both from the medical and ancillary staff working in them, and sometimes from the families of the residents (those who often have to take on the burden of care). As a result, only 21 per cent of government expenditure on people with learning difficulties in 1985 was on community care (Audit Commission, 1986b). At the central government level, there has generally been a lack of clear direction in policy and a reluctance to tackle the problems of implementation caused by inappropriate mechanisms for the financing, planning and implementation of community care. The only exception has been the *All Wales Strategy* for people with learning difficulties (Welsh Office, 1983). This strategy is deeply imbued with the ethos of normalisation, and the objective is to build up comprehensive community services to give people with learning difficulties the right to normal patterns of life within the community (and, therefore, to prevent inappropriate hospital admissions). Additional finance has been made available, clear lines of responsibility have been drawn, and a monitoring and evaluation system has been set up.

Despite this recent initiative there is a long way to go before the gaps identified by Griffiths are filled. For example, the run-down in the hospital population has been much slower than envisaged in the 1971 White Paper. In 1980 it was estimated that in England and Wales 15,000 people could be discharged from hospital immediately if appropriate community services were available. There has been a considerable growth in alternative residential provision by local authorities and other agencies but this has still been at a rate well below that anticipated in the White Paper. In 1984 total provision was still only just over 40 per cent of the number of hospital places (Audit Commission, 1986b). Furthermore, the variations in provision between areas was large, with some local authorities spending six times the amount per head of population than others (Audit

Care for People with Learning Difficulties 149

Commission, 1986b). Nevertheless, local authorities' provision of special housing schemes for people with learning difficulties has been the major focus of policy, and it is to this that we now turn.

Special housing provision

Type of provision

There is a lack of systematic information about housing provision for people with learning difficulties. The most useful survey was carried out in England and Wales during 1981 (DoE, 1983). Three hundred and fifty-five housing schemes for people with learning difficulties and thirty-one schemes designed for both people with learning difficulties and mentally ill people were identified. These provided accommodation for just under 2,000 people with learning difficulties. This compares with the 40,000 adults who, at that time, had been in mental handicap hospitals in England for more than one year. Two-thirds of the schemes were based in council housing and one-third in property belonging to housing associations and voluntary organisations. However, these figures must be treated with caution, since they do not include schemes owned by social services departments or other non-housing agencies.

When thirty-five of the housing schemes were examined in more depth it was found that most of them had originally been conceived by social services agencies who had approached housing agencies with fairly specific demands for accommodation. The reason for the approach is clear.

With the exception of the largest hostel, the organisations involved wanted ordinary houses which were like others in the area. There was a general view that whatever type of scheme was intended, including hostels, ordinary residential houses were needed, partly because small-size schemes were preferred and partly to ensure that it was not in any way conspicuous. (DoE, 1983, p. 52)

The use of ordinary properties is helped by the fact that people with learning difficulties are not regarded as needing special adaptations to dwellings in the same way as, say, physically handicapped people, although of course some people with learning difficulties, particularly those with severe problems, also have some physical disability. However, few schemes seem to be designed specifically for them. In fact, of the schemes surveyed by the DoE, 90 per cent were in existing accommodation and only 10 per cent in new, purpose-built accommodation.

Nevertheless, almost all the schemes were planned to involve social support. Where such support is to be provided by the residents themselves through mutual support and group living, the accommodation has to be conducive to it. This also applies to support provided by volunteers or paid staff, whether they are resident on the premises or not. Therefore it is primarily the need for social support that may lead to changes to mainstream housing and which constitutes the 'special' element of provision.

It is common to divide schemes into categories such as hostels, group homes, cluster units or core and cluster. These categories are confusing, though, because it is impossible to define them precisely and they hide important differences. It is more accurate, if more complicated, to categorise schemes on the basis of the following variables: objectives of the scheme (is the provision temporary rehabilitative or permanent, and what is the degree of dependency of the people who are to be housed – for example, profoundly or mildly handicapped?); size of the scheme (the number of residents per scheme in the DoE survey ranged from two to thirty); type of accommodation (rooms, shared flat, individual flat, bedsit, or house); and arrangements for social support (staff on premises, communal support, staff close by in core unit, or visiting staff).

The alternatives given are not exhaustive and some schemes will involve more than one category; for example, they may contain some rooms and some individual flats. However, such a categorisation is more useful than simpler ones and it does bring home the wide variety of provision that has emerged. It is not possible to identify the number of schemes that would fall into each of these categories because of the lack of any comprehensive survey; similarly, there has been little attempt systematically to evaluate these different forms of provision and to compare their effectiveness. This is partly due to the difficulties of devising an appropriate evaluative framework. In particular, measuring the outcomes of provision can be difficult, since so many of the variables defy quantification; it can also be costly and insensitive, as well as methodologically unsound, to use research techniques such as questionnaire surveys with some people with severe learning difficulties. In practice, therefore, one is forced to rely on the professional judgements of those involved in provision and on the essentially subjective judgements of researchers looking at individual schemes.

The Campaign for Mentally Handicapped People (Tyne, 1978), has devised a checklist which can be used as a guide for evaluating the 'quality of life' in residential settings for people with learning difficulties. The checklist covers a wide range of items from day-to-day requirements related to sleeping, washing and dressing, to items concerned with the personal identity of residents such as privacy, personal relationships, participation in activities, and facilities for personal development and growth. It is based, following Maslow (1954), on a hierarchy of needs, with 'basic' day-to-day requirements such as eating meals being considered before higher-level needs for personal identity and development and growth. The checklist provides a useful guide to items which should be considered in any assessment of residential environments, especially as it gives a lot of emphasis to higher-level needs which stem from an acceptance of the principle of normalisation. In looking at the items, it is envisaged that the evaluator will take into account the facilities in the scheme, such as whether there are single bedrooms to give privacy, as well as the way in which the project functions, for example whether staff knock on the door to respect the privacy of residents or just walk into a room. It is also envisaged that account should be taken of the perceptions of residents in each of these areas, for example whether they consider the facilities or the behaviour of staff to constitute an unwarranted invasion of privacy. This obviously relies on a subjective judgement by the person carrying out the evaluation, and is therefore unlikely to provide an objective measure of the quality of life in different kinds of scheme. Nevertheless, the checklist has been used by the Campaign for the Mentally Handicapped in a study of a number of projects in London (Tyne, 1978) and by Gulstad (1987) in four projects in Scotland.

In terms of type of provision, the accepted wisdom is that many existing schemes are too large and do not create a family-type environment. Tyne (1978, p. 6), for example, concludes that

larger living units often experience difficulties in adequately providing for the very basic needs of life (food, warmth, clothing, sanitation) and almost always fail to provide adequately for people's needs for a personal identity (privacy, security, friendship).

There is also much criticism of the lack of privacy in many of the schemes where residents are forced to share rooms. In the case studies undertaken by the DoE, just less than half the schemes had one or more bedrooms which were shared. Yet it was concluded that 'the majority view, however, was that residents should have a room of their own if at all possible' (DoE, 1983, p. 4).

Where single rooms were not provided, cost considerations were said to be the reason. Tyne (1978, p. 6) further concludes that

> very few living units of any kind (hospital, local authority, private or voluntary) make adequate provision for the mentally handicapped adults to develop and grow.

Tyne also points to the lack of managerial and professional support for staff in many projects and their lack of appropriate decision-making powers to make projects work effectively.

Research on schemes has shown that the small scale of provision, its diversity, and the ineffective implementation of the principles of normalisation, reflect the difficulties which housing, health and social service agencies have faced in implementing a community care strategy for people with learning difficulties. These are evidence of a lack of political will which shows itself in a shortage of resources and the absence of effective mechanisms for translating the rhetoric of community care into reality. This becomes evident when the planning and finance of schemes and their management is discussed in more detail.

Planning projects

In the DoE study it was found that the role of housing agencies in planning and setting up schemes was minimal and largely reactive. Whether the initiative came from the voluntary or statutory sector, 'The initiative for most of these schemes had come from the agencies who were later to provide the support and in most people's view this was the way it should be' (DoE, 1983, p. 42).

Most arrangements are made on an *ad hoc* basis, depending on local circumstances, and the long-term availability of housing stock on a large scale being offered to or requested by any social services department is a rare occurrence. In some cases, of course, the housing and social support agencies are one and the same. This usually occurs where a voluntary organisation active in the field of mental handicap finances a housing project itself or forms a housing association specifically to provide housing for this group. However, in most cases housing and social support are provided by two different agencies. In the voluntary sector this is usually a voluntary organisation and a housing association. In the statutory sector it is a housing department and a social services department which, outside metropolitan areas, will be in different tiers of local government. In addition, collaboration is needed with health authorities if housing provision is to be co-ordinated with other forms of provision. This is essential if the philosophy of community care is to be put into practice and if people with learning difficulties are to be removed from long-term hospital care or prevented from entering it in the first place. Health, social services and housing agencies need to collaborate in the identification of people with learning difficulties who need care and in the appropriate form it should take.

The organisational links needed to plan effectively are complex, and housing agencies have had a very marginal status. For example, from its initiation in 1976 the joint planning machinery, which has been the primary mechanism for implementing the policy of community care for people with learning difficulties, has largely excluded housing. However, liaison is improving, especially with the change of rules for joint finance which occurred in 1983 in England and Wales and 1985 in Scotland. This meant that, for the first time, housing projects could qualify for financial support. Progress has been patchy, and many housing organisations still have no formal links with social services or health agencies. The result, by and large, has been that housing agencies have sat back and waited for others to make the running and have reacted on an *ad hoc* basis to requests for involvement in specific projects.

In the statutory sector, involvement largely means making mainstream housing available for conversion for use by people with learning difficulties. The DoE study found that housing departments were often not involved in the conversion process because this related to the requirements for social support which was judged to be the responsibility of other agencies. In the voluntary sector the involvement of housing associations in the development process is greater, partly because of the funding arrangements, which will be outlined later. But even here collaboration is dependent on initiatives taken by individual organisations. Where the housing association was set up by a support body and where it specialises in projects for people with learning difficulties, links can be strong. However, problems of segregation can then occur, with projects being isolated from mainstream housing provision. The difficulty in collaboration occurs when the principle of normalisation is taken to imply integration with the mainstream provision of local authorities and of non-specialist, community-based or general needs housing associations.

In his report on community care, Griffiths (1988) argued that housing agencies should restrict their involvement to the provision of 'bricks and mortar'. However, this view is based on the false assumption that there is a clear dividing line between responsibility for provision of the 'bricks and mortar' and for the provision of social support. In practice, the two are inextricably bound together, as will be shown later in the chapter; their separation could create severe practical problems as well as reinforcing the popular view, reported in the DoE study, that the passive attitude of most housing agencies is acceptable. This view gives these agencies an excuse to avoid responsibility for meeting the housing needs of people with learning difficulties. When requests are made for accommodation, the response is likely to be made without regard to any strategy of provision, and without any knowledge of the requirements of people with learning difficulties or of the range of services available to them. It can also contribute to a situation where housing agencies can feel little commitment to the project and may not realise what is required of them for its continuing management.

There are signs that some forward-thinking local housing authorities are beginning to develop a strategy, in collaboration with other agencies, on services for people with learning difficulties. For example, in Glasgow, the Housing Department took the initiative in 1985 by establishing a high-level inter-agency Special Needs Strategy Group with five sub-groups. These are multi-agency groups whose remit is to formulate a strategy for a specific group such as people with learning difficulties. The aims are to ensure that the housing needs, aspirations and related service requirements of all special needs groups in the City of Glasgow are met to the maximum extent possible. This involves reviewing needs and existing provision and policy, co-ordinating the inputs of different agencies, prioritising research, policy development and implementation, and monitoring the effectiveness of action.

There are also signs that housing agencies are becoming more involved in the joint planning machinery. On its own, joint planning may not necessarily lead to a unified care strategy for people with learning difficulties, since managers, by simply adding housing to what is universally described as an already imperfect system, are not likely to devise an effective comprehensive plan for the needs of such people in all their different aspects. However, many criticisms of joint planning seem to stem from over-optimistic assessments of the likelihood of rational-comprehensive planning in a situation where agencies with differing responsibilities and objectives are involved. In practice, joint planning provides a forum in which the plans of agencies are discussed, criticised and reconciled. As Glennerster *et al.* (1982) comment, 'Hard bargains were struck and compromises reached, sometimes facilitated by the existence of the financial inducement of joint finance.'

Hunter and Wistow (1987) argue that the achievement of joint planning fell well short of the ideal of strategic client group planning, but did result in more effective communication between different agencies and led to what they call 'parallel planning', with the plans of different agencies being drawn up on the basis of consultation and an exchange of information.

The frustration felt by many people at what was perceived as the failure of joint planning to achieve substantial progress resulted in the setting up of a working party by the DHSS in 1984 to review the existing arrangements. The report, *Progress in Partnership* (Working Group on Joint Planning, 1985), stressed the importance of identifying specific tasks, placing responsibility for fulfilling them on named individuals, and strengthening lines of accountability. It also made a number of specific recommendations to increase the importance of the joint planning machinery and to widen its scope by focusing on 'total resource planning' rather than on incremental changes at the margin.

In its investigation into the implementation of community care, the Audit Commission (1986b) reinforced the emphasis on simplification of existing responsibilities and methods of accountability and suggested a re-organisation of the responsibilities of the agencies involved in order to achieve this. The Commission called for a more rational organisational structure, local responsibility, and more clearly defined authority and accountability for delivering a balanced, community-based care service for different client groups. It also recommended that local authorities should be made responsible for the long-term care of people with learning difficulties, except for the most severely handicapped who require medical supervision, and that the resources necessary to do this should be transferred from the health service.

Griffiths (1988) rejects such a radical restructuring of responsibilities in favour of a more incremental approach. However, he also sees local authorities as the primary focus of responsibility for community care, and recommends that they be given resources from existing health and social security budgets. He therefore envisages changes in the current structure for financing community care.

Financing projects

Joint finance (or support finance as it is called in Scotland) provides a strong incentive for co-operation between agencies and an inducement for housing organisations to enter the planning arrangements. However, the resources that have been made available are small (building up from minimal levels to only 1 per cent of NHS and 3 per cent of planned personal social services spending in 1985/6 in England, while expenditure in Wales and Scotland has been even lower). Combined with the marginal role of housing authorities in the joint planning process, this means that few housing schemes have been financed in this way.

Essentially, joint finance is the 'top slicing' of the NHS budget to provide health authorities with funds to support selected personal social services capital and revenue expenditure. Until 1983, support for schemes was available for only a limited period and on a tapered basis – that is, social services (or housing) authorities had to make their own contribution to schemes and finally to meet all the costs from their own budgets. The exact arrangements for joint finance vary between England, Scotland and Wales (see Hunter and Wistow, 1987, for details).

The joint finance arrangements were considered by the government to have made little impact on the need for a rundown of long-stay hospitals and the build-up of alternative, community-based forms of care and shelter. Therefore, in 1983, the government made joint financing provisions more generous for this purpose and introduced the 'care in the community' arrangements to enable health authorities to make lump-sum or continuing payments from their budgets to other agencies to enable people to be transferred from hospital.

Payments can be made as a 'dowry' on each patient transferred to enable local authorities to provide care for that person. This can provide a valuable source of finance for local authorities, but Hunter and Wistow (1987) argue that many health authorities are reluctant to transfer resources and that the overall level of funds available may be insufficient to provide adequate alternative forms of care.

Other financing arrangements can be divided into those for statutory agencies and those for housing associations. They need to cover the capital costs of acquiring and converting property, the provision of furniture and equipment, and management and support costs. We consider each of these briefly in turn.

Where a local housing authority is involved in the acquisition and conversion of properties, the usual arrangement is for capital costs to be met from the total capital allocation for housing. In other words, special provision has to compete directly with other items of expenditure such as the modernisation and major repair of existing public housing, the building of new public housing, and the provision of improvement grants for privately owned property. Given the well documented and substantial reduction in local authority capital spending since 1979 (Murie and Leather, 1986), it is not surprising that most local authorities are more concerned to keep their existing stock in a habitable condition than to become involved in schemes for people with learning difficulties. This means that a substantial proportion of capital costs must often be borne by social services departments and voluntary organisations (Gulstad, 1987). A mix of funding arrangements is thus produced which depends on agreement between the parties.

The position is simpler for housing associations, since most of the capital cost can be met from Housing Association Grant (HAG), in the same way as for schemes for mainstream housing (see Chapter 4). The provision of equipment and furniture is a separate stage which is financed differently from other capital costs. Many arrangements can be found, including funding by voluntary organisations, by social services departments, by the residents themselves, by donations, or by housing associations. The only general rule seems to be that local authority housing departments rarely meet these costs. The sums involved at this stage are not large compared with the costs of acquisition and conversion, but, as the DoE study reports, because of the lack of any one system of financing, 'in many cases this stage of the scheme causes more trouble and difficulty than the original acquisition of the houses' (p. 75).

Once the properties are completed, the funding of day-to-day management and support costs for schemes is the most complicated area of all. Where a scheme involves a local authority housing department and a local authority social services department, the usual arrangement is for the housing department to cover the costs of managing and maintaining the accommodation, while the social services department covers the cost of social support, charging such expenditure to mainstream budgets. Where a voluntary organisation provides social support in a project with a local authority housing department, it, too, usually bears the cost, and it is here that problems start. Most voluntary organisations find it difficult to secure sufficient resources from donations and often have recourse to urban programme funding, which currently finances many existing projects. The major problem with this solution is that funding is not only restricted to specifically designated urban areas, but it is temporary, only being made available from central government for up to a seven-year period. The voluntary organisation is then faced with the options of finding the resources itself, persuading a statutory body to provide funding, or closing the scheme. The temporary nature of funding and the uncertainty this creates is a barrier which prevents many organisations from starting schemes. It also gives rise to considerable problems with staff morale and denies security of tenure to residents. It seems likely, moreover, that changes in priority within the urban programme, which is drifting away from social projects towards more economically oriented ones, will reduce the amount of finance available from this source.

Housing associations also have had problems in funding social support costs, even though they have been able to claim a special management allowance for this from the Housing Corporation. Before 1977 in England, the Housing Corporation would only sanction projects in which support costs did not exceed twice the management allowances paid for mainstream housing projects. The limit has since been raised to six times the management allowance. In Scotland each scheme is examined and judged individually.

However, many projects continue to have difficulty in covering costs from these sources and require 'topping up' funds from other sources, for example the local authority social services department. Schemes classed as hostels can claim hostel deficit grant, a discretionary grant from the DoE which can cover housing costs such as wardens' salaries.

Some social support costs can be met from charges to residents. As most residents are dependent on income support, the amount charged is usually set on the basis of what will be covered through social security payments. This is complicated because there are two major forms of payment. First, residents eligible for income support can claim board and lodging allowances. As explained in Chapter 4, these cover the costs of meals and accommodation plus a small amount for personal expenses. The ceilings laid down for payment vary by region and also by type of accommodation. Residents with learning difficulties are usually eligible for a level of funding which contains an element for care and support. Alternatively, residents can claim housing benefit, which may cover some communal service charges such as the upkeep of a communal lounge. Whether residents are better off claiming housing benefit or board and lodging allowance will depend on the facilities in their particular scheme and on the regulations governing benefits, which are continually changing. It may also depend on the discretionary judgement of particular housing benefit and DSS staff, which can vary widely.

This account of the mechanisms for planning and financing projects gives some idea of the complexity and fragility of the arrangements. The numbers of different agencies involved in the planning process and the inadequacy of the arrangements make any comprehensive planning impossible. The financing arrangements are so complex and change so often that a lot of effort is needed to generate the funding to enable projects to be set up. The current arrangements provide little incentive for the provision of community care facilities. For example, income support arrangements are more generous for those in residential care than in community care. This results in a disincentive to provide community care and has been a major factor in the recent large increase in private residential provision for older people.

The central government system of funding local authority expenditure and the controls exercised by central government over local authority expenditure, have acted as a futher disincentive to expenditure on community care. The need to control overall expenditure has been seen by central government as the primary objective, so that some of the local authorities at the forefront of new initiatives have been penalised by central government for excessive levels of spending; this has led to a disproportionately high burden of cost being borne by local taxpayers. As the Audit Commission concludes, 'local authorities are often penalised through the grant system for building the very community services which government policy favours' (1986b, p. 2).

The conditions attached to some funding arrangements have a major influence on the form that projects take. For example, the difficulty of finding enough funds to cover social support costs has meant that there has been a bias towards schemes with low levels of support, inevitably catering mainly for people with less severe difficulties. As the DoE comments, 'There are serious disincentives at present to projects designed for more dependent people' (DoE, 1983, p. 72).

There have been many calls to change the current system of planning and financing. For example, the National Council of Voluntary Organisations (NCVO) has called for a community care fund, which would be

> a central fund specifically designed to promote diversity in the field of community care, complementing other funding sources, and encouraging inter-agency collaboration including voluntary action. (Purkis and Hodson, 1982, p. 46)

Glennerster *et al.* (1982) suggest that reforms of the local planning machinery should be accompanied by an increased use of local client-group plans and budgets as a basis for more systematic local planning. However, it is relatively easy to design an ideal system, but more difficult to see how it can be implemented given the lack of political will, the shortage of resources, and the conflicting interests of the main parties involved.

Managing projects

Because of the mixture of agencies and functions involved in the day-to-day management of housing for people with learning difficulties, it is imperative that the rights and duties of the parties are clearly laid down in a management agreement. This may seem obvious, but it is surprising how often such a basic step is not taken. The case of one project where no such agreement existed is outlined in the DoE report:

> In this case the property was leased to a voluntary organisation and there appeared to be complete confusion, indeed contradiction, about who was responsible for certain aspects of setting up and maintaining the scheme. (DoE, 1983, p. 45)

The general rule on the distribution of responsibilities is that housing agencies are responsible for the maintenance and upkeep of the building and management functions such as the collection of rents, while a social services agency or voluntary organisation is responsible for the organisation and provision of social support. Often both parties are involved in the selection of residents, although the social support agency may have the key role because of the need to select and prepare residents appropriately for the support available in a particular scheme. Obviously this is a vital job, and is perhaps the single most important factor in determining the success or failure of a scheme.

Thus housing agencies primarily have responsibility for the maintenance and management of the properties, although they are often also involved in other areas such as the selection of residents with the support agency. For most housing agencies the project then takes its place alongside mainstream housing and is slotted into the existing procedures. For example, repairs are reported and carried out in the normal way. Housing management and maintenance are often carried out in a remote and bureaucratic way, with the emphasis being on impersonal standardised procedures with little room for personal discretion. This is changing with current trends towards the decentralisation of housing management (see Chapter 8), but it has not gone far enough to meet the individual needs of people with learning difficulties, whether they are living in special projects or in mainstream housing.

People with learning difficulties in mainstream housing

The emphasis so far in this chapter has been on the provision of special housing projects for people with learning difficulties, largely because it has been the primary policy emphasis. However, many such people live in ordinary houses and receive social support from their family, friends or statutory and voluntary organisations. Some interpretations of the concepts of community care and normalisation would lead to an aim of keeping these people in their present situation for as long as possible and to provide appropriate social support in their homes. For people with learning difficulties already living in various forms of residential care, the aim should be to transfer them to as 'normal' an environment as possible. In some cases this means mainstream housing provision, whether in the public or private sectors. In this situation, people with learning difficulties need both social support and adequate housing.

Social support

One of the key elements of the current government's philosophy towards social policy – epitomised in the market model introduced in Chapter 2 – is the view that the family should take primary responsibility for the provision of care and support. Where this fails, or in order to supplement family provision, help should be provided through the voluntary work of friends or neighbours. The state should step in only as a last resort, when these informal sources of help are inadequate. In practice the amount of voluntary help available for people with learning difficulties is severely limited. In general, friends and neighbours, even if willing to help, can only provide certain forms of care at particular times of the day or week. The tasks are usually practical in nature and rarely involve carrying out personal activities. Thus, a neighbour may do shopping or feed the cat, but rarely help with dressing or washing, or help a person with learning difficulties to manage their money (Willmott, 1986).

This is partly a realisation of the neo-conservative view, mentioned in Chapter 2, that family life is the building block of society. It reflects the assumptions, first, that members of families *ought* to care for each other; second, that state benefits undermine this interdependency; and third, that reducing the cohesion of the family might undermine the solidarity of society as a whole. In this situation community care essentially means family care. But even within the family, the burden of care tends to fall on the immediate household, who do not usually receive much help from other relatives. In a study of families with children with severe learning difficulties, Wilkin (1979) found that, although there was often some sort of mutually supportive relationship, other relatives rarely provided care that was relevant to the day-to-day domestic routine. Thus, although neighbours and other relatives often provide a limited degree of emotional and practical support, this does not prevent the major burden of routine care falling on the immediate family of the person with the learning difficulty.

Within the immediate family, the burden of care falls unequally. Wilkin (1979) found that large proportions of mothers caring for children with learning difficulties received no help with child-care or domestic tasks. Carey (1982), in a study of carers of children with learning difficulties in North Wales, found that the contribution of fathers to child-care and domestic tasks never approached half the total workload; where help was given, it was often with the less onerous and more pleasurable tasks such as play – it was rarely with routine chores such as cleaning and tidying the house or dressing the child.

The pattern of caring for adults with learning difficulties living at home is very similar (Bayley, 1973; City of Bradford MDC Social Services Department, 1983). The major difference is the increasing age of the main carer. In the Bradford study the average age was 57, and 41 per cent of main carers were aged 60 or over. The infirmity or death of carers is one of the major reasons for the common occurrence of people with learning difficulties being admitted to residential care for the first time in middle age.

In a review of the literature on carers, Parker (1985) concludes that the costs of caring can be substantial. Carers may be forced to give up work, or lose time if they continue in paid employment, and may suffer reduced earnings and lost opportunities for promotion. When added to the need for increased expenditure to meet the care needs of a person with learning difficulties, the economic cost to the family can be substantial. However, the costs are not solely economic. Parker (1985, p. 64) concludes: 'While any directly causal link between caring and physical ill-health is, as yet, unproven, there is clear evidence of the toll imposed on the mental well-being of carers'.

There are important gender differences in the costs of care. Not only are women more likely to have to take on the burden of care, but when they do they seem to suffer more economic, physical and

emotional costs than men in a similar situation. In present circumstances the move towards community care for people with learning
difficulties is adding significantly to the already disadvantaged
position of many women, and is leading to their exclusion from
mainstream economic and social life.

Despite growing evidence of the problems faced by carers, support for the carer from the statutory health and social services is
limited in two major ways. First, constraints on the resources
available for such services, justified by reference to the needs of the
economy, mean that relevant services are in very short supply.
Second, the assumption underlying the provision of most conventional services is that the dependent person is the recipient rather
than the carer. Thus where a family member takes on the care of a
person with learning difficulties, statutory services are likely to be
reduced to a minimum on the assumption that care is available.
Thus carers rarely get help from services such as home help, meals
on wheels, community nurses, or health visitors. Statutory services
are generally seen as a substitute for family care, rather than as
complementary to it.

Where support is available its impact is lessened because the
separate packages of care usually on offer are inflexible and poorly
co-ordinated. Such care is rarely tuned to the particular needs of
individual people with learning difficulties. In addition, statutory
support is likely to exacerbate gender inequalities because there is
evidence that male carers are more likely to receive it than female
carers (Parker, 1985). This reflects the continued entrenchment
within the welfare state of stereotyped views about the different roles
that are 'natural' to, and appropriate for, men and women. Similar
inequalities applied until recently to social security benefits, and only
one state benefit, the Invalid Care Allowance, exists specifically to
support carers. This is subject to stringent rules of eligibility, and
married women carers have, until recently, been ineligible for
support. As a consequence, the Equal Opportunities Commission
(1982) has estimated that only 0.5 per cent of carers received the
allowance. However, the number of people claiming should rise
significantly now that the regulations have been changed, following
a ruling by the European Court of Human Rights, to allow married
women to claim. This does not, of course, remove the problem that
the majority of carers are still women, who receive very little in the

way of 'holiday' from their caring role, let alone any organised opportunities to pursue a career in the paid labour market.

In the past few years there have been a number of innovatory community care schemes designed to overcome difficulties associated with the provision of conventional services, and to prevent admission into residential care. Most examples have been designed to provide support for older people and so will be described in the next chapter. One scheme that has been considered in relation to people with learning difficulties is the 'Crossroads' care attendant scheme for severely physically disabled people. Paid care attendants relieve informal carers at appropriate times of the day and carry out tasks normally done by them such as dressing or washing the disabled person. Although the schemes have not been adequately evaluated, they appear to have provided considerable relief to carers of physically disabled people and could possibly do the same for carers of people with learning difficulties. A scheme for such people is being tried in South Glamorgan. Other forms of provision, such as sitting services or respite care through fostering and family placements, could also prove useful to carers of people with learning difficulties.

Housing

The primary aim of housing policy as part of community care for people with learning difficulties living in mainstream housing should be to ensure that their housing is adequate and properly maintained. Given that these housing needs are no different from most other people's, the primary mechanisms for achieving them should be through mainstream housing policies. Nevertheless, people with learning difficulties have three sets of needs which may not be shared by a majority of other people. First, they are likely to have very low incomes because of their difficulties in gaining well-paid employment. Even where people with learning difficulties are living with their family, the economic impact on the carer is likely to result in the household having a lower income than they otherwise would. Second, the need to provide practical and social support to the person with learning difficulties may mean that extra space is required to allow, for example, a care attendant to have appropriate working space while allowing other members of the family to enjoy privacy. Third, where people with learning difficulties are living on their own, they may have difficulty in coping with the running of the house and the organisation of repairs. Where they are living with a family, the pressure on the main carer may also cause problems in dealing with these matters. The problems may be worse in the owner-occupied sector than in the public rented sector, where it is the job of housing managers to deal with most of these functions.

Each of these needs may be experienced by people with learning difficulties and their families, but some may not experience any of them. The precise need and its relative importance will vary considerably from one person or household to another, and it is this kind of sensitivity, and therefore flexibility, which mainstream housing policy has to adopt.

The question of low income and its impact on the housing situation of people with learning difficulties and their families is obviously a problem shared by many in the housing system. In part, the solution to this lies in state intervention in the labour market, but it also has to be seen in general government policy towards the housing system as a whole. Policy has had as its primary aim the supporting of owner-occupation for those who can afford it and the relegation of public rented housing to a residual role catering for those who cannot become owner-occupiers. It seems that, in such a system, many people with learning difficulties and their families are likely to find themselves in the public rented sector and, therefore, their housing circumstances will be inextricably bound up with conditions in that sector and the way it is perceived by society as a whole. This latter point is important because normalisation may not be achieved if people with learning difficulties are in a sector which is universally stigmatised, even if their physical housing conditions are on a par with others in that sector.

The need for help in managing and maintaining a house, and for facilities to enable support to be provided, are factors that can only be dealt with on an individual basis. Their close relationship with other items of practical and social support serves to stress the necessity for co-ordinating these two sets of policies. It may seem easy to divide responsibility between housing and support agencies and to confine the housing agency's role to the provision and maintenance of shelter, as Griffiths (1988) has suggested. In practice, however, this clear-cut division of responsibility breaks down in the public rented sector, largely because of the housing agencies' resposibility for determining access to their stock. People with learning difficulties may present themselves on the waiting list for accommodation or may apply for a transfer in the usual way. However, their need for social support means that they are unlikely to have their needs met through the usual methods of allocation. For example, some people with learning difficulties may have to be near to their family or friends for social support. Few allocation systems based on points take such factors into account. Another example is of a person with learning difficulties being discharged from residential provision and applying for mainstream accommodation. In this case the housing department has primary responsibility for ensuring that the person is able to cope in the house they are allocated and that appropriate support is provided.

The problems are intensified when a person with learning difficulties becomes homeless and applies for housing to a local authority housing department. As discussed in Chapter 5, under the terms of the Homeless Persons Act 1977, the local authority has a statutory duty to find permanent accommodation for vulnerable people such as these. Again the housing authority has the responsibility for ensuring that temporary or permanent accommodation is provided and is in the best place to ensure that appropriate social support is available.

In these situations housing staff need to be trained in how to deal with the needs of people with learning difficulties and to be aware of the support services that are available. This has implications for training policy, and it means that housing staff must be ready to deal with people with learning difficulties on an individual basis. This is contrary to the received wisdom of current practice because, from the outset, housing management in the public sector has been regarded as an administrative function which can largely be reduced to a set of standardised procedures (see Chapter 8). The pressures on public housing at the present time mean that, if it is adequately to cater for 'special needs' groups such as people with learning difficulties, housing management must consciously adapt to take on a more social orientation and to treat people as individuals (Clapham, 1987).

The same general point applies to agencies dealing with people with learning difficulties and their families in the owner-occupied sector. For example, procedures for the administration of improvement grants are not flexible enough to meet their individual needs.

In short, the co-ordination of housing and social support for tenants is difficult because of financial constraints and bureaucratic inflexibility in the public sector, and such co-ordination for owner-occupiers is difficult because there are only a few housing agencies which offer the kind of service to help them with any housing problems. Our review of these issues indicated an important need for housing initiatives to be included, along with social support, in innovatory schemes for people with learning difficulties.

Conclusion

Community care for people with learning difficulties has consisted both of care *in* the community and care *by* the community. The former has involved the provision of 'special' schemes of housing and social support, while the latter has been concerned with the role of kinship, friendship and neighbourliness in caring for people with learning difficulties. Our analysis of care in the community has shown that the planning and funding mechanisms for special schemes are so complex that their number is limited and the form they take is mostly determined by what can be funded rather than by the needs of residents. The insecurity of much funding through the urban programme, housing benefit or income support creates a climate of uncertainty among staff and residents, and makes long-term planning difficult. In addition, there is little evidence that many existing special schemes allow people with learning difficulties to develop to their full capacity or enable them to be integrated into mainstream life. Some progress in this regard could be made through making schemes smaller, by providing more privacy for residents, and through appropriate methods of management and support. Nevertheless, it is doubtful whether 'special' provision reserved for the 'special needs' of people with learning difficulties can ever ensure their integration into mainstream society. The very definition of the needs as special ensures that people are excluded from 'normal' life.

Community care has also meant care by the community in the sense that the burden of care has been placed on individual household members, usually women. Although this may have resulted in the better integration of people with learning difficulties into the community, it has often led to the exclusion of carers, who may be forced to withdraw from employment or to lead a very restricted social life. Domiciliary services, which could ease this problem, are badly co-ordinated and not geared to meet the multi-faceted needs of people with learning difficulties and their carers. Thus, apart from the limited commitment to carers evinced by the state, the inadequacy of domiciliary support is leading to many people with learning difficulties being faced with the inadequate alternatives of inappropriate residential care or very limited domiciliary care.

Apart from the context of 'special' schemes, there is little co-ordination between housing and other social services in the provision of community care. Existing domiciliary services have few links with housing agencies, and even the innovatory schemes outlined earlier rarely have a housing component. Housing agencies do not usually have the expertise to deal with people with learning difficulties and their families, and the prevailing definition of housing management as consisting largely of the administration of a set of standardised procedures is likely to make the individualised service needed by people with learning difficulties difficult to achieve.

Additional problems are arising because housing policy is increasingly leading to the concentration of disadvantaged people, including people with learning difficulties, in the public rented sector, at the same time as physical conditions in the sector are deteriorating, the standard of service to tenants is declining, and the stigma attached to being a council tenant is increasing.

It is obvious that people with learning difficulties and their families have not been well served by a social policy which stresses the primacy of the market and provides a residual set of services for those unable to compete. Although the immediate causes of this unsatisfactory situation lie in inappropriate organisational and financial structures, these problems are soluble if there is a political will to deal with them. What has prevented this happening has been the priority of the interests of capital in corporatist bargaining procedures. Irrespective of consumer demand, or even of pressures exerted by a professional elite, the consequence has been increasingly tight control over public expenditure, which has dictated the financial and organisational mechanisms that are available to those implementing community care. Coupled with central government adherence to a belief that the family should take primary responsibility for the provision of care, this has resulted in substantial burdens being placed on many people with learning difficulties living in the community.

The seeds of an alternative approach which stresses the rights of people with learning difficulties and their families to enjoy full citizenship and to be integrated into society can be found in the concept of normalisation. This provides a guiding principle by which forms of care can be evaluated. From this concept a number of criteria can be identified by which policies for housing and social support to people with learning difficulties and their families should be organised. Services should be decentralised in order to be flexible and responsive, and involve collaboration between different services, including housing, to break down the existing boundaries between different forms of care. They should also be responsive to consumer demand and accountable to public scrutiny. Services should recognise the existence of informal family care and should support informal carers. They should also be flexible and responsive enough to recognise the needs of individual people with learning difficulties and their carers. Further, they should be organised in such a way as to reduce stigma and not to lead to exclusion from the mainstream of life. In order to achieve this, the superior corporate bargaining power of business and professional elites must be challenged by a more open, participatory structure of democratic decision-making that is sensitive to the needs of people with learning difficulties and which strikes a different balance between the needs of the corporate sector and the needs of people with learning difficulties, with the latter being given more prominence.

7

Housing and Community Care for Older People

The reasons for the move towards a policy of community care for a variety of different groups of people have been similar. Thus, for older people, as for people with learning difficulties, the major impetus has been a desire to move away from institutional care. In an important study of residential care for older people, Townsend (1962) painted a bleak picture of institutional life and recommended a move towards community care. In doing this, Townsend had existing forms of provision on which he could base his proposals for expansion, the most important of which were domiciliary services (especially the home-help service) and sheltered housing. Provision of both of these has expanded considerably in the intervening period, and they have become the cornerstones of community care provision for older people. Butler, Oldman and Greve (1983) estimated that 5 per cent of the population over 65 lived in sheltered housing, and this figure has increased considerably in the last few years. In 1980 it was estimated that 871,115 people received a home-help service and that 89 per cent of these were over retirement age (Dexter and Harbert, 1983).

The search for, and development of, appropriate forms of community care provision has been given added impetus by the increase in the numbers of older people. Between 1931 and 1981 the numbers of people aged 65 and over in Britain more than doubled, reaching fully 15 per cent of the total population. Although the overall numbers of older people are not expected to rise much up to the end of the century, the number of people over the age of 85 as a proportion of the older population is expected to rise from just over 8 per cent in 1984 to 11 per cent in 2001 (Central Statistical Office, 1986). This is important because average levels of dependence and the need for a range of social services and support tend to increase with age. Only 5 per cent of the population above retirement age are in some form of institution; the rest, therefore, live 'in the community'. The growing proportion of older people in the population has been brought about by declining mortality in all groups and a long-term downward trend in fertility, which has reduced the proportion of children in the population. It has given rise to increasing talk about the 'burden' of older people on the economy and has contributed to the common view of old age as constituting a 'problem' for society to deal with.

The objective of this chapter is to examine the different forms of community care for older people. Most emphasis is placed on sheltered housing because of its pre-eminence in the policy debates and its unique mixture of housing and social support. However, other housing and social support initiatives are reviewed and an assessment of their impact is made. In housing provision, the major initiatives are amenity housing, care and repair schemes, and private retirement homes. In the field of social support, they are area-based initiatives such as the Kent Community Care Project and community alarm systems. Although these special initiatives are important, they are on a relatively small scale and have to be seen in the light of the wider trends in the housing system discussed in Chapter 2, such as the polarisation of housing tenure, and the reduction in financial support for public housing, which provide the context within which special initiatives operate.

Throughout the discussion of these policies and programmes the underlying assumptions about the nature of old age and the needs of older people will be examined. This is necessary because of the importance of social policy in contributing to the meaning of old age, both to older people themselves and to society at large. Biological ageing affects people at different chronological ages and to varying degrees. This means that 'old age' is a social construct rather than a biological category, the origins of which include politically determined retirement policies which assign the status of 'old age' on the basis of chronological age rather than physical or mental ability. There is no necessary relationship between age and dependency, but retirement policies impose a dependent status by enforcing withdrawal from the labour market, and forcing the vast majority of older people to rely on state welfare benefits. In principle this could be seen as a reward for a lifetime's contribution to society.

In practice, the scale of provision suggests this is not the case, for in societies where status is largely defined in relation to the productive economy, 'old age' is likely to be characterised as low status, and older people will be regarded as 'dependent' and as a 'burden' on the productive economy.

The way social policies are designed and delivered can serve to challenge, or alternatively to reinforce, this negative image of old age. In other words they can reinforce the primacy of the economic system (following the market model in Chapter 2) by stigmatising those not involved in it, by exacerbating images of dependence, by providing inferior forms of care, and by stressing the separation of older people from the mainstream of society. Alternatively they can emphasise the importance of the citizenship rights of older people (following the social democratic model set out in Chapter 2) and foster positive, self-enhancing images of old age which emphasise the integral role of older people in society. A key element of the latter approach is the recognition that the so-called 'special needs' of older people are caused by factors such as low income or physical disability which are shared by many other people. Furthermore, the needs of older people are not uniform but vary considerably from one individual to the next.

In Britain, reflecting the primacy of the interests of capital in corporate bargaining procedures, social policy has tended to adopt the first approach and reinforce negative images of old age. Victor (1987, p. 13) argues:

> The perception of the elderly as a homogeneous group with particular needs different from the rest of the population has dominated social policy formulation for later life. Such policies are essentially ageist in approach, for they contain the implicit assumption that the elderly can be treated as a distinct social group isolated from the rest of society. Social policies are already related to age ... rather than specific needs such as chronic disability.

Such policies are often justified by reference to the theory of disengagement, which states that ageing involves a gradual but inevitable withdrawal or disengagement from interaction between the individual and their social context (Cumming and Henry, 1961). By disengaging from society, it is argued, individuals are preparing themselves for death. Yet there is no systematic evidence to suggest that older people generally wish to, or actually do, disengage from interaction, and the theory has been heavily criticised for its negative view of old age and for its implicit assumption that social policy should promote disengagement (see Estes *et al.*, 1982). Despite this criticism the theory has been very influential in policy debates, and has been used as a rationale for policies which have sought to separate older people from society and to reinforce negative images of old age.

Reflecting the importance of the social construction of old age, the following description and analysis of housing and support policies for older people will place particular emphasis on the underlying assumptions of policy and their impact on the meaning and image of old age. We conclude by assessing the impact of these policies, which leads us to make a case for a more integrative policy framework affording importance to a full range of citizenship rights for older people.

Sheltered housing

Sheltered housing in the public sector is a form of provision designed to meet the need for good-quality rented housing and for social support (private sheltered housing is considered later in the chapter). It consists of small housing units (one or two rooms with kitchen and bathroom being usual) which are specially designed for use by older people. Important features include whole-house heating, grab rails on common-access stairs and passages, easy-to-reach light switches and power points, and special bathroom features such as non-slip floors and hand-holds beside the WC and bath/shower. In addition, the accommodation must be at ground or first-floor level unless lifts are provided. Consideration is also given to the location of the dwellings, which are usually sited close to public transport and to local facilities such as shops and a post office. The dwellings are usually grouped together, with the average size of schemes being about thirty dwellings. Sometimes the dwellings are linked by a heated corridor, and there may be either common entrances or individual access to the units.

Townsend (1962) argued that the grouping together of dwellings was necessary in order that social support to the tenants could be more easily organised. This is done primarily through a warden who is usually resident on the site and who is linked to the tenants through a warden call system. The main duties of the warden are usually to deal with emergencies and to act as a 'good neighbour' towards the tenants. However, there is some disagreement about what this should mean in practical terms, as will be discussed later. Communal facilities are also provided as part of sheltered housing. These usually include a common room (sometimes with a small kitchen), a communal laundry, and a guest bedroom.

The management of sheltered housing

The key issues in the management of sheltered housing are, first, the allocation of tenancies, which determines who receives the benefit of the provision, and, second, the organisation of social support, the most important feature of which is the role of the warden. These are now examined in turn.

Surveys of allocation policy have shown the great variety of procedures employed (see, for example, Butler *et al.*, 1983; Wirz, 1981; Clapham and Munro, 1988). Particular problems are caused by the nature of sheltered housing as the provision of both housing and social support, and the consequent difficulty of assigning relative priority to housing, health and social needs. In practice most emphasis in the allocation process is placed on health criteria (Clapham and Munro, 1988). In a recent Scottish survey, 59 per cent of sheltered housing tenants said that one of the reasons they wanted to move into sheltered housing was because of bad health (Clapham and Munro, 1988). However, despite the emphasis on the health status of entrants to sheltered housing, the profile of tenants has been shown in some surveys not to be very different from that of older people as a whole (Butler *et al.*, 1983). This is because most housing agencies take account of the 'balance' in a particular scheme between 'fit' and 'frail' tenants. In other words, allocations are often made to relatively 'fit' tenants in order to prevent schemes being completely filled with 'frail' tenants. The reasons usually given for this are to prevent schemes becoming institutionalised, to enable the 'frailer' tenants to be helped by the 'fitter', and to limit the demands on the warden. The idea of balancing schemes is very controversial and poses fundamental questions about the concept of sheltered housing.

It also shows the belief among policy-makers and managers of sheltered housing that this form of provision is suitable for older people with a wide range of needs and abilities. In some local authorities and housing associations older applicants are steered towards sheltered housing and are given few opportunities to exercise choice between different forms of provision. In extreme cases, an application for housing from an older person is automatically assumed to be an application for sheltered housing, and an older person may not realise that they are being considered for sheltered housing until they are visited shortly before an offer of accommodation is made. In most cases, older people are not given the information necessary to make informed choices between different forms of provision. The result is that many older people are allocated sheltered housing when they are not in need of its unique communal facilities and the support of the warden, but are seeking the housing elements of the package. Older people on full housing benefit are unlikely to refuse an offer of sheltered housing because the extra costs of the communal facilities are paid for them, even if they are not met by other tenants through rent pooling, and the facilities themselves (including the services of the warden) do not have to be used if they are not wanted or required. The warden is the key figure in the provision of social support to sheltered housing tenants (Heumann and Boldy, 1982). The stereotype of a sheltered housing warden is of a middle-aged married woman; in fact, all the survey evidence strongly confirms this picture. Butler *et al.* (1983) found that 69 per cent of their sample of 237 wardens in England and Wales had no formal qualifications after leaving school, and only 24 per cent said that they had experienced any form of training either before or after starting their present job. A similar picture was found in a survey of 89 wardens in Scotland carried out in 1986 (Clapham and Munro, 1988). However, the number who had received some form of training from their current employer was 47 per cent, reflecting the increasing efforts being made to improve training, particularly by the large specialist housing associations. Despite this fairly recent emphasis on warden training, the general picture is of a relatively unskilled group of people recruited more for their correspondence to the stereotypical caring female than the possession of any qualification or formally taught skill. The low pay and long working hours of many wardens reflect the poor status traditionally given to the female caring role in the family.

The role which wardens are expected to perform by their employers is congruent with their lack of formal skills and low status. The generally accepted view in housing organisations is that a warden should be a 'good neighbour'. This is a very vague term which in practice is interpreted in different ways. Nevertheless, it implies that the warden does not need specific skills but is there to 'keep an eye on', be an advocate for, and a friend of tenants, only becoming involved in an emergency or to carry out small tasks which residents are not capable of doing themselves. According to Boldy (1976), health and social service organisations are more likely to interpret the warden role as that of a 'provider' – that is, someone who is part of the overall provision of care in a locality. This goes further than being a 'good neighbour' and places emphasis on the social and nursing care provided by a warden and the provision of support through the performance of regular practical tasks such as putting tenants to bed or doing their shopping.

Wardens report that tenants and their relatives often expect them to carry out duties which they are either discouraged from doing or expressly forbidden from doing by their employers. In the Scottish survey, one-third of wardens admitted undertaking such tasks regularly (Clapham and Munro, 1988). The most common examples were domestic care tasks which would normally be carried out by a home help, or personal care or nursing tasks such as bathing or administering medication. About half of the wardens in the sample had regularly administered medication, and two-thirds had carried out personal care tasks such as putting tenants to bed. However, only about one-third of wardens had performed either of these tasks in the past month, which would seem to indicate that the majority of wardens did not carry them out regularly.

The tension inherent in the warden's role is shown by the ranking of tasks shown in Table 7.1. A list of nine tasks was presented to wardens, to sheltered tenants and to tenants of amenity housing (which is specially designed housing for older people which does not include a warden service). Each was asked to name the three most important tasks a warden should do, and they were analysed by ranking the tasks according the the number of times they were mentioned. The major differences in rankings occurred for help with small jobs, which was ranked low by wardens and tenants of sheltered housing, probably because they were aware that wardens were not supposed to carry out such tasks, but ranked reasonably

Table 7.1   *Ranking of tasks carried out by wardens*

	Wardens	Sheltered tenants	Amenity tenants
Someone to help in emergencies and answer the alarm	1	1	1
Someone to offer emotional help and support	2	7	8
Having someone friendly around to talk to	3	2	3
Someone to offer advice when it is needed	4	4	4
Someone to help security and prevent vandalism and crime	5	8	7
Someone to encourage people to talk to each other and arrange social activities	6	5	6
Someone to keep an eye on residents	7	3	2
Someone to look after the building	8	6	9
Someone to help out with small jobs such as shopping or cleaning	9	9	5

Source: Clapham and Munro (1988).

highly by amenity tenants, who were unlikely to have a clear idea of what wardens actually did but who perhaps saw this as what they would find most useful. The other major difference occurred in the case of emotional help and support, which was ranked highly by wardens but lowly by tenants. This may reflect an increasing professionalisation of wardens and a desire to define the warden's role as a form of residential social work. Cunnison and Page (no date), in a study of sheltered housing in Hull, found that half of their sample of wardens gave this support, which they saw as reinforcing the tenants' sense of individual and group identity. However, the wardens reported that this activity was not appreciated or rewarded by their employers, and the low ranking given by tenants to such activity may show that it does not reflect their needs.

The most important task carried out by wardens, as ranked by all parties, was answering the alarm and helping out in emergencies. In a survey of sheltered housing in England and Wales, Butler (1985) found that 23 per cent of sheltered tenants had experienced an emergency in the previous four years. In the Scottish study 37 per cent of tenants reported that they had had an emergency in the past year, and 13 per cent of all tenants had had more than one emergency (Clapham and Munro, 1988). Not surprisingly, the incidence of emergencies varied according to the physical capabilities of the older person and whether they lived on their own. But even among relatively able tenants who lived with a spouse, one in five reported having had an emergency in the last year. Eighty-eight per cent of all the emergencies were due to illness or a fall.

When emergencies occur, alarm systems are not always effective in getting help, because of difficulties of use; other methods of summoning help such as the telephone or attracting a neighbour's attention by shouting or knocking on the wall can be just as effective. On the first point Butler found that 7 per cent of tenants in his survey who had experienced an emergency would have liked to activate the alarm system but were unable to do so. The reasons for this may have been an inability to reach pull cords or switches, the failure to wear personal devices, or the alarm not working. The Scottish survey found that despite the increasing use of community alarm systems and relief wardens for the period when a warden was off-duty, in five of the twelve case-study schemes there were regular times when there was no one to answer the alarm (Clapham and Munro, 1988). For these reasons it may not always be possible to use the alarm to summon help. Nevertheless, in most emergencies (82 per cent in the Scottish sample) the alarm was satisfactorily used. However, the importance of alarm systems has been questioned by Butler. He argues that the stereotypical picture of older people being 'frail' and subject to the frequent occurrence of emergencies is exaggerated. The picture of an old person lying on the floor injured for hours after a fall is a very striking and emotional one which, he argues, has unduly influenced policy. He examined the self-reported emergencies in his sample and found a large number not to be genuine emergencies. Also, in many cases, the alarm was not the only practicable means of summoning help. He argues that only 6 per cent of the tenants in his sample suffered genuine emergencies in which the alarm was the only practicable way of summoning help.

In short, the warden is considered to be pivotal to the success of sheltered housing, but there is substantial conflict concerning the role she should carry out and the value of key tasks such as dealing with emergencies, particularly in the light of the spread of community alarm systems discussed later in the chapter.

The other unique elements of sheltered housing are the communal facilities which usually comprise a common room, a communal laundry and a guest bedroom. Usage of laundry facilities is usually fairly high and home helps in particular find it useful. Other facilities are less well used. The guest bedroom is used by only a few tenants and then not regularly, but in many schemes where the dwellings are small its removal would mean that tenants would not be able to have visitors to stay.

The common room seems to be used largely for organised social activities and not often by tenants on an informal basis. Middleton (1984) describes communal lounges as an anachronism provided in the past to compensate for a lack of private space in schemes with only bedsitting accommodation. Because bedsits proved so unpopular with tenants, most recently-built schemes have been in the form of self-contained flats which leave little need for communal provision. In some sheltered complexes people from outside the scheme are permitted to use the facility, but this can often be resented by tenants, especially where the common room is designed as an integral and central part of the scheme.

Evaluating sheltered housing

Sheltered housing is a combination of housing provision and social support. The housing elements of the package are not unique because some housing units are built to the same basic design guidelines. Evaluation of sheltered housing should therefore focus on the social support elements, both in terms of their cost-effectiveness compared to other forms of social support and in terms of their relationship to the housing elements. Much of the recent criticism that has surrounded sheltered housing has revolved around this latter point. Butler *et al.* (1983) found that half the old people moving into sheltered housing had never heard of sheltered housing before the move, and only 20 per cent had actually sought this type of accommodation. After an investigation of the moving process as experienced by tenants, they concluded:

> From our interviews it was clear that of paramount importance was the desire for a more manageable house or flat in a particular location, either close to where they already lived, or closer to a relative. The number who specified that they were seeking the particular features of sheltered housing – a warden, an alarm, the

company of other elderly people, and a commonroom – were very few indeed. (Butler *et al.,* 1983, p. 197)

The same picture emerged from the Scottish survey, with few tenants naming the special facilities of sheltered housing as being important in their desire to move.

Nevertheless, the vast majority of sheltered housing tenants seem very happy where they are. When tenants were asked in the Scottish survey to list the three best features of living in sheltered housing, the factors relating to the housing elements predominated, as Table 7.2 shows. The unique features of sheltered housing, such as the communal facilities, the alarm and the warden, together only accounted for 23 per cent of all mentions. The most vulnerable group of tenants (single people with low capacity for self-care) were slightly more likely to value the unique features of sheltered housing than the average. This is reinforced by the fact that the more vulnerable people make more use of communal facilities. For example, they are more likely to experience an emergency and need to use the alarm system to summon help. They are more likely to use the common room and to appreciate the friendliness of sheltered housing compared to their previous accommodation. Furthermore, although the point has not been confirmed by any recent research, it

Table 7.2   *Three best features of living in sheltered housing as identified by vulnerable group and all tenants*

	% of mentions by vulnerable group*	% of all mentions
Factors relating to the house itself	25	29
Friendliness	25	17
Warden	15	13
Location of the scheme relative to local amenities	13	17
Alarm system	12	6
Peace and quiet and privacy	7	9
Communal facilities	0	4

*Single high-dependency group of tenants.
Source: Clapham and Munro (1988).

is generally accepted that this group takes up much of the time of the warden.

Despite this evidence that more vulnerable people appreciate the unique features of sheltered housing to a greater extent than the less vulnerable, it was found in the Scottish survey that 29 per cent of tenants were not vulnerable in any way. Alexander and Eldon (1979) found that two-thirds of the sheltered housing tenants in their sample were totally independent. Forty-two per cent of the Scottish sample of sheltered housing wardens stated that, in their opinion, some of their tenants were too fit for sheltered housing. As outlined in an earlier section, this situation occurs because of the practice of controlling allocations to ensure a mix of 'fit' and 'frail' older people in a scheme. This is said to be necessary in order to prevent schemes becoming 'institutionalised'. However, there is no evidence that the level of dependence of the tenants in a scheme adversely influences its atmosphere or friendliness. In the Scottish survey no relationship was found between tenant assessments of friendliness, or measures of their satisfaction with the scheme and the average level of dependence. Fisk (1986) argues that the physical environment of a scheme is more important in determining the atmosphere than the level of disability of the residents. Additional factors such as the attitude of the warden also seem to be more important than the level of dependence of the tenants in determining the atmosphere of a scheme and the level of satisfaction of tenants.

Another argument for 'balancing' schemes is that it is necessary to prevent an undue workload on the warden, who is said not to be able to cope with too many dependent people. The strength with which this argument is usually put by those responsible for the management of sheltered housing shows just how rigid the conventional wisdom about sheltered housing can be, as it is an example of fitting the client to the service rather than flexibly gearing the service to fit the client.

The practice of 'balancing' schemes is at the heart of the contradictions inherent in the concept of sheltered housing and of the difficulties involved in trying to strike an appropriate balance between the housing and social support elements of the package. The present standardised package only works if a substantial proportion of older people allocated to sheltered housing do not need it. This waste of resources is indefensible at a time when many older people are without the basic elements of care. The answer would seem to be, on the one hand, to provide more effective housing for those who can and want to remain in ordinary housing and, on the other hand, to adapt sheltered housing to cope solely with those who need and want its unique facilities. This would probably mean increasing the level of support in sheltered schemes, and it would possibly have implications for their design and the facilities provided, as well as for the training of wardens.

The case for this solution is made stronger because, despite the attempts to 'balance' individual sheltered housing schemes, it seems that the average dependence level of schemes is increasing (Clapham and Munro, 1988). This is causing many local authorities and housing associations to consider the introduction of very sheltered housing. Basically, this is sheltered housing with increased social support facilities and staffing. Most commonly this involves an enhancement of the facilities by the provision of meals, and greater social support, either by increasing the number of wardens or by the addition of more practically orientated care assistants. The lack of a single model does not mean that provision is any more flexible, but that different approaches are being pursued in different organisations and no one approach has achieved universal acceptance.

Some local authorities have stopped short of adopting a model of very sheltered housing but have upgraded the provision of social support within sheltered housing. The most common ways of doing this have been by providing extra help for the warden, either through an effective system of relief wardens based in the scheme or sometimes on a peripatetic basis, or by providing a community alarm system for when the warden is off duty.

This drift towards upgrading social support elements of sheltered housing means that it is moving further away from being a form of *housing* provision. The argument that older people with few physical incapacities are better off with good-quality mainstream housing and domiciliary care rather than in sheltered housing has gained sway. The experience of local authorities such as Warwickshire shows that very sheltered housing, as envisaged by Townsend (1962), cannot serve as an alternative to institutional care for a large number of people. For example, very sheltered provision does not seem to be suitable for people suffering from dementia to any appreciable degree. Very sheltered housing, therefore, seems likely to be used as a complement to existing forms of provision.

The traditional model of sheltered housing has also been criticised as being based on a stereotypical view of older people as being vulnerable and in need of support. The isolation of older people in the age-segregated environment of a sheltered housing scheme has also been criticised, and has led Victor (1987) to argue that in practice it is an effective method of disengaging older people from their wider environment.

These criticisms have particular relevance where the standard package of care is inflexible and where the assumption is made (in the practice of balancing schemes) that it is relevant to the needs of a very wide range of older people. These criticisms are less applicable where only those older people in need of the support facilities of sheltered housing are allocated places, and where the support is flexible and adapted to the needs of individual residents. In this way provision can be related to the actual needs of individuals rather than being based on a preconceived stereotypical view of what older people in general want.

The acceptance of this view would, in the present circumstances, lead to a general drift towards very sheltered housing through the upgrading of support to meet the needs of existing and new tenants. Thus sheltered housing would become less of a form of housing provision in that there will be even less cause to allocate it to older people whose main need is for adequate housing. A variety of solutions needs to be found to meet the varied housing needs of older people.

Housing provision for older people

The slowly changing role of sheltered housing, from a form of housing provision towards a social service, has given impetus to an already accelerating trend to look for other solutions to the housing needs of older people. In the public sector this has taken the form of the identification, provision or adaptation of dwellings specifically suited to the needs of older people. Reflecting the government's emphasis on supporting market provision through owner-occupation, however, two major initiatives have developed to meet the needs of the growing number of older owner-occupiers. The first of these are 'care and repair' schemes, which have been devised to deal with the difficulties which many older owner-occupiers have in keeping their properties in good repair. The second is the increasing provision of retirement homes by private developers, sometimes with the support of public or voluntary organisations.

Each of these three special forms of provision will be considered in turn, followed by a discussion of the impact of general housing policies on older people.

Designated rented housing for older people

Many local authorities have designated dwellings as being particularly suitable for older people, because of factors such as their size, location and design features. In England, older people with physical disabilities may be allocated wheelchair housing (for those largely confined to a wheelchair) or mobility housing (for those with less serious disabilities). However, the most interesting form of provision is amenity housing, which is found in many areas of Scotland. Amenity housing consists of the housing elements of sheltered housing. In other words it is a specially adapted dwelling which contains whole-house heating, special bathroom fittings, grab rails on common-access stairs and passages, and easy-to-reach light switches and power points. The dwellings may be specially built or converted mainstream housing and may be grouped or scattered among the ordinary stock.

Not much is known about how much amenity housing exists in Scotland and who lives in it. The official statistics show that there are 8,529 units, but this figure is grossly inflated, as many of the units so classified in these statistics do not conform fully to the official guidelines, although they may be specially reserved or specially adapted for older people. In many cases this reflects a flexible and pragmatic approach by local authorities towards the housing needs of older people and also the undue rigidity of the design guidelines. Nevertheless the concept of amenity housing is relatively flexible in that existing dwellings can be converted to amenity standards, and so some older people can have their existing houses adapted. Although this will not be possible in all cases, since some dwellings may be too big or unsuitable in design or location, many existing dwellings could be converted to amenity standards.

A survey of tenants of a sample of amenity houses in Scotland (Clapham and Munro, 1988) showed that they were on average fitter and younger than tenants of sheltered housing and were less likely to live on their own. In general, tenants moved into amenity housing to improve their housing conditions by getting a 'small, warm home'. However, some quite vulnerable older people lived in amenity housing and, where the appropriate level of domiciliary social support was available, they seemed to be very satisfied with their situation. However, the lack of effective co-ordination between housing and social work authorities meant that a small number of tenants did not receive the level of social support they thought was appropriate.

The high satisfaction felt by tenants of amenity housing shows that it can be a valuable alternative and complementary form of provision to sheltered housing for many older people. It provides good quality, suitable and unsegregated housing for older people living in unsuitable housing conditions, in many cases without having to move too far away from family and friends. However, it is not a widely known or understood form of provision among older people, and no effective mechanism has been found for linking it with domiciliary services.

Care and repair schemes

There are now a number of initiatives variously called 'staying put' or 'care and repair' designed to enable older owner-occupiers to stay in their own homes whilst ensuring that they have basic amenities and the dwelling is in a good state of repair. These initiatives have emerged from concern about the poor housing conditions experienced by some older people living in the private sector. Older people are much more likely than younger people to live in pre-1919 housing and to experience problems with the lack of basic amenities or poor housing conditions. In the 1981 census, 6 per cent of people over retirement age were living in homes without exclusive use of a bath or inside toilet, compared to 1 per cent of younger households. In the 1981 House Condition Survey, 41 per cent of elderly owner-occupiers in England were living in houses that were unfit or needed more than £2,500 (at 1981 prices) of repairs, compared to 22 per cent of owner-occupier households with a younger head (DoE, 1982).

Despite this evidence of the large number of older people living in sub-standard housing, the uptake of improvement and repair grants appears to be low. Older people are influenced by the same factors which tend to reduce take-up in general, such as the complexity of the present system, the valuation gap (where the amount spent on improvement or repair is not matched by an increase in the market price of the property), and the difficulty of finding the personal contribution needed. There have been many calls for reform of the present system to ease these problems. However, there was widespread antipathy to government proposals put out as a Green Paper in 1985, but it has proceeded with more limited reforms (see Chapter 2). Also, it has supported the development of schemes specifically targeted at older people. These schemes are organised to provide an agency service to older people by advising them on the grants available and helping them through the repair or improvement process by liaising with builders and other agencies. Some schemes also attempt to enable older owner-occupiers to 'unlock the equity' of their homes by taking out mortgages on the property to pay for repairs and improvements. Repayments of the capital can be deferred until the house is sold or the owner dies.

This approach is based on a set of assumptions about the factors which inhibit older people from improving or repairing their homes. First, there is an assumption that some older people may not be aware that their house is in need of repair, or know about the feasibility of making improvements. General studies of householders' awareness of the condition of their houses have been at variance with professional judgements (see Kintrea, 1987). Second, there is an assumption that older people experience difficulties in applying for improvement grants and getting work done, and that agency services are the best way of helping them. In a survey of 243 applicants to the Anchor Housing Trust's Staying Put scheme, Wheeler (1985) found that 28 per cent did not know about the existence of repair or improvement grants and a further 46 per cent knew about the grants but did not apply, mainly because they thought they would not be eligible or because they did not consider the idea. Twenty-nine per cent said they found difficulty in dealing with builders and would, therefore, probably benefit from the agency services.

Third, there is an assumption in schemes that require older people to make a financial contribution that they can afford to do so. Sixty-one per cent of the Anchor sample said they had difficulty in paying for work on their homes, which is hardly surprising considering the low incomes of many older people. Forty-two per cent of the sample were on supplementary benefit and 69 per cent had savings of less than £1,000. For schemes such as 'Staying Put', where a loan is

188   *Housing and Social Policy*

raised and repaid on sale or inheritance, the assumption is that older
people wish to convert their wealth for immediate use in this way.
Two-thirds of the Anchor sample who carried out repairs and
improvements took out an interest-only mortgage to help fund the
work. However, only 30 per cent of applicants to the scheme went
ahead with work, although only 13 per cent of those not going ahead
mentioned the expense or a reluctance to borrow as a reason.

Other schemes such as the Ferndale Project in South Wales have
concentrated on carrying out small items of repair to keep a
property wind- and watertight, and to maintain essential services
such as electricity supply and water. Because the project was backed
by Shelter and the Help the Aged Housing Trust, only a nominal fee
was charged for the work, which thus involved a heavy subsidy.

The wide variety of schemes means that they are very difficult to
evaluate as a whole. However, it seems clear that they are a valuable
addition to the policy instruments designed to improve the condition
of the housing stock in general and help the older owner-occupier in
particular. Nevertheless, the initiatives do have their limitations.
Schemes which rely on using existing grants in addition to mortgages are only really feasible for better types of property. In general,
building societies offering the mortgages do not relax their usual
lending criteria. It could, therefore, be difficult to get a mortgage for
a particularly run-down property or in an area where house prices
are falling. This type of scheme is favoured by the government
because it places the major responsibility on the individual rather
than the state to ensure that housing is improved or kept in good
repair, and therefore it is in congruence with the market model
outlined in Chapter 2. Schemes which rely on subsidising the cost of
repairs or improvements outside or in addition to the existing grants
system would be expensive if applied widely. Both approaches are
limited by the adoption of an area focus, and neither offers a
satisfactory alternative to reform of the overall improvement and
repair grant system.

Private retirement homes

The last few years have seen a considerable increase in the number of
properties specifically built for owner-occupation by older people.
These vary from schemes which have the full facilities of sheltered
housing, including an alarm system and a warden, to units of

accommodation considered to be suitable for older people but without any special facilities.

Many of these schemes are built by private housebuilders and managed either by private companies set up by developers, by housing associations or voluntary organisations. Some schemes, however, are provided by housing associations as 'leasehold schemes for the elderly'. These were to extend sheltered provision for sale to those who cannot afford the full purchase price. Thus a subsidy (usually of 30 per cent) was provided through the Housing Association Grant system, leaving owners to pay 70 per cent of the current market value. Shared ownership or equity sharing schemes are also available from some private developers.

There is little research as yet on retirement homes. The only major study was carried out in 1982 and was funded by the Department of the Environment (Fleiss, 1985). This study predated the boom in provision, so that its sample may be unrepresentative of current provision. All of the schemes in the survey were similar to public sheltered housing schemes in that they had communal facilities and a resident warden linked to the tenants through an alarm system. The research found, not surprisingly, that the sample of sheltered housing owners was significantly different from samples of sheltered housing tenants, in particular because almost all of them owned their previous home outright and 45 per cent were in the employer, managerial and professional socio-economic groups. In addition they were less dependent than the average of all older people (Fleiss, 1985).

The evaluation of this type of accommodation must be along the same lines as that of rented sheltered schemes. A major difference which has been instrumental in altering the form of provision is that sheltered owners invariably bear the full cost of running the scheme, which includes the costs of upkeep of the communal facilities and the wages of the warden. The DoE study showed that these costs varied substantially. However, about half of the owners thought the charges were unreasonably high, and this, along with high initial purchase prices, was the main reason given by those who withdrew from purchase.

Consequently, many private developers have cut management charges by reducing the level of communal facilities and by changing the role of the warden into that of a caretaker whose main job is to look after the building and grounds. This is possible because of the very low dependence level of owners. For most schemes there is a screening process which results in most dependent people being excluded. Owners face restrictions on resale to prevent dependent people entering schemes, and there is a clause in many agreements that the owner has to move on if they become too dependent. It remains to be seen whether this will be enforced and what will happen in such schemes if owners should become dependent.

The move away from the model of sheltered housing means that many recent schemes are merely newly-built housing aimed at older people. The large number of sales of units in such schemes means that they meet a demand from relatively well-off older owner-occupiers to move into a new dwelling which is designed with older people in mind, where all maintenance is taken care of and there is an alarm system for emergencies. They are, therefore, an important addition to the housing options available to some older people, although they are not a realistic option for more dependent people or for those in lower-value property or with low incomes.

The impact of general housing policy

These developments in the field of housing provision for older people must be seen in the light of trends in the housing system as a whole. In particular, the continuing decline of the private rented sector and the increasing government support for, and the resulting growth of, the owner-occupied sector, have a profound impact on the housing situation of older people.

According to the 1981 census, 30 per cent of pensioner households lived in the private rented sector. Forty-one per cent of households in the sector contained at least one member of pensionable age. The low return to landlords in the sector has resulted in a housing stock which is generally in a poor condition, so that more than one in six privately rented dwellings are unfit and nearly half need repairs of more than £2,500 (DoE, 1982). This compares with figures of one in twenty and one in five respectively in the owner-occupied sector. In addition, 12 per cent of households in the privately rented sector lacked sole use of a bath or inside WC in 1981, compared to 2 per cent of owner-occupiers. Previous attempts to revive the sector have not managed to reverse the decline, and even if recent legislation succeeds in this objective, it is unlikely to be to the benefit of lower-income groups. The provision of improvement grants has not succeeded in improving the relative position of the stock in the sector because of the low take-up by private landlords.

The growth of the owner-occupied sector has meant that many more people with relatively low incomes are becoming owner-occupiers. It also means that an increasing proportion of older people are outright owners. Nevertheless, in 1983, 63 per cent of single pensioner owner-occupiers had an income below 140 per cent of the supplementary benefit level, and experience of the 'care and repair' initiatives showed that low income is the primary reason for older people having difficulty in keeping their homes in good repair. The number of older people experiencing these difficulties is likely to increase, because low-income owner-occupiers are likely to have low incomes in old age and not to have had the chance to build up savings to fund improvements and repairs. They are also more likely to live in older, cheaper property which is likely to be in worse condition or built to lower standards, causing repair problems.

As we saw in Chapter 4, the drive to increase the penetration of the market into housing provision has meant that most government help and subsidy for owners is aimed at reducing the cost of entry into the sector rather than at the running costs incurred in home ownership. Thus help is concentrated in the early years of home ownership rather than at the later stages of the life cycle, when running costs may be particularly hard to bear financially. The expectation is that some older people will be able to solve any problems by trading down to a smaller, more modern house, and others will be able to take advantage of the growth in private retirement homes. Both these options, however, are most likely to be available to higher-income groups, and do little to address the housing and income problems associated with poverty in old age.

In line with the prevailing ideology, with its emphasis on individual return for individual effort and individual responsibility, there is also increasing interest in schemes for 'unlocking the equity' stored in owned homes. Interest-only mortgages for repairs and improvements are now becoming more freely available. These maturity loans, as they are known, only involve repayment of the capital when the house changes hands – for example, on the death of the owner. Interest repayments can be paid by the state if the owner is in receipt of income support. But for older people with an income above this level, the repayments can be onerous, especially since the recent withdrawal of MIRAS subsidy on loans for the improvement and repair of houses. Mortgage annuity schemes are an alternative form of borrowing which enable people over the age of 70 to take out a substantial mortgage on their homes (usually around 75 per cent) in order to purchase an annuity from an insurance company which is used to pay the interest on the loan and to provide a regular income. The loan is usually restricted to £30,000 because of the upper limit on tax relief, and the income which this generates is relatively small, although it increases with the age of the borrower. There is, at present, no central government policy to support these schemes as an answer to the difficulties of low-income, older owner-occupiers (rather it has been left to provide sector agencies to take the initiative and devise appropriate schemes). Nevertheless, such schemes would seem to be the most likely way of dealing with what will probably be an increasing problem.

The market solution to housing for older people is, however, likely to lead to two problems. First, individuals' abilities to tap into such schemes, and to reap the benefits which can be derived from them, are likely to vary considerably according to the value of the properties they own. This will not only perpetuate lifetime income inequalities into old age but will also sustain inequalities in wealth, generated by national and regional differences in house price inflation. Second, such schemes will reduce the importance of the inheritance of housing wealth, which is an increasingly important way in which wealth is transferred from one generation to another (except, of course, for the very wealthy.) The impact of this on the overall distribution of wealth could be significant, although the impact on inequalities in wealth is difficult to predict without knowing the distribution of the take-up of the schemes.

Finally, the residualisation of public housing is likely to have a substantial impact on older people. Older people are over-repre-sented in public housing compared to other households, and the nature of local authority allocation policies (with their common emphasis on waiting time as a key factor in deciding on priorities for making allocations) has ensured that older people have been over-represented in the most popular stock (Clapham and Kintrea, 1986). However, those remaining in the sector are likely to receive a poorer standard of service in future as subsidies are completely withdrawn, and the physical fabric of the stock is likely to deteriorate further as funds available for repairs decline. The reduction in capital allocations, combined with losses from the sector either through the right to buy or through disposals to private landlords or other agencies, will mean that public sector tenancies will be increasingly difficult to obtain.

Innovations in social support

Domiciliary care

Domiciliary social support is provided through a wide range of services (home helps, meals on wheels, chiropody, occupational therapy and district nursing, among others) and is delivered by a variety of agencies including social work, health and voluntary organisations. The difficulties involved in co-ordinating these services and gearing them to meet the needs of individual older people are immense, and there is little doubt that this results in an over-standardised and inflexible service.

For example, the most important single service, in terms of the number of older people receiving it, is the home help. Hunt (1978) found that 9 per cent of older people had received a home help during the previous six months. Although there is little systematic evidence about the tasks performed by home helps, it is evident that, in many cases, they perform only a limited number of domestic tasks such as regular cleaning, washing clothes and shopping. This leaves many tasks for which older people receive little help, particularly heavier domestic tasks such as spring cleaning, interior decorating and gardening, as well as personal care tasks such as bathing, which seem to fall between the home help and the district nurse. Fisk (1986) argues that the type of tasks now most often carried out by home helps are those activities which older people are more likely to be able to manage themselves; some older people have services performed for them which they are able to do themselves, but receive no help for other tasks which they cannot carry out themselves. Many of these, such as interior decoration, gardening and small-scale repairs, are routinely undertaken for occupiers in sheltered housing and many retirement homes. There is no reason why this kind of caretaking service could not be provided to more people in public housing. This should be increasingly possible as caretakers are becoming recognised for the important services they provide in public housing and they are becoming more widely used.

The question of the co-ordination of services and their flexibility to meet individual needs remains. In an attempt to achieve this, a number of new initiatives in domiciliary services have been tried, although none of them has involved co-ordination with housing services. The best known initiative is the Kent Community Care Project, and similar projects exist in Gwynedd and Gateshead. The aim of the Kent project is to provide a flexible system of domiciliary care geared to the needs of individual people in order to prevent their having to move into residential care. A project worker assesses the needs of individual older people and can then organise effective support by 'buying in' services from an agency, within a limit of two-thirds of the cost of residential care. All of the projects seem to have been successful in reducing admissions to residential care while providing a flexible and satisfactory service to older people.

Community alarm systems

There has been a rapid increase in the number of community alarm systems in recent years, as housing and social work authorities have sought to extend the ability to summon help in an emergency beyond just sheltered housing tenants. There is now a wide variety of alarm systems being promoted by the many companies in this field. The most sophisticated of these provide for two-way communication by telephone or radio with a central control point. Some schemes have mobile wardens who can respond to an emergency when alerted by the central control. Others rely on friends or neighbours living locally to respond when called. While these initiatives can be important for older people who perceive themselves at risk, both systems have disadvantages. With mobile warden services there are problems of access to the older person's home in an emergency. Carrying keys around in a van leads to security problems and means that older people cannot bolt their door. There are also problems in responding to calls within a reasonable period of time, especially in rural areas where the population is spread widely. For example, the Central Region scheme in Scotland, which uses geographically organised mobile teams, aims for a maximum response time of 30 minutes. Even though, in practice, the average response time is 12–15 minutes (Age Concern, 1985), this can be a long time for an older person who may be lying injured on the floor.

With systems relying on neighbours or volunteers to respond, there may be problems in providing full cover. There are also doubts about the wisdom of relying on untrained people to respond effectively to emergencies. With both types of scheme there have also been some problems with the reliability of the alarm equipment.

The major criticisms of community alarm schemes have been concerned with whether the large sums of money spent on them could not better be used to provide other services such as increasing the provision of home helps. It is argued that older people themselves have not expressed a great demand for alarm systems and that their growth has owed more to the marketing skill of the manufacturers as well as the widespread conception of older people as being frail and at risk of sudden illnesses or falls. Tinker (1984) found that 12 per cent of a sample of older people with a community alarm system had had an emergency in the previous year and contacted someone. However, as outlined earlier, Butler (1985) argues that many events classified as emergencies turn out not to be so on closer examination, and that even in genuine emergencies it is often possible to call for help in other ways. These criticisms hold less weight if provision of alarms is targeted on older people who are particularly vulnerable to illness or falls. However, as Butler points out, once the major investment is made and the central control equipment has been installed, there is an incentive to maximise its coverage to as large a number of people as possible, regardless of their need. For example, Glasgow District Council has decided to install a community alarm system in all one-bedroom flats regardless of whether they are occupied by older people or whether they are in need of it. It is possible with the Glasgow approach that many older people living in poor housing conditions or confined to the house because of difficult outside steps will have an alarm installed rather than have their major problem overcome by other means.

The provision of a community alarm system can provide valuable support to an older person who is at risk of illness or falling. However, systems would seem to be of most benefit when they are locally based, so that call-out time is reduced and continuity of response and a more personal service can be offered. One way this could be provided would be to link systems with sheltered housing schemes which have twenty-four-hour cover. The blanket coverage of older people inherent in many of the systems is an example of the standardisation of services and the waste of resources involved in their use in inappropriate circumstances.

Informal care

The number of older people living with other members of their family has declined substantially since 1962, while the proportion living on their own or only with a spouse has increased. In the 1979 General Household Survey only 8 per cent of people over the age of 65 lived without their spouse and with children or children-in-law.

For older people with spouses, most help and support is given by the spouse. For older people without spouses, despite the small numbers living with family, the main carers are female relatives, particularly daughters and daughters-in-law. These latter tend to be left to carry the burden of care and to receive little help from other female relatives or from their own spouses (Parker, 1985). The financial, physical and social burden of caring on women carers can be considerable, as was outlined in the previous chapter. Some are forced to give up work completely, others to take a reduction in earnings. The physical and psychological stress involved in caring can also be substantial (Parker, 1985) and can lead to some women being effectively isolated from society. Neighbours are sometimes a source of help, particularly in keeping an eye on older people, being a source of companionship, being on hand in an emergency, or helping with practical tasks such as doing some shopping or collecting a prescription. However, some older people are reluctant to seek help from neighbours, especially when it cannot be reciprocated or when the matter concerned is considered to be personal or private (Willmott, 1986).

Despite these different forms of informal care, some older people remain isolated and without support. The 1980 General Household Survey (OPCS, 1982) showed that about one in six of all older people saw relatives or friends less often than once a week. This proportion rose to one in five of those over 80 and of single people. In all, 5 per cent of older people did not speak to relatives, friends or neighbours as often as once a week.

Conclusion

Community care for older people is relatively well developed when compared to care for people with learning difficulties, but there are many evident problems. Sheltered housing, which was treated as a panacea for the problems of older people in the 1970s, has proved to be an uneasy mixture of housing and social support elements. This has created tensions between its different elements and has generated conflicts over its role and management. Griffiths (1988) has argued that housing organisations should only be responsible for the 'bricks and mortar' of sheltered housing while social services agencies should be responsible for the social support elements of the package. The Wagner Committee on residential care (1988) also made the distinction between social support and shelter in residential care, arguing that the two elements could be separated conceptually and organisationally, with support services traditionally associated with residential care being provided in non-residential (i.e. community) settings. To this end they recommended further training for sheltered housing wardens, their integration into the mainstream of social support services, and their employment by social service rather than housing organisations.

These reports seem likely to give added impetus to an increasing tendency to downgrade the importance of the housing elements of sheltered housing and to give an increasing emphasis to social support. This is already happening in practice, partly as a result of deliberate policy, but mainly as a result of the increasing needs of tenants. In so far as it is a reflection of demand, the upgrading of social support in many sheltered housing schemes, and the adoption of the model of very sheltered housing, are undoubtedly positive developments which, with an appropriate allocation policy, should ensure that the unique features of sheltered housing are available to those most in need of them.

This orientation of sheltered housing towards a social service role, together with the growing realisation that it is not the answer to the problems of all older people, has led policy-makers to concentrate on providing good housing conditions and appropriate domiciliary care outside the sheltered complexes. The two problems with these developments are that they are piecemeal and that they epitomise the difficulties of co-ordinating housing, social services and health agencies. The piecemeal nature of the new initiatives is evident in the area focus of the care and repair and social services initiatives, which are limited to the relatively few older people living in particular areas. The other initiatives such as amenity housing or private retirement homes are also limited in scope, targeting existing tenants and better-off owner-occupiers respectively. Those in private rented housing and the majority of owner-occupiers are unlikely to benefit from these developments. The provision of community alarm systems, on the other hand, which sometimes occurs on an indiscriminate basis, is an example of a single element of service provision which is completely unco-ordinated with any other and which is not therefore provided as part of an integrated package of care.

The inherently limited impact of these initiatives shows the constraints imposed by selectivist 'special needs' policies directed towards older people. Much more could be achieved by examining the workings of the housing market and dealing with disadvantage within it, rather than by relying on a piecemeal approach. Similarly, reforms to the basic structure of the personal social services in Britain, together with increases in funding, might do more to improve social support services to older people than the setting up of area-based initiatives. Directing special policies to meet the perceived 'special' needs of older people may be a way of separating them out as the 'deserving poor' who are to be given more help than other 'undeserving' groups such as the unemployed. This can lead to the absurd situation where an older person and an unemployed person may be owner-occupiers living next to each other, both of whom are unable to afford to keep their homes in good repair because of low income, but where only the older person will be helped through a 'care and repair' scheme.

In short, despite the extra help which may ensue, the categorisation and labelling that is necessary to make such 'positive' discrimination work can be harmful to older people. It serves to differentiate them from mainstream society, and can give rise to negative images of old age. It is old age which is seen to be the problem rather than the real problems of physical frailty, low income or social isolation. Many older people may not suffer from any of these problems, and among those who do, individual needs will vary considerably. The association of these problems with the label 'old age' hides the fact that many of them are also experienced by younger people.

Nevertheless, 'special' provision does have its place and perhaps represents the most likely way forward, given present economic and political constraints. The care and repair schemes and the Kent Community Care Project represent important steps forward in providing flexible, integrated and responsive services to older people. The major challenge now is to integrate the social and housing initiatives to provide a more complete policy response to the

wide variety of needs of older people, and to broaden the programmes to make them available to more older people and to others
who would benefit from them.

In the current political climate, affording primacy to the needs of
the economy and emphasising individuals' responsibility for their
own and their family's well-being, the most likely area of expansion
will be in schemes for 'unlocking the equity' stored in the homes of
older owner-occupiers. The income thus derived can be used to buy
social support as well as to meet housing needs. Private provision,
which is already evident in residential care, may well then spread to
the provision of domiciliary services. This may result in a better
standard of care for those able to generate substantial income in this
way, but others may be forced to rely on relatives or to resort to
inferior and stigmatised public provision.

8

Housing Management and Social Policy

One of the major themes of this book has been the increasing promotion of housing as a marketable commodity through central government policy. This process has been accompanied by attempts (most notably in the Housing Act 1988) to restructure the provision of rented housing to make it conform more closely to this model. The aim in this chapter is to describe recent changes in the structure and functioning of rented housing, and to assess how these changes influence the ability of the housing system to respond to social concerns.

We focus primarily on trends in public rented housing, but we refer also to the private sector, not least because a key objective underlying the changes in housing policy is to transfer the ownership of some public housing to private landlords and to introduce the 'discipline of the market' into public provision.

A key concern of current policy is the nature and effectiveness of housing management. Since recent changes in housing provision have far-reaching implications for the way in which rented housing is managed, we devote most of our discussion to the development of housing management and to the current debate over the nature of the housing profession. In essence, we explore some consequences of the reorganisation of the public sector for the current nature, and future role, of housing management, focusing particularly on housing management's contribution as an instrument of social policy.

The housing manager's effective performance of a socially oriented role must involve collaboration with other social service agencies. This quest for integration has been a principal concern in social policy for many years (Hill, 1983). Numerous official and semi-official reports have argued the need for the co-ordination of services, and policy mechanisms such as corporate planning and joint consultative committees have been set up in an effort to achieve what has proved to be an elusive goal. The reasons for the failure to achieve integration have often been sought in the nature of professionalism and in the organisational structures set up to provide social services. We argue that these factors have to be seen in the light of wider trends in welfare provision, which can themselves create a general climate within which integration can flourish or die. Integration at a local level between housing and other social services, for instance, will be more difficult if decision-making is being concentrated at central government level, where it is more sensitive to corporate influences than to consumer demand. In the same way, integration at any level will be more difficult if the social policy emphasis in housing is being reduced. Collaboration between housing managers and other social service agencies has to be viewed in the light of trends in the housing system as a whole, as we now go on to show.

Trends in the housing system

In Chapter 2 it was argued that there has been a restructuring of the housing system away from the direct provision of housing through local authorities towards a market-based system where state intervention is increasingly focused on the promotion of subsidised privatisation. This reflects the ideological shift from an emphasis on housing as a right of citizenship to housing as a marketed commodity. However, to secure its legitimacy, the state retains a role by intervening in the market to support those whose unfitness or frailty prevents them from achieving a minimum level of provision. This has largely occurred through the direct provision of housing by local authorities and housing associations, either through new purpose-built dwellings for 'special needs' groups or through those parts of the public sector stock which remain after sales to sitting tenants or private developers are completed.

One result of this trend is a deep division between the two major tenures of owner-occupation and public rental, with the latter acting as the 'social arm' of housing policy. This is reflected in the characteristics of the tenants in the public sector (as shown in

Chapter 3), with disadvantaged households being increasingly concentrated in this part of the housing system.

While public housing is increasingly viewed as a residual sector,
acting as a safety net for the minority who cannot sustain ownership,
definitions of eligibility remain wide. The sector accommodates
those whose major problem is a lack of income, as well as those who
cannot compete in the private market because of learning difficulties
or who, because of physical handicap or the need for practical or
social support, have particular needs not catered for by private
developers. What these people have in common is that they are also
likely to be in contact with other branches of the welfare state,
particularly social security, health or social services agencies. With
the adoption of the policy of community care and the reduction in
institutional care, the number of people in this category is likely to
increase. Central government is aware of this and has attempted to
concentrate the declining public sector new-build programme in
housing for these 'special needs' groups.

Whilst public housing has become increasingly identified as the
major social arm of housing policy, power over policy within the
sector has become increasingly centralised. Through a wide range of
legislation, financial instruments and policy initiatives, central
government has sought to limit the powers of local housing authorities. Controls over the amount of new build through the system of
capital allocations and the right given to council tenants to buy their
homes at a discount, have ensured a decline in the size of the sector.
But central government has also been able, either directly or
indirectly, to influence the level of rents and to reduce (in most case
remove) payments from local taxes to housing revenue accounts (see
Chapter 4). Central influence over local housing management issues
has been less direct and has mainly involved the promotion of a
decentralised model of management through the Priority Estates
Project or by advising on the future of estates through Estate
Action, which can provide grants to improve rundown estates.

Other measures seem designed to bypass local authorities and to
reduce their role in housing. For example, the housing association
movement has been relatively well protected from cuts in capital
allocations and (as we saw in Chapter 2) its share of net capital
spending has risen. This is an important development because
central government has greater control over housing associations
through the Housing Corporation than it does over local housing

authorities. Capital spending priorities can be determined by central government, while the amounts to be spent on management and maintenance are centrally determined. Associations are subject to monitoring of their activities by the Housing Corporation, which involves checks on their policies and practices. If considered unsatisfactory, associations can be subjected to a number of sanctions, including, as a last resort, being closed down.

The publication of the White Paper, *Housing: The Government's Proposals* (DoE, 1987) heralded a significant change in the Government's approach to housing policy. As we saw in Chapter 2, there is still a major concern with the expansion of owner-occupation, but more emphasis is being placed on restructuring the provision of rented housing. Perhaps partly in recognition of the limits to which owner-occupation can be extended down market (even with the generous subsidies available), the government is determined, wherever possible, to substitute the private for the public sector in the provision of rented housing and to restructure the remaining public provision to bring it more closely into line with private provision and more in tune with the market model.

The mechanisms which the government has used to bring about these changes were also outlined in Chapter 2. They include the right of council tenants to opt for an alternative landlord (or, more accurately, the right of prospective landlords to bid for the ownership of council properties); Housing Action Trusts (to enable central government to take over the management of council housing in areas considered to be badly managed); decontrol of private lettings; and reforms to the housing association movement (decontrol of rents, reductions in Housing Association Grant, and emphasis on the use of private sector finance). In Scotland, a quango called Scottish Homes has been formed by a merger between the Scottish Special Housing Association and the Housing Corporation in Scotland.

In combination, these measures could result in a major reduction in the municipal housing stock, although the likely scale and pace of change cannot be known at present. The government would prefer to see transfers made to commercial private landlords, but the prospects of a major revival in this sector do not seem great. Most properties to be transferred may go to housing associations, though it seems unlikely that existing ones would be capable of swallowing up much of the council sector within the next decade. Perhaps because of this, a number of local authorities are in the process of setting up new housing associations to take over their entire stock. In sum, these changes will mean that rented housing, even where it remains within the public sector, will be increasingly 'commercial' in outlook and subject to the 'disciplines of the market'. This will inevitably have an impact on their housing management practices.

In the public sector, centralisation of decision-making has been combined with a decentralisation of housing management. This apparent paradox is resolved by looking at the functions that have been either centralised or decentralised. Strategic decisions have been taken away from the pluralistic local authority system and brought closer to the corporate sphere of decision-making, while central control over the implementation of these decisions has been strengthened. This has been seen by many as a direct attack on local government and an attempt to remove it from the field of housing provision and management. Parallels can be made with proposals in education to give more powers to schools and parents while centralising decisions over the curriculum and resources.

Undoubtedly this process means that the role of local authorities as providers and managers of housing is diminishing. There has been some talk of this being replaced by a strategic and enabling role. In other words, local authorities should become regulators of the housing system, promoting new development where it is not already occurring, dealing with difficulties of access, and so on. These are all functions which it is argued can be successfully carried out without owning and managing housing stock. However, in practice local authorities have few of the powers needed to perform this role adequately, and there seems little prospect of them being given these powers by central government, at least in the short term.

In summary, recent trends in the housing system are leading to the equation of public rented housing with a residual 'social' role, coupled with the fragmentation of housing management between many different kinds of organisations, and a reduction in the role of local authorities as providers and managers of housing. At the same time there has been a centralisation of policy-making combined with some decentralisation and reduction in the scale of housing management. This has been coupled with an attempt to make public rented housing more commercially oriented. These trends, if they continue, will substantially change the context within which housing management takes place. Already they have had a considerable impact on housing management practice, and it is to this, and to the debate about the practice and philosophy of housing management – which has taken place for at least as long as local authorities have been providers of rented housing – that we now turn.

The development of housing management

The aim of this section is to review the development of housing management as a profession, in order to shed light on those factors which may constrain or encourage its use as an instrument of social policy. Much of this introduction to housing management is based on the work of Kemp and Williams (1987), to which readers should refer for a more detailed account.

The origins of 'housing management' as a profession are often traced back to the nineteenth-century voluntary housing movement (referred to in Chapter 2) and in particular to the work of Octavia Hill (Clapham, 1987; Malpass, 1982; Power, 1987). If that term is intended to mean management for purposes other than just income generation through renting housing, this historical precedent must be acknowledged. Certainly, Hill introduced a new, intensive style of management, for which she claimed great results. And although she relied upon the voluntary work of middle-class women rent collectors (fully in keeping with prevailing Victorian notions of charity), towards the end of her life she saw the value of paid, trained, professional workers (Brion and Tinker, 1980). Moreover, in helping to increase the employment opportunities open to women (albeit within a sphere seen as 'women's work') she was a positive force in developing housing management as a profession.

Property management as a separate activity did exist on a wide scale before the First World War (Kemp, 1986). In order to minimise the 'troubles and anxieties' involved in the management of working-class homes, many private landlords chose not to carry out this task personally, but instead employed an agent to do it. The contracting out of management tasks ranged from just rent collection to all its aspects, including the selection and eviction of tenants (Daunton, 1983). Property management was carried out by a range of different types of exchange professionals, including house agents, auctioneers, and surveyors, between whom there was a constant and at times bitter struggle for pre-eminence. While some firms, mostly house agents, specialised in property management, for many it was simply another source of income to supplement their main activity, such as surveying or valuation (Kemp, 1986).

Octavia Hill's methods of housing management were rather different in style and orientation from those of her contemporaries; they repay detailed study because they illustrate many of the key characteristics and expose many of the tensions in housing management (see Wohl, 1977, for the best review of her work). There are four key points about Octavia Hill's methods that we wish to emphasise here. First, we should note that Hill was as much, if not more, concerned with her tenants' moral condition as with their housing condition (see Hill, 1875). Housing was, in a sense, a medium through which she could seek to improve the moral welfare of the poor. Indeed, it was her view that moral improvement was the key to housing improvement, since this, rather than the wider structural forces of society, accounted for the existence of housing problems now that legislation existed to prevent the building of slum property. She was firmly opposed to subsidies or state provision of rented housing.

Second, it was a basic premise of Hill's management philosophy that it was necessary to deal with the tenant and the dwelling together. She argued that the physical improvement had to go hand in hand – indeed, was contingent upon – the education and moral improvement of the tenant and, for that matter, the slum landlord. Her contemporaries in property management also made distinctions between types of tenant when deciding whether to redecorate a dwelling or to allow a limited amount of arrears to accrue (Englander, 1983; Kemp, 1987), but their purpose for such action was different from Hill's. Hill sought to offer rewards for good behaviour, while her contemporaries rewarded those tenants whom they wished to keep because it was in their long-term interests to do so. Thus Hill operated with a moral imperative, other property managers with a commercial one.

Third, Hill's moral imperative entailed the strict enforcement of punctual rent payment. Arrears of rent were not tolerated. In this she was considerably less flexible than many mainstream property managers of this period (Daunton, 1983), who adjusted their methods to the realities of working-class financial insecurity. It was common for landlords to allow arrears to accrue, for example, during downturns in trade, in the hope and expectation that they would be paid off when conditions improved (see Englander, 1983). It was necessary for them to do so simply because fluctuations in incomes and employment were so widespread.

Fourth, despite Hill's achievements in advocating the social responsibilities of housing management, it is not clear whether the success she claimed to have achieved was the result of 'improving' her tenants or simply of weeding out the 'undesirables'. Since Hill saw it as her moral duty to evict forthwith those of her tenants who fell into arrears, and given that fluctuations of employment and income levels were endemic, the latter rather than the former might account for most of her success in keeping bad debts to a minimum. Nevertheless, Hill herself (1875, pp. 50–1) claimed that though her tenants were 'of the very poor', none had continued 'in what is called distress except such as have been unwilling to exert themselves'. This suggests that she may have been somewhat out of touch with the harsh realities of everyday life for the indigent, 'undeserving', late Victorian poor. Certainly, it is doubtful that her approach to management could have worked at the time on a wide scale if the poorest of the poor were ever to be properly housed (Kemp and Williams, 1987).

In short, Octavia Hill's method was imbued with a view that housing management was a social work-orientated activity which could act as an agent of social change. This was interpreted as seeking to enforce a fairly strict moral code of behaviour and to make tenants into respectable and useful members of society. A very personal style of management was used in which a housing manager, at least in theory, had a personal relationship with each individual tenant. Housing management was closely linked with social work, and Octavia Hill was involved in the early years of both the professions, which shared the emphasis on an individualistic and moralistic approach.

While Hill's management methods gained a lot of publicity at the time, partly as a result of a series of articles that she wrote (collected together in Hill, 1875), she appears to have had very little impact on the way in which the majority of rented housing was managed prior to 1914, which was dominated by commercial criteria. In fact, the same could almost be said of the management of public housing in the twentieth century. Although many have advocated the use of Octavia Hill's management methods, in practice few local authorities have used her system on a large scale.

Following the First World War, the rented housing market was restructured, with private renting declining and local authorities slowly emerging as the main providers and managers of housing to rent. This has inevitably had a considerable impact on the nature of housing management as an activity and as a profession, although there were important continuities with private sector practice in the early years after World War I.

After the First World War, the newly formed Ministry of Health (which was given responsibility for central direction of local authority house building) was particularly concerned to ensure the rapid production of 'homes fit for heroes to live in' (Swenarton, 1981), and it gave local authorities much advice aimed at facilitating the speedy and cheap production of council houses. But it gave very little advice about how the newly built houses should subsequently be managed. In the little guidance that it did give, the Ministry argued that each council should be free to devise its own management scheme in the light of local circumstances. Moreover, in setting out the nature of the new task that the 1,500 local authorities were taking on, the Ministry provided a definition of tasks that was in fact no different from those carried out by the private sector. Thus, if there was to be anything 'social' about management by local authorities, it was left unstated (Kemp and Williams, 1987, p. 13).

The way in which housing management has been carried out in practice since 1919 has been influenced to a significant extent by the changing way in which local authority housing has been perceived and the role it has played in the housing system (see Clapham, 1987). In particular, the overall social class of tenants has determined the changing emphasis between a commercial and a social welfare approach. This is particularly evident during the period from 1919 to 1939. In the 1920s council housing was orientated towards the better-off working class and even the lower middle class, rather than to the very poor or those most in need (see Bowley, 1945; Daunton, 1984). Partly this was the product of notions about who was deserving of the 'privilege' of a council tenancy, but, more importantly, it was also because the rents on the new council homes were high and beyond the reach of the poorest households. Thus the poor were largely excluded from council houses, while an intense housing shortage and the high quality of the dwellings meant that the better-off workers were often very keen to accept a council tenancy. In part because councils were accommodating the better-off, 'respectable' working class, housing management was not seen as a problem to which particular attention should be devoted or about which central advice should be given.

During the 1920s the housing shortage abated, building costs fell, and local authorities gradually began to house poorer tenants (see the case studies in Daunton, 1984). After about 1933, council house building was devoted to rehousing those displaced by slum clearance and to reducing overcrowding. This meant opening up the public sector to tenants who were much poorer than those in the earlier period (Byrne, 1974). As a result, councils were increasingly forced to confront the problem of reconciling prudent estate management with local social policy (Ryder, 1984). This led to a new concern about how housing management should be provided and to the setting up of a sub-committee of the Central Housing Advisory Committee to examine the management of municipal housing estates (CHAC, 1939). In its report, the CHAC noted that because rehousing after slum clearance, as specified in the Housing Act, 1930, had introduced an entirely fresh principle in housing administration – that the very poorest were to be rehoused – this meant that much 'closer supervision' of the new class of tenants was necessary (CHAC, 1939, pp. 24–5). The CHAC proposed an interventionist style of management which was much more in line with the aims of social policy than the practice of 'interested detachment' that the authorities had followed before 1930.

After the Second World War, the more intensive, socially-orientated style of housing management was itself subject to criticism. As we have seen, until the mid 1950s both Labour and Conservative governments gave council house building a general needs orientation. One consequence of this return to a wider role was that, as in the 1920s, it was often not the poorest tenants who were rehoused by the local authorities. Hence the interventionist and paternalistic management style that emerged in the 1930s no longer seemed as appropriate in the 1950s. Thus, in 1950, one borough treasurer questioned whether the council tenant got 'too much management' of a kind which produced 'a distinct danger of quite respectable normal people being unduly harassed by visits and inquisitions' (quoted in Kemp and Williams, 1987, p. 16). The Central Housing Advisory Committee, too, acknowledging the changed orientation of council housing since its 1938 report, argued in its 1959 report, *Councils and their Houses,* that 'tenants today are much more representative of the community as a whole and are, for the most part, independent, reliable citizens who no longer require the support and guidance which was often thought to be necessary in the past' (CHAC, 1959, p. 2).

As well as the question of housing management style, there were also the related issues of how housing management should be organised and what division of labour was appropriate for the task. In practice, debates about these issues were closely bound up with the struggle for professionalisation in housing management.

In the public rented sector, housing management has only very slowly and incompletely become professionalised. In 1916 an Association of Women House Property Managers was set up by followers of Octavia Hill (Power, 1987) which operated in the private and voluntary sectors. It made an attempt to become firmly established in the new local authority housing sector, but with little real success. There were a number of reasons for this, largely related to the Association's advocacy of the so-called 'Octavia Hill system' of management. This method laid great stress on the role of women as housing managers; it entailed a generic approach to dealing with the various tasks involved in management, and it involved considerable emphasis on social work and on 'improving' the tenants. This approach was not, however, very appropriate to the kinds of tenants whom local authorities were housing in the 1920s. It was also a very expensive form of housing management because such an intensive style inevitably limited the number of properties each worker could manage.

Moreover, the generic approach, which involved a variety of management tasks being performed by one individual, would probably have required the setting up of separate housing departments within local authorities. Although some councils did do this after the First World War, others allocated the various tasks among existing departments within the authority – for example, rent collection and accounting to the Treasurer's Department, and repairs to the Surveyor's or Engineer's Department. These departments had their own professional bodies, which had a technical rather than a social welfare orientation, and were dominated by men. Thus the pre-existing organisational and professional structure of local government favoured the fragmentation of housing management, and produced what Power (1987) has called a property rather than a people (social policy) orientation.

When the Institute of Housing was set up in 1931 (in competition with the Society of Women House Property Managers), it was dominated by men from these other professions, and it advocated a property-oriented and fragmented approach to housing management. Although, in its evidence to the Central Housing Advisory Committee investigation into the management of municipal housing estates, the Institute recognised that the 'social work' aspect of management was a legitimate one, it saw it as a subordinate function most appropriately carried out by women (CHAC, 1939).

After the Second World War, the differences between the two professional bodies diminished. Indeed, in 1955 the two organisations set up a joint committee, and in 1965 they merged to form the Institute of Housing Management (now named the Institute of Housing). In its evidence to the 1959 CHAC investigation into housing management, the Institute of Housing argued that the debate was no longer simply one about what style of management should prevail. Instead, it argued, it was important that unified housing departments be established and that generic housing managers be employed. Thus while the Institute did not advocate the social welfare model favoured by the women's society, it did now accept the view that tenants should look to one housing manager about their tenancy rather than have the various tasks parcelled out among the different departments in the council. The two key principles which the Institute wished to see established (unified housing departments and generic housing managers) were important prerequisites for the establishment of housing management as a profession in its own right, separate from the other professions in local government.

The 1960s and 1970s saw effective movement towards unified housing departments and generic housing management. It also saw an increase in the scale of housing management, mainly because of local government reorganisation, which reduced the number of local housing authorities (from over 1,300 to 442 in Great Britain) and significantly increased their size. Although a major factor behind these organisational changes was a perceived need to increase managerial efficiency, the result was to make tenants more remote from their council landlord and to depersonalise the landlord/tenant relationship. Personal contact between landlord and tenant was futher weakened by the trend away from the traditional door-to-door rent collection in favour of payment at council offices and Post Office giro collection.

So the housing management profession started as an instrument of social policy as exemplified by the methods of Octavia Hill. Since then there have been tensions between a social policy role and a commercial role (exemplified in the distinction between the management of people and the management of property), with the balance between them being determined largely by the socio-economic imposition of the council sector. When the poorest tenants are housed, the social policy orientation is predominant, whereas when the sector caters for a wide variety of needs, the commercial role is predominant. It remains now to see what the current balance between these is and what this means for the potential of housing management as an instrument of social policy.

Current trends in housing management

In the 1980s the reduction in public capital programmes has meant that management issues have achieved more prominence relative to development issues in debates on housing policy. At the same time the increasing social polarisation between housing tenures, resulting in a concentration of deprived people in the sector, has (as in the 1930s) provoked a reconsideration of the style and structure of housing management and has prompted demands for a more socially oriented approach (see Power, 1987). This debate has resulted in a new consensus about the appropriate organisational structure of management, as the fairly widespread move towards decentralisation shows. However, this has not resulted in a standard response and a unified view of what housing management should be. Rather, different emphases have emerged, and they are being pursued to varying degrees.

There is an increased awareness of the need to improve the effectiveness of housing management procedures (Audit Commission, 1986a; Maclennan *et al.*, 1988). The widespread move towards the decentralisation of housing management can be viewed as a means of achieving this end. There has been particular criticism of existing repair systems which have largely operated on a centralised basis. They have proved to be too remote and rigid a system to provide an efficient service. A number of surveys of tenants have all pointed to an inefficient repairs service as being the major complaint by tenants about housing management (MORI, 1985; Maclennan *et al.*, 1988). When the service is decentralised, which means localising repair teams and giving tenants better access to housing staff in order to report repairs and to keep an eye on progress, the service seems to improve, as does tenant satisfaction (Power, 1987). The same appears to be true when decentralisation takes the form of a tenant management co-operative. Control over the repairs service is one of the most important reasons for tenants wanting to form a co-operative, and is perceived by members as one of the major advantages of a co-operative. The Department of the Environment-sponsored Priority Estates Project (PEP) has attempted to demonstrate the value of locally based, intensive housing management as a way of providing a more efficient and effective service (Power, 1984). Although there are variations between the different projects, the key to the PEP approach has been to decentralise management to the level of the estate, to involve tenants in decision-making, and to pay meticulous attention to the basics of the housing management task, such as ensuring that rubbish disposal is carried out and taking determined action to enforce tenancy conditions. The PEP method seems to represent a conscious attempt to reintroduce what are seen to be some of the methods of Octavia Hill (see Power, 1987).

Decentralisation of housing management often seems to be accompanied by the adoption of a welfare orientation to the service. The welfare model involves the provision of a service adapted to the needs of disadvantaged people. It frequently contains two elements: the provision of a wider range of services than has been usual in housing management, and a reinforcement of social control. The former often involves the provision of welfare rights advice, debt counselling services and housing advice. It has also involved welfare benefit take-up campaigns. This trend has been accelerated not only by the increasing reliance of those who remain council tenants on state benefits, but also by transfer in 1982–83 of the administration of housing benefit for income support recipients from the local offices of the DHSS to local authorities (see Chapter 4).

The second element of the welfare model of housing management (social control) can include taking more determined action to enforce tenancy conditions, such as those relating to the punctual payment of rent and to the penalties associated with arrears. It can also involve taking steps to avoid the occurrence of anti-social behaviour such as racial attacks. This can be done through liaison with other agencies, such as the probation service, the police, or local community relations councils, and can be combined with action to alter the population balance on particular estates or parts of estates by amending housing allocation and eviction policy. More recently, following the publicity which surrounded Coleman's (1985) research on some London estates, this approach has also involved attempts to reduce crime by making changes to the built form by, for example, removing walkways. The rationale behind a welfare approach is that the worst problems of some council estates are caused by a breakdown in informal social control. It is argued that this needs to be rekindled before any progress can be made in improving conditions in local areas. An important element of the approach, therefore, is that it views the needs of a local area as a whole, mobilising the appropriate combination of agencies to meet these distinctive clusters of needs. It has led to some important and innovative attempts to achieve collaboration at the local level between different agencies, which will be described later.

An alternative approach is the adoption of a conception of housing management which aims to create the conditions and opportunities required to devolve power to disadvantaged people. From this perspective, locally based housing management can be a means for enlarging the control people exert over their lives, by involving them in the management process. This varies from merely keeping tenants informed of what is happening, to forming a co-operative in which tenants have a large degree of control over the management of their houses. In between, there is a wide variety of different methods used to involve tenants in management, and the degree of influence which tenants have also varies considerably. Nevertheless, the existence of organised tenants' groups and the recasting of housing management practice to work with them has been brought about by a realisation that it is essential to mobilise local people and to gain their support if public sector neighbourhoods are to be renewed effectively.

These new directions in housing management, which aim to improve its efficiency and effectiveness and to give it a more socially oriented role, are not mutually exclusive; indeed, in practice, individual initiatives rarely fall neatly into only one of these categories. Moreover, it is easy to overestimate the extent to which change has taken place, since many local authorities and housing associations still appear to be unmoved by changes in their environment and are proceeding very much as before. Even so, the pace of change in both the style and the organisational locus of housing management has been significant and shows little sign of easing up as the public sector comes to terms with its role as a residual social welfare sector.

The Housing Act 1988 will have an impact on these trends. In particular, by leading to the fragmentation of the public rented sector and the introduction of commercial criteria into housing management, the Act will modify the welfare role to take into account the commercial pressures that will fall on public landlords. This may mean that the emphasis on efficiency and effectiveness of management will be given added impetus, but it also suggests that the social welfare role of management will increasingly be viewed as a means of imposing social control rather than giving power to public sector tenants. Whatever the future holds, the adoption of any socially oriented role for housing management has implications for the relationship between housing and other social services, and it is to this that we now turn.

The potential for collaboration

Recent changes in the housing system mean that public housing agencies are being pushed towards an essentially social service role. As previous chapters have shown, this is bringing housing organisations into close contact with other social services, requiring co-ordination between the different activities and the various agencies which supply them. The results of poor co-ordination are evident in the chaos that surrounds the policy of care in the community and in the effect this has on people with learning difficulties and their carers. Where there is a lack of effective co-ordination, it has generally been coupled with poor working relationships between housing managers and social workers, brought about in part by a misunderstanding about the nature of each other's role and powers. The question to be addressed in this section is whether recent and likely changes in the housing system have improved, or will reduce, the potential for co-ordination.

To facilitate discussion, a useful typology of co-ordination put forward by Sargeant (1979) will be employed. This distinguishes between three different levels of activity:

1 'Strategic collaboration' over service development and resource allocation.
2 'Operational co-ordination' involving the setting up of formal procedures to ensure the integration of complementary services.
3 'Ad hoc case co-ordination' between practitioners regarding the care and treatment of individual clients or households.

Strategic collaboration

The re-orientation of local housing authorities to a social welfare role and the trend towards housing 'special needs' groups makes strategic collaboration increasingly necessary. Yet Hudson (1986) has dismissed the possibilities for strategic collaboration because of the lack of any real planning capacity in either housing or social services authorities. Hambleton (1986) also points to the abandonment of both the housing and the social services planning machinery. He shows how the system of Housing Investment Programmes (HIPs) was introduced in 1977 in an attempt by central government to encourage local authorities to develop effective local housing strategies which reflect local assessments of housing needs. Although progress along these lines was uneven, in some cases it was substantial. However, with the election of a new government in 1979, the objectives of the system changed and it became an instrument for central government to make substantial cuts in local authority capital expenditure on housing. Housing authorities in England and Wales now lack a formal mechanism for strategic policy planning. There is little doubt that the increased central direction of policy associated with the change of function of the HIP system has led many local authorities to doubt the worth of strategic planning when constraints imposed by central government prevent their plans from being implemented. The Audit Commission (1984) has criticised the way in which the public expenditure planning process, which operates on an annual basis, prevents local authorities from making efficient use of their capital expenditure.

Hambleton (1986) outlines three attempts between 1962 and 1979 to introduce a strategic planning system between central and local government for the personal social services. But since 1979 what Hambleton refers to as 'the general deterioration in central/local relations' has meant that no new formal system of planning has emerged in that field. In contrast, policy planning in the health service has been relatively successful and long lasting. This may reflect the government's need for such a system in order to maintain the accountability of a service which lacks any effective local direction. Nevertheless, the existence of a formal policy planning system and the information which such a system makes available to policy-makers seem likely to be major factors in making collaborative planning possible.

Nevertheless, the main mechanisms for collaborative planning are the joint planning and joint financing arrangements between health and local authorities that were introduced in 1976. These have been described as 'weak and ineffective' (Hambleton, 1986). As outlined in Chapter 6, the amount of money allocated through joint financing has been very small, and the impact of the planning framework on the participating agencies has been marginal. The result has been a lack of effective collaboration in the policy of community care and its implementation.

As we have seen, the government is attempting to achieve a much greater plurality in the ownership of rented housing, by encouraging the growth of housing associations and private commercial landlords at the expense of local authority housing. The increasing fragmentation of ownership and management that are likely to result from these policies will make collaboration more difficult, not least because of the greater number of agencies involved.

In the 1987 White Paper on Housing (DoE, 1987) the government argued that local authorities should in future act as enablers in the housing market rather than as providers of housing. The implication of this was perhaps that they should take on a more strategic role, encouraging other agencies to meet housing needs and helping them to do so. This is crucial if strategic collaboration is to be achieved in an increasingly privatised housing market. Yet little thought seems to have been given to what this task would or should involve, nor to how they ought to go about performing it. For example, if the local authority is to stimulate desirable activities, is it also to discourage undesirable activities? What powers would a local authority need to act as an enabling organisation, and do they possess them already? What kinds of information would local authorities need in order to perform the role effectively and how should they set about obtaining this information? The lack of thought apparently being given to these issues seems to lend support to the view that the enabling role referred to in the White Paper is to be a very limited one and is being used, at least in part, as a cover for reducing local authority ownership of rented housing. Without the creation of an effective strategic role for local housing authorities, the emerging fragmentation of rented housing management and ownership will severely limit the capacity for successful collaboration at the local level.

The centralisation of key decisions about the direction of housing policy and the consequent distribution of resources provides the opportunity for collaboration at a higher level. For example in Scotland, Scottish Homes could be in a position to collaborate with other strategic organisations with a similar scope of operations. However, the only other agency operating on a similar scale is the Scottish Development Agency, which deals with economic regeneration. There is no equivalent agency in the social policy field. Scottish Homes, therefore, would seem to have as little chance of success in achieving co-ordination as government departments themselves have had in the past. Nevertheless, the concentration of strategic planning activity at this level seems to imply a desire to concentrate this activity closer to the corporate sphere of decision-making in order to insulate it from pluralist influences.

Operational co-ordination

Despite the lack of any effective strategic collaboration, there have been several examples of operational co-ordination between housing, personal social services and health authorities. Many of these initiatives have taken place at the neighbourhood level between housing and personal social services authorities. The trend towards the decentralisation of housing management has enabled these initiatives to take place where housing and personal social services are both run by the same tier of local government. For example, in Islington both services have been decentralised into neighbourhood offices designed to serve a small area. More usually, however, decentralisation has proceeded separately, and housing departments have been more actively moving towards this model of organisation than social services.

In social services, the policy of decentralisation has been more controversial and has been linked with the concept of community social work, an idea that has been important in thinking about the social work task since the publication of the Seebohm Report in 1968. The Barclay Report in 1982 gave added impetus to the concept and sketched out in more detail what the approach entailed. The essence of this trend appears to be a focus on the needs of a small 'patch' as the basis for the provision of social work services. This local area focus means that social work has to be largely generic because of the limited opportunities for specialisation in a situation where the range of problems is very wide and the number of staff is small. The small area focus also enables the problems of individuals to be seen within the context of the local community. This means that solutions can potentially be found by encouraging people in the local area to take collective action or by mobilising local informal care networks. It also opens up the possibility of recognising problems in the area and of attempting to change them in ways developed by, and acceptable to, the local residents. This, at least, is the essence of the 'patch' approach as discussed by Beresford and Croft (1984), in which professionals are viewed as enablers, while initiative, in theory (though not always in practice), flows from the commodity.

The acceptance of this area focus and the adoption of a community-orientated approach is bound to lead social workers based in local neighbourhoods to confront the housing problems of their clients. With the growing incidence of social problems within the public sector, they are likely to come increasingly into contact with housing managers. However, the slow spread of the 'patch' approach to social work, and the organisational split between housing departments and social services, have meant that this has not been widely accompanied by organisational change.

Nevertheless, there have been some interesting and innovative projects at a local level. One example of this is the Barrowfield project in the East End of Glasgow, where a combined housing and social work office was opened on the estate under a co-ordinator funded through the Urban Programme (see Clapham and Smith, 1988). Together with local residents, it was possible to take a comprehensive view of the problems which local people faced. Initiatives could be started which cut across organisational boundaries and tackled problems as they were perceived by local residents. It then proved possible to integrate, for example, solutions to problems of disrepair with those of local unemployment, and difficulties in paying the rent with those of claiming welfare benefits and obtaining money advice.

Another approach to operational co-ordination has been to focus action around a particular event, such as the closure of a long-stay hospital for people with learning difficulties. In some cases this has led to good examples of co-ordination between health, personal social services and housing authorities. For example, in their evidence to the Griffiths review of community care, the King's Fund Institute (1987) pointed to innovative examples of co-ordination, such as the Southwark Mental Handicap Consortium, set up to provide community provision for people discharged from Darenth Park Hospital, which was scheduled for closure. It consisted of representatives of the two health authorities covering the area, the social services department, local voluntary organisations, the Southwark Adult Education Institute, and three housing associations.

Co-ordination at the operational level, where the objectives are clear-cut and practical, seems easier to achieve than strategic co-ordination in the field of community care. However, only limited progress has been made because of the problems with the joint planning machinery identified in Chapter 6. Further progress may be difficult if government policy results in a break-up of the council housing stock and a large number of publicly subsidised bodies providing rented housing.

Ad hoc case co-ordination

Co-ordination at the individual case level has been hampered by the poor relations between housing managers and social workers, and by their widely divergent approaches, which stem from their different professional ideologies. Although social work and housing management may have started out with a similar approach, the overriding concern in housing management with the administration of standardised procedures has made effective collaboration with social work (with its client-orientated perspective) difficult. It has contributed to the widespread suspicion and misunderstanding which undoubtedly exist between many members of these two professions. A common example of a clash between the two approaches arises when the social worker is concerned to push a client's case for a transfer to another house to ease a problem, while housing management is attempting to ensure that standardised procedures are strictly enforced to ensure equity between tenants. The very concept of a 'case' is in many ways alien to most housing managers, and may only occur in specific functions such as the recovery of rent arrears.

Nevertheless, housing management is being pushed into a more social welfare-orientated role, which almost invariably means acting more often at an individual level. For example, the procedures usually employed in allocating tenancies in general needs housing – that is, the application of standardised procedures and allocation criteria based on quantifiable measures of housing need – are not applicable in letting a special needs scheme for people with learning difficulties. In the latter case, there should be a detailed analysis of the needs and resources of the individual person and an assessment made of how they will cope in a particular scheme.

If, at the same time, social work moves fully towards a community-orientated frame of reference in which the individual is seen in relation to the local environment and local social networks, it may be possible for housing managers and social workers to liaise more easily at the level of an individual 'case'.

Conclusion

The increasing prominence afforded to property rights relative to citizenship rights in housing policy and practice, particularly at central government level, has given impetus to the social polarisation of housing tenure and has helped to relegate public housing to a residual welfare role. At the same time, considerable changes are occurring in the form and structure of the public sector. Housing management and ownership is beginning to be devolved to a wide variety of different bodies, including housing associations, co-operatives, quasi-private trusts and commercial private landlords. The rent regime for these agencies is being changed to allow rents to rise to, or nearer to, market levels, and an increasing role is envisaged for private finance. These changes are intended to bring the non-market provision of rented housing more into line with market provision by introducing competition between housing agencies and by initiating financial arrangements which rely to some extent on the need to attract private investment.

The fragmentation of public rented housing may also reflect the desire to remove it from the local political domain by restricting the role of local housing authorities. These are still to have statutory responsibility for many functions, though, such as ensuring accommodation for homeless families. Nevertheless, without a stock of housing or effective powers to make stock available, it will be considerably more difficult for local authorities to discharge their statutory duties, even with nomination rights to some housing association accommodation. It seems likely that the costly and inadequate system of housing families in bed and breakfast accommodation could become even more prevalent.

The rationale behind this shift in the responsibilities of local authorities is that, instead of owning and managing stock, they should increasingly perform a strategic housing role. Yet, as we have shown, nowhere is this role spelled out, and there has been little discussion of the powers necessary to make progress in this direction. In the absence of such guidelines we can only conclude that the changing conception of local government's involvement is part of a deliberate move to undermine the powers of local representative democracy.

The intended removal of housing from the local political sphere, and the centralisation of key decision-making at central government level can, therefore, be seen as attempts to make housing provision more responsive to corporate demands and more able to resist the demands of local electorates as a whole and of council tenants in particular. At the same time, the ethos of public rented housing is being changed to place more emphasis on market values so as to strengthen the ideological hold of property rights over citizenship rights in the sector.

The impact that all this will have on the social welfare role of public sector agencies is, at this stage in the process, difficult to predict. Housing management has been slowly edged towards a more welfare-orientated role, and attempts have been made at the local (operational and individual case) level to overcome some of the barriers to better co-ordination with other social service agencies. The imposition of more market-orientated values, and the wider variety of agencies who may be involved in managing public sector housing, may alter the direction of change and make co-ordination even more difficult to achieve. The precise direction of change is likely to depend to some extent on the relative growth of non-profit housing associations compared with more commercially orientated organisations, and on the speed and degree to which council housing is actually hived off to new ownership. It will depend, too, on how much housing associations will be forced to rely on private financing now that they are officially part of the 'independent' sector (DoE, 1987). At the time of writing, it is difficult to foresee either the scale and speed of change which the new legislation will bring about, or the impact which the changes will have on service orientation and delivery. Nevertheless, it seems clear that the pursuit of social policy aims will be more rather than less difficult in the future.

9
Conclusion

In this book we have identified a range of ways in which housing policy advances the aims of social policy more generally. Our conclusions, therefore, begin by drawing together the achievements of housing as social policy, emphasising two key themes of the text. The first theme is the co-ordination of housing with a range of other social services to provide a more or less integrated package of care to particular individuals and groups. A second theme illustrates how trends in housing policy express a tension between the social democratic and market-orientated models of welfare provision. The second part of this chapter shows how the analysis of housing as social policy provides an interpretation of the power structure of society. In particular we suggest that the powerful dual politics thesis requires some revision in the light of recent trends in housing policy. Finally, we offer a prospectus for the welfare element of housing provision, placing it at the heart of a revitalised social democratic model of social policy.

Housing as social policy

Service overlap and integration

Each chapter has drawn attention to one or more areas of overlap between housing and social policy and to the strengths and weaknesses, problems and potential, of the integration of housing with other welfare services.

Chapter 2 began by exposing the tension within housing policy caused by the changing relationship between the mix of social, environmental and economic ends to which such policy must be directed. Our analysis showed that, in the last decade, economic and political considerations seem to have outweighed the social arguments for direct state intervention in the housing system. Currently, housing is at the leading edge of a move away from a model of welfare demanding state intervention to secure a range of citizenship rights, and towards a subsidised market model which specifies economic prosperity as the guarantor of individual well-being.

Chapter 3 questioned the wisdom of this new orthodoxy by drawing attention to the enduring character of housing inequalities in late twentieth-century Britain and by showing how housing disadvantage exacerbates, and reproduces, other forms of social inequality. Our findings here suggest not only that housing is an important indicator of deprivation, but also that housing policy can *create* the problems with which other social services must cope. By the same token, however, we argue that housing is an important point of intervention for social policy, and therefore that housing policy can, and indeed should, be a vehicle for pursuing social goals. The next four chapters considered what has, and could be, achieved in this respect in the fields of assistance with housing costs, homelessness, and care and shelter for people with learning difficulties and older people.

We showed in Chapter 4, for instance, that under the social security reforms implemented in April 1988, the means tests for housing benefit, income support and family credit were harmonised, whereas previously they had all been different. Apart from introducing greater coherence into the social security system, this harmonisation has meant that local authority housing benefit administrators are now much more easily able to identify whether or not housing benefit recipients have an unclaimed entitlement to income support and family credit, which are administered by the DSS. Thus local housing authorities can now more effectively encourage the take-up of welfare benefits.

However, Chapter 4 also highlighted the important interrelationships between DoE policy on local authority and private sector rent levels, and DHSS (now DSS) policy on housing benefit payments. We showed that the DoE policy of reducing Exchequer subsidy to council housing, by pushing up local authority rents, has helped to increase significantly DHSS expenditure on housing benefit. The DHSS has then used this increase in the cost of housing benefit as a

226 Housing and Social Policy

justification for cutting the 'generosity' of the scheme. Similarly, we pointed to the apparent disagreement between the DoE and DSS over deregulation of private sector rents under the 1988 Housing Act – a policy which is expected to result in significant rent increases and hence a rise in the cost of the housing benefit scheme. This is an example, therefore, where inadequate policy co-ordination at central government level can have deleterious consequences for low-income tenants.

In Chapter 5 we discussed some of the difficulties that result from placing homeless people in bed and breakfast accommodation prior to their being temporarily (or permanently) rehoused. We examined some of the stresses and dangers that arise from extended stays in this type of accommodation and we saw how, for homeless people, such stays can disrupt their children's education, make it more difficult for them to gain access to health care, and increase the cost of obtaining a balanced and nutritious diet. In these ways, the disadvantage that homeless people experience because of their lack of permanent shelter can be exacerbated and can also reduce their opportunities to benefit from the social rights that other people take for granted. At the same time, these problems themselves often result in additional demands being placed upon other social welfare services that, arguably, would not result if the homeless were rehoused directly into permanent accommodation in the first place.

Chapters 6 and 7 showed both the difficulty in co-ordinating housing with other social services and the impact on disadvantaged people and their families which a lack of co-ordination can bring. Attempts to implement the policy of community care have been characterised by inconsistency, confusion and conflict between different services and the organisations who deliver them. Contradictions occur, for example, between the general policy of moving people out of institutions, and the comparatively high level of DSS payments to people in private residential care which provide a countervailing financial incentive. Moreover, there is no secure funding mechanism or adequate level of finance for community care, both of which are needed if alternative forms of shelter in the community are to be provided.

Although there are some good examples of the necessary co-operation between different professions and agencies in meeting the closely related care and shelter needs of older people, or people with learning difficulties, these are rare. Even in relatively successful forms of provision, such as sheltered housing, there are inevitable tensions on a practical level between social work and housing agencies, and at a more general level concerning the balance of emphasis between shelter and care. This failure of the state to provide adequate community care services has resulted in substantial burdens being placed on family members (usually female).

The Audit Commission (1986b) and more recently Griffiths (1988) have drawn attention to these problems in implementing a community care policy and have suggested ways in which different forms of provision could be integrated more effectively by changing existing attitudes, responsibilities and funding mechanisms. Chapter 8 points to the difficulties of integrating housing and other social services at a time when council housing is being dismantled and responsibility for the provision and management of rented housing is being split between a wide variety of public and private agencies. Ironically, this has occurred at a time when the housing management profession is edging its way towards a more welfare-orientated role, and attempting to overcome some of the organisational and professional barriers to closer co-ordination. The fear is that the recent housing legislation will check this trend and make co-ordination even more difficult to achieve.

The state and the market

The shifting of the burden of care from the state to the family can partly be explained by the failure of implementation outlined above, but it also reflects the steady erosion of a social democratic model of welfare provision in favour of a market-orientated vision of social policy. We introduced these models in Chapter 2, where we showed how the different strands of housing policy have been more or less closely aligned with one or other model during the present century. Chapter 3 considered how these trends have contributed to the reproduction of three enduring forms of inequality, relating to class, gender and 'race'. Focusing particularly on the shift towards the market model observed in the last decade, this review suggests that, far from eradicating systematic or excessive inequality, attempts to 'free up' the housing market have helped sustain some fundamental social cleavages. Chapters 4 to 7 gave further illustration of what this policy trend means in human terms.

This shift from a social democratic to a market-orientated model of social welfare has, for instance, been evident in the provision of assistance with housing costs, which we examined in Chapter 4. Since 1979 there has been a shift away from general price ('bricks and mortar') subsidies, such as the Exchequer grant to council housing, to income-related subsidies in the form of housing benefit and tax relief to owner-occupiers. This shift to individualised assistance has played a key role in the privatisation of housing that has been taking place since 1980. What this serves to demonstrate is that while the market model has extended further into housing provision than it has into other areas of social welfare, it has not been in a 'pure' form. Rather, the shift to the market in housing provision has been sustained and made possible by extensive state subsidies to individual owners. Despite rhetoric about the 'self-reliance' and 'independence' that is said to accompany home owner-ship, market provisioning in housing is crucially predicated upon state intervention (of a kind which is universally available and devoid of the stigma associated with means testing, but which carries greater benefits for those who are better off).

In Chapter 5 we saw that the shift to a more market-orientated approach to housing provision has been accompanied by a marked growth in homelessness. Although provisions for this in the 1977 Housing Act currently remain intact (at the time of writing they are subject to review), their limited coverage has been underlined by an increase in the number of households living on the margins of the formal housing market that are not eligible for rehousing under the legislation. Childless couples and the able-bodied young, in particular, have been labelled as undeserving of assistance and largely left to fend for themselves in the housing market. Ironically, this growth in homelessness has been attributed by the government both to the 'dependency culture' supposedly encouraged by public subsidies and to inefficiencies in the management of local authority housing departments. In the present political climate, homelessness is rarely recognised as an outcome of inequalities generated by the market.

Chapters 6 and 7 went on to explore in more detail this further consequence of adopting the market model, and examined the categorising or labelling of groups as 'more' or 'less' deserving of state-provided shelter and welfare. These chapters identified two groups among the 'more' deserving (those perceived as unable to compete in the market due to frailty, handicap or illness): people with learning difficulties and older people. These groups do receive 'special' subsidies and 'special' provision, which are undoubtedly important and helpful to them. There are, however, two obviously undesirable consequences of this form of service allocation. First, it means that many of the routine needs of fit and independent older people and of people with slight learning difficulties are ignored in mainstream housing policy. That is, to qualify for state assistance, one has to submit to the imagery or stigma associated with labels like 'elderly' or 'mentally handicapped', even if one's lifestyle, needs and aspirations do not quite fit into the package of care offered. Second, the creation of categories of 'special' need is a socially divisive measure which confers inappropriate stereotypes on large numbers of individuals and can lead to the creation of a social hierarchy among those deemed more or less deserving of public subsidy.

The culmination of this process is evident in Chapter 8, which examined the social and management implications of an increasingly 'residual' public sector in the housing system. Although home-owners are, except in the very lowest income band, subsidised to a greater degree than public tenants (through tax relief on mortgage interest), there is a widening gap in status between those who own their homes and those who continue to rely on the local authority for shelter.

Nevertheless, from the evidence examined, we find little in principle to favour the unmediated market-orientated model of social policy. Indeed, our review of the housing service – where the process of privatisation has been effected most rapidly – suggests quite the contrary. While few would quibble with the criticisms that have been levelled at large unwieldy public sector bureaucracies, it is clear that considerations other than economic efficiency are required to guarantee socially effective forms of resource distribution.

It is important to recognise, too, that advocates of the market model have tended to compare the inefficiencies of the existing public sector with an ideal model of the market that exists in theory but not in practice. It is hardly surprising that the public sector is found wanting when such an unrealistic comparison is made (Hindess, 1987). In fact, the market also exhibits considerable deficiencies. Indeed, as we saw in Chapter 2, one of the reasons for favouring state intervention in the first place was evidence of inadequacies and inequalities in the market as a distributive mechanism. These underlay the introduction of building by-laws and public health legislation in the mid-nineteenth century, while one of the main factors behind the subsidisation of public housing in 1919 was the failure of the private sector to provide decent housing for working people at rents they could afford. Today, too, the private housing market is rarely characterised by perfect competition, consumers do not have full information, and choice is constrained by what producers supply and by buyers' wealth and income.

In view of this, we conclude by setting out a practical agenda for what housing as social policy *could* look like were some relaxation of (or compensation for) the market mechanism to be allowed. However, it is important, first, to reconsider our understanding of some broader aspects of the power structure of the kind of society in which these changes would be set.

Dual politics in practice

At the outset of this book we identified a number of theoretical perspectives on the power structure of advanced liberal democratic societies. We also suggested how each of these perspectives would interpret the meaning, character, aims and effectiveness of social policy in such societies. From this review we identified the dual politics thesis, as advanced by Cawson (1986) and Saunders (1986a), as the most useful or authentic starting point for our own analysis. We chose it, however, not as a definitive statement of 'reality' but rather because it seemed to 'work' best when applied to our understanding of the organisation of social policy in modern Britain. We still regard this thesis as the most helpful starting point for the conceptualisation and analysis of the role of housing as social policy. In the light of previous chapters, however, we would propose some modifications to the thesis. In the light of these modifications, our conclusions and recommendations are somewhat different from those suggested by earlier advocates of the dual politics approach.

The thesis as we specified it, following Cawson and Saunders, proposed a consistent and necessary relationship between the kinds of resource bargaining that are possible (corporate/plural), the level of state activity at which that bargaining takes place (central/local), the aims of state intervention encouraged by that bargaining (the protection of property or citizenship rights) and the interests served by such intervention (class interests/consumption sector interests).

Having examined these relationships in the context of the social aspects of housing policy, and in the context of the housing service in interaction with other welfare services, it seems necessary to qualify this framework.

First, our review suggests that corporate interests penetrate local as well as central government bargaining, and that the demands thus exerted on policies vary according to the *kind* of corporate bodies drawn into the bargaining process. Certainly, where business interests are concerned, most pressure has been exerted centrally (that is, at the point where financial control over social policy has been concentrated) and the interests served may be thought of in class terms. Nevertheless, as the process of contracting out state services, and of opting out of state provisioning (e.g. in health, education and housing) continues, we may expect to see corporate business interests applying increasing pressure on local governments (affecting, for instance, land-use planning and rent levels in the 'independent' sector). This 'trickle-down' of corporate influence has, moreover, already taken place where the corporate interests of welfare professionals is concerned and there is the ever-present problem that multi-agency collaboration will lead to a consolidation rather than a dispersal of the power of the professionals.

Second, because of the increasing centralisation of strategic decisions (especially those related to finance) that has accompanied attempts to infuse social policy with a market philosophy, the scope assigned by the dual politics thesis for pluralist bargaining at a local level may increasingly be limited. Advocates of the market model actively seek to diminish the role of local politicians in public life, bypassing local government through support for bodies such as housing associations, and appealing directly to local people as service consumers. The centralisation of power that has accompanied this may, therefore, be read partly as an attempt by the political centre to minimise the extent of local resistance to the shift towards market provision. One interpretation of the effect of this process is that the opportunities for consumer groups formally to participate in or control the process of service provision will be restricted. The alternative argument is that consumer choice as exercised through purchasing power may be regarded as a more authentic measure of local demand than that articulated through local government officials (since public participation in representative democracy is only partial).

Either way, it seems unlikely that social policy interventions at a local level work to protect citizenship rather than property rights as the dual politics thesis requires. Chapter 8 confirms this, showing that local authorities are charged first to advance the cause of the market and only then, and only through a diminishing segment of the housing system, to meet a limited range of special needs. It seems, then, that both centrally and locally, the protection of property rights takes precedence over the extension of citizenship rights. This is because, according to the market model, economic independence – a supposedly valuable source of independence from the state and from political interests – is seen as the key to securing a full range of other citizenship rights.

Third, the dual politics thesis, with its emphasis on social cleavages which derive from the politics of production and consumption, underplays the salience of 'race' and gender as enduring axes of inequality that cut across the boundaries of class and consumption sector. Whether power is centralised or localised, wielded through corporate bargaining or by a plurality of interests, and whether it is organised to protect the rights of property or to extend the rights of citizenship, it is shot though with the influence of racism and patriarchy. Black people and women have, on average, a weaker position in the labour market than their white and male counterparts, and this immediately places them at a disadvantage in an increasingly market-orientated housing system. At the same time, black people and women have had restricted access to the services of the welfare state (as illustrated by Cohen, 1985; Gordon, 1986; Williams, 1987), and this has occurred as much in terms of access to public housing as in terms of the receipt of other welfare benefits. Crucially, moreover, this relative exclusionism has been part of a catalyst promoting feminism, black consciousness and anti-racism as forms of protest, resistance or collective bargaining that cannot be subsumed within the conventional political categories (central/local, corporate/plural, class/consumption sector) of the dual politics approach.

Finally, this all raises the question of who social policy serves. This book suggests that there is a tension between consumer interests, corporate interests (as exercised by business interests and by welfare 'professionals' – and not always in the same way) and the interests of capital at every level of the state. The notion of a relationship between mode of bargaining, level of state activity, the kind of rights protected and the type of interests served therefore begins to break down, and we are left with a model in which the competing interests of business and welfare professionals squeeze out the interests of consumers and electors (especially where these interests cannot be translated into purchasing power), and marginalise the role of pluralist bargaining in the process of resource allocation.

This blurring of the distinction between the two arms of dual polity (central/local, corporate/plural, and so on) in late twentieth-century Britain reflects above all the increasing penetration–culturally as well as politically and economically–of a market model of welfare provision. Some consequences of this are considered in the final section.

Prospectus

Our discussion, reflecting opinion in the literature and in political discourse, has been organised around two key models of welfare: the market model popularly associated with the rise of the new right; and the social democratic model which was partially realised in the ideals of the post-war welfare state. Housing policy in the twentieth century can be understood in terms of the shifting political popularity of these very different welfare 'ideals'. Furthermore, the social content of housing policy in the future depends crucially on which of these models prevails. To explain why, we began with the observation that, although both these models claim to embrace three key elements of social justice–equality, freedom and democracy–their understanding of what these concepts mean, and of how they should be realised, is quite different.

Neo-liberal (and, to a lesser extent, neo-classical) economics, which are an important element of Britain's new right, interpret *equality* as equality of opportunity in economic terms. Providing the market is operating efficiently, inequality of outcome is not only tolerable but also necessary and even desirable. *Freedom,* from this perspective, is freedom for individuals to compete in the economy. Friedman (1962), for instance, argues that capitalism maximises economic freedom and that this in turn promotes 'political' freedom–namely, the freedom to choose and make decisions about one's life. From this perspective, and from that of a second strand of the new right–libertarianism–this means that *democracy* is only a secondary (overly politicised and not very effective or representative) indicator of consumer demand. The notion of democracy is, in effect, important only to allow governments to legitimise their attempts to preserve a status quo in which individuals are freed from the power of the state in the organisation of both public and private life. This anarchistic tendency is tempered by the authoritarian influence of traditional Toryism (a third element of the resurgence on the right) which is in principle supportive of a strong state as a means of preserving order, hierarchy, social control and social responsibility. This view, however, embodies that strong element of Tory thinking which has always opposed the extension of democratic rights among all social groups and throughout the class structure.

The social democratic views of equality, freedom and democracy are quite different. *Equality,* equity, or some equivalent principle of egalitarianism, is seen as valuable in its own right, as a means of encouraging social integration, diminishing social conflict, and pursuing social justice. Plant (1984) provides a particularly illuminating account of this 'democratic equality' (which is also concerned with legitimate inequality), contrasting it with the more limited visions of both equal opportunity and equality of outcome. This view of equality means that *freedom* can never be absolute in a libertarian sense, since to ensure that freedom means the same thing for all citizens, some kinds of action must be limited. In theory, the route to balancing equality with liberty is rooted in *democracy,* though we shall argue that this principle is the least developed, yet potentially most powerful, theme within the traditional social democratic model.

While both these models of welfare have received considerable scrutiny in the last forty years, we have shown that it is the market model which currently attracts most political legitimacy and, in many areas of social welfare, most public support. Deakin (1987) shows just what a powerful hold this model has, by drawing attention to the tenacity of views concerning the over-generosity of public services, to the extent of concern about the 'mistakes' of the paternalistic welfare state and to the notable absence in modern politics of sustained discussion of the concepts of welfare and the aims it should satisfy. It is clear from what we have written, moreover, that many modern criticisms of the welfare state are well-founded. Equally, though, our evidence suggests that the popularity of the market model rests on a series of claims which a modified social democratic model can not only match but improve upon. At a time when the relationship between civil society and the state is coming under increasing scrutiny in politics and social theory (see Keane 1988a, 1988b), we conclude by seeking a way out of the statist/privatisation dualism, proposing a revitalised citizenship 'theory', and suggesting how housing as social policy could help to put this theory into practice.

As a starting point we examine four claims associated with the market model, suggesting that the aims they embody cannot be realised without the development of a more democratic notion of citizenship and of the role of the state in securing the rights associated with it. The four claims we examine relate to the principle of economic efficiency, the ideology of inequality, the integrity of the individual, and the sanction of the electorate.

Economic efficiency

First, it is claimed by advocates of the market model that it is only by securing economic efficiency that the broader set of rights associated with citizenship can be extended throughout the population – not necessarily equally, but certainly without producing excessive inequality. Traditionally, the social democratic model, indebted to the work of Marshall (1950), has opposed this view, regarding collective responsibility for welfare as essential to offset the inequalities generated in a market economy. State intervention was regarded not just as desirable, but also as necessary, to ensure that economic prosperity enhances rather than undermines individuals' rights as citizens. From this perspective the inegalitarian underpinnings of the market model are regarded as inferior to, and less enlightened than, the aims of the social democratic alternative. State-subsidised welfare would therefore be seen either (at best) as part of the moral advance of modernism or (at worst) as a necessary use of economic prosperity to buy consent. For many years, in fact, the major criticism of the welfare state was not the right-wing assertion that state-subsidised welfare undermines economic prosperity, but rather the left-wing charge that the welfare state was structurally incapable of overcoming the basic inequalities generated by the relationship between capital and labour.

The tension between the objective of expanding state welfare provision and stimulating a market economy was not considered important in the 1950s when, for example, Crosland (1956) was arguing that the expansion of state welfare provision could be funded from economic growth without harming the economy or resulting in excessive increases in taxation. Today, however, the cost of welfare dominates the legislative agenda across the political spectrum, and concern for economic efficiency is as important in reformulating the social democratic model of welfare as it has been in developing the market model. As Turner (1986, p. 49) observes, 'The world in which Marshall originally framed his view of citizenship no longer exists', and the economics of welfare are likely to remain a key concern for all governments, who are equally faced with the challenge of competitiveness brought by the internationalisation of capital and labour. Few governments can now regulate or control their own economies, and national efficiency in world markets *is* important if welfare rights are to be guaranteed to all. In this sense, the claims made by advocates of the market model are valid, and would not be opposed by advocates of the social democratic alternative.

Where our analysis suggests that the market and the citizenship models must part company is not, therefore, over the principle of economic efficiency in itself. It is rather over the use to which that productivity is put, for the late 1980s are witnessing reductions in public spending, even against a background of economic prosperity and a well-funded public purse. Today, the social democratic 'solution' is, or should be, as committed as the market alternative to a vigorous economy, but couples this with an emphasis on the importance of collective responsibility to those unable to exercise their right to work or to accumulate wealth through the market. Any contradiction between these two aims can be minimised by formulating social policy in a way that maximises its positive impact on the economy using social policy interventions, wherever possible, to stimulate economic activity.

Inequality

A second source of the market model's appeal is its claim to have replaced a stultifying, initiative-inhibiting quest for equality with an ideology of (limited) inequality, which supposedly increases individual incentive and nurtures the work ethic. Here, there is a very real area of disagreement–or crisis of values–in the welfare debate concerning who should benefit from the wealth generated by a national economy. Our discussion of assistance with housing costs shows that, under the market model, those with most wealth and status already benefit most from subsidies associated with housing provision. The argument used to justify this makes reference to incentive and the work ethic, as well as to the self-regulating capacity of the market, which is expected to prevent moderate inequality becoming excessive. However, after almost ten years of this kind of approach, there is little evidence that such self-regulation has significantly reduced housing inequality. The market model, in short, may offer wider opportunities to a privileged sector of the working population, but achieves this at the expense of any collective obligation to those who, for social, economic and political reasons, are excluded from the labour market or the wealth-creating sectors of the economy. Deakin (1987) therefore argues that there is a moral reason for resurrecting the social democratic model, arguing that rights to welfare should be put back at the centre of social policy as a means of discharging society's moral obligations to the poor and as a way of moving towards a more closely integrated society.

Apart from the issue of who should benefit, there is also a debate concerning whether, even if deemed morally desirable, a 'strategy of equality' could succeed, for the charge of undesirability is a relatively recent, if increasingly significant, source of attack on the egalitarian underpinnings of the welfare state. A more common challenge, both from the left and the right, is that it is impossible to achieve the kind of equality embedded in the welfare ideal. It is frequently argued that the welfare state benefits the middle classes rather than the poor, that it has redistributed wealth only between the rich and the very rich, and that it is over-bureaucratised and too inefficient to meet public needs. However, Hindess (1987) has criticised authors such as Le Grand (1982) who appear to demonstrate the failure of the strategy of equality, arguing that, for a range of political and economic reasons, such a strategy has never been tried in Britain, and so can hardly be deemed to have failed. A similar observation is made by Ashford (1986), who points out that the ideal of the welfare state was compromised from the start in Britain. The 'strategy of equality', therefore, could still be an important element of social policy and, as shown in Chapter 3, housing has a particularly important role to play in this.

Liberty

A third tenet of the market model, and perhaps the key to its appeal, is its emphasis on the autonomy or 'freedom' of the individual. The principles of individual liberty and freedom—cast both in economic and political terms—are at the centre of this model's appeal. It is by encouraging individual effort and by celebrating (and rewarding) individual achievement that neo-conservatism has made its greatest popular gains. The left has been successfully defined, and condemned, as uncompromisingly and unappealingly collectivist both in terms of managing the economy and in terms of controlling people's lives. Building on some very real problems associated with state-administered socialism, neo-conservatism has, in Keane's (1988a) opinion, popularised 'a distorted interpretation of the virtues appropriate to civil society—self-interest, hard work, flexibility, self-reliance, freedom of choice, private property, the patriarchal family, and distrust of state bureaucracy' (p. 7). Thus the individualist rhetoric invoked to legitimise the market model has not only played down the collectivism of traditional Toryism, but also masked a key theme of the social democratic model, which is *its* recognition of individuality, and its respect for the integrity of individual rights.

Citizenship, argued Marshall, (1950 p. 10), is fundamentally about the 'rights necessary for individual freedom'. While it is commonly claimed by the right that the principles of individualism (or liberty) and equality are incompatible, Hindess (1987), Plant (1984) and Turner (1987) all argue that this is a false opposition. They show that there are many kinds of freedom and many forms of equality, and that there is 'no reason to suppose that reduction of significant inequalities necessarily involves the loss of important freedoms, or that the preservation of important freedoms requires inequalities that would otherwise prove unacceptable' (Hindess, 1987, p. 164). What they are ready to recognise, however, and what the market model denies, is that because the exercise of rights is so bound up with the availability of wealth and resources, 'a fair distribution of the *worth* of liberty is therefore going to involve far greater equality of income and wealth as well as the provision of services' (Plant, 1984, p. 26; our emphasis). In short, the difference between the market and citizenship models is not that one is individualist and the other collectivist, but that one defines individuality in terms of economic independence, whereas the other is concerned with social and political interdependence: one gives primacy to economic rights; the other balances these economic rights with a set of social obligations.

Many examples have been given in this book of the burdens that individual freedom in the purely economic sense can bring to many people who are not in a position to take full advantage of the opportunities it can present. Individual freedom in those narrow terms is also individual responsibility. The objective of the social democratic model is to support individual freedom and responsibility with collective social obligation towards those whose burden of responsibility is too great. A major problem with some social policy interventions traditionally pursued by the left is that they have ridden roughshod over the individual freedoms of those receiving them and have fostered dependence rather than independence. A mixture of bureaucratic insensitivity, professional arrogance and political paternalism has sometimes turned programmes that were designed to enhance the freedom of their recipients into ones that are perceived as oppressive and which require beneficiaries to adopt a supplicant 'client' role or to conform to negative stereotypes. This is not a criticism of the principles underpinning the social democratic model, but rather of the way in which they have been implemented. Given sufficient attention to the importance of individual freedom in the design of social policy interventions, these practical faults could be rectified.

Democracy

A final source of appeal of the market model is its declared sensitivity to public demand. This is part of a strategy whereby both (selected) corporate interests and local representative democracy are being excluded from decision-taking on the grounds of being unrepresentative or élitist. Instead, faith is placed in the public's freedom to choose, usually through the exercise of purchasing power in some guise or other (a preference for home ownership, choice of private health care, and so on). Yet this alternative indicator of local demand ignores the extent to which such 'preferences' are actively shaped from the top down with financial incentives. It ignores the extent to which consent is dictated rather than won. For instance, tax subsidies on mortgage interest payments and a running down of local authority housing stocks underlie a lot of the current support for owner-occupation, and much the same tactics appear to be in place to assist the development of private medicine.

The argument for consumerism takes a very unrealistic view of consumer power in markets, such as housing, which are dominated by a few powerful producers—both private housebuilders and local authorities—who can determine effectively the quantity and price of the product. In our view responsiveness to consumer demand is important and should be increased by measures to empower consumers. But this should be pursued as a complement to representative democracy rather than as an alternative to it. Both should have their place in a 'new' citizenship model which argues for 'a differentiated and pluralistic system of power, wherein decisions of interest to collectivities of various sizes are made autonomously by all their members' (Keane, 1988a, p. 3).

While the social democratic model by definition places greater faith in representative democracy than does the market model, at all tiers of the state, it cannot be denied that the development of welfare provision in Britain has often compromised this principle. As we have noted in discussing the development of public housing, paternalism largely precluded consumer participation, and institutionalisation eclipsed original thinking (trends which Ashford, 1986, detects throughout the British welfare state). As Turner (1986) points out, citizenship is about the conditions of social participation, and to that end there is merit in pursuing democracy in its own right, as well as as a means to an end. This, in our view, is the greatest potential of the citizenship model as applied to housing provision as an element of social policy.

Of course, the principle of democracy is always a danger to those in power, since it 'implies conferring a capacity to make real choices' even though these 'may not always be to the liking of those who believe they know best' (Deakin, 1987, p. 187). Nevertheless, we agree with this view that a social policy based on democracy has something 'important to contribute about institutions and their responsiveness to the needs of their customers, which neither the

advocates of choice through the market nor the dwindling band of
state centralizers can match' (Deakin, p. 188).

To summarise, those keen to revive and re-invigorate the social
democratic model of welfare and social policy emphasise at least
four key components which are not generally acknowledged to be
part of this model by the political right. First, the model can be
regarded as compatible with the principle of economic efficiency on
a national scale (i.e. it can be put into place without damaging
Britain's role in the international economy). Second, the model
makes a moral case for reasserting the principle of egalitarianism
(while resisting the notion that this is a way of forcing people to be
the 'same' as one another in terms of lifestyle, material possessions
or cultural attributes). Third, there is an inherently greater and a
better balanced respect for the integrity of the individual than in the
market alternative. Finally, and above all, the citizenship model
offers the prospect of more effective and accessible forms of representative democracy. It remains for us to suggest what the implementation of such a model might mean for housing policy and,
indeed, how housing policy might itself play a part in putting such a
model into practice. We shall illustrate this for each of the above
points in turn.

Stimulating the economy

First, it is clear that housing policy has not always given due weight
to the need to support a productive economy. For example, it is clear
from Chapters 2 and 3 and from the work of Duncan (1986) and
Dickens *et al.* (1985) that state intervention has not always provided
an incentive for efficient production of housing. This partly reflects
the limited accountability demanded by local government of those
contracted to build public housing, but it also reflects the inability or
unwillingness of successive governments to curb speculative profits
from land development. The result has been the concentration of
house-builders on profits from land development and the relative
neglect of improved efficiency in the house-building process.

However, the need for an integration of housing and economic
policies has other dimensions. For example, there is a need to
concentrate new housing investment in areas of economic growth
(or to concentrate economic growth in areas where there is a surplus

of housing). Also, housing mobility could be made easier to aid labour mobility. At the moment it is hindered by local authority (and housing association) allocation rules and by massive house price differentials between different parts of the country.

There has also been a neglect in policy terms of the economic spin-offs from local housing regeneration projects. Economic activity can be stimulated in particular localities by integrating housing and environmental works to develop a strategy which aims to provide skills for local people and to create appropriate mechanisms (such as community businesses) to harness skills and to use housing investment as a stepping stone to other activities. In other words, housing investment can be used to pump-prime local economies, and the lack of integration of housing policy with other elements of economic and social policy, of which there are many examples in the preceding pages, has led to these opportunities being missed.

Current Labour Policy

Against inequality

Second, under a social democratic model, housing policy would aim towards some degree of equality, if only by reducing the magnitude of existing inequalities. It would, therefore, challenge rather than legitimise the kinds of inequality identified throughout this book, confronting rather than ignoring the plight of groups who, for many reasons beyond their own control, are unable to compete in the labour market, and whose 'special' needs are not simply related to building adaptations or medical care. Deakin's (1987) notion of welfare pluralism as a means of achieving this is appealing, in that it defuses politically contentious arguments about *who* provides services, and directs attention to the best combination of market, state and voluntary effort required to ensure that some level of servicing is widely available.

This formulation also shifts attention away from state provisioning in kind as a means of achieving equality and towards the iniquities embedded in housing finance and subsidy systems. The crucial ingredient in any strategy to reduce inequality in housing is a subsidy system which does not heap largesse on one particular tenure (owner-occupation) at the expense of others, and which is progressive (that is, it channels assistance to the poorer rather than to the richer households). Reform of the present iniquitous system (outlined in Chapter 4) is well overdue and should be the cornerstone of a social democratic housing policy. Following D. Harris (1987), however, we also recognise that there is an important place for state provision in kind (though this need not necessarily be along the lines of traditional council housing), not only because of its potential to create a sense of 'community' membership, but also because, in a society which tempers individual rights with social obligation, one may, for instance 'have a right to education, although not a right to income which may or may not be spent on education' (D. Harris, 1987).

A re-assertion of the role of housing as a universal or 'general needs' welfare service has, therefore, a moral as well as a material rationale. The two major criticisms of this sort of provision are, first, that public provision in kind can be divisive and stigmatising and, second, that it represents an extension of state control over ordinary people's lives and thus runs counter to the principle of liberty. However, the third and fourth elements of a revitalised citizenship model suggest that such fears could be unfounded (though this is not to say they have been unfounded in the past).

Individual and society

The social democratic model is deeply concerned with the integrity of the individual, and those who work to re-establish it are as keen to avoid the corporate socialism of the 1970s as they are to replace the supremacy of the market in the 1980s. Thus, while the model is centrally preoccupied with problems caused by systematic inequalities in the distribution of effective citizenship rights, and while it therefore recognises entrenched social cleavages related to class, 'race' and gender, it offers an important policy alternative to the 'special' needs vision of welfare that is increasingly in vogue. The model recognises the reality of group inequalities but works to diminish these in ways that avoid the stigmatisation that has so often been associated with benefit dependency. In housing, therefore, we have argued throughout the book for the importance of catering to 'disadvantaged' groups through mainstream housing programmes, thus avoiding forms of social categorisation that make those so labelled more rather than less marginal. This kind of integration may not only be socially desirable but also more effective in targeting resources, as we indicated most clearly in our discussion of the housing needs of older people.

Further, individualism is particularly important in housing because most of the costs and benefits of housing accrue to the user and not to the community at large. The home is a crucial element in family life and an important factor in generating a person's positive self-meaning, not only in itself, but also because it is the place where so many of the important features of life take place. Social democratic housing policy can recognise this by seeking to expand the control which individual households exercise over their home, and over their housing situation in general. Restrictions on this individual freedom are only justified where they are important to the achievement of other social goals such as equality. However, many current restrictions do not meet this criterion. For example, excessive restrictions are often placed on households' use of their housing through tenancy agreements in the public sector. Individual choice in matters as diverse as the colour of a bathroom suite or the type and size of house to be rented is often very limited.

In the private rented sector, a household's use of the dwelling is usually even more constrained, reflecting the sanctity of landlords' private property rights. Much could be achieved here through the application of a model tenancy agreement to all private lettings. In both public and private renting there is a need for an effective system for settling disputes between landlords and tenants which is easily accessible to both parties. This need could be met both through an expanded network of aid and advice centres specialising in tenancy relations, and through a system of informal housing courts which would be more specialised, flexible, and easier to use than the present legal arrangements. These courts would also be of use to owner-occupiers who may encounter problems with loan repayments or mortgage conditions.

Individual choice is generally greater in the owner-occupied sector than in rental sectors, although it is, of course, crucially dependent on the constraints of income and wealth. A reformed housing finance and subsidy system which channels help to those at the lower end of the income scale would, therefore, be a crucial way to increase the individual choice of a large number of people–an expanding population of low-income owner-occupiers–whose choice is most constrained.

These are only examples of policies and programmes which could follow from an emphasis on the integrity of the individual and on the importance of housing and the home to individuals and their families (for fuller discussion see Clapham, 1989; Smith, 1989a). However, they show the value of adopting such an approach through the concept of citizenship rather than through market provision, which, as outlined in the book, has many deleterious effects.

Public participation

Finally, and most crucially, the revival of the social democratic model is seen as a means of extending the right to, and effectiveness of, public participation in service provision. This promise is advanced by Deakin (1987), Turner (1986), Harris (1987), Smith (1989a) and most other advocates of the 'new' citizenship model. Adequately reconstructed, the concept of citizenship embraces 'a genuine commitment to infusing welfare services with opportunities for participation in flexible and decentralised structures rooted in local communities' (D. Harris, 1987, p. 146). What is required, argues Deakin (1987, p. 188) is

> smaller rather than larger units of government, but with closer linkages between them, so that the effects of the separation of functions between the elected and non-elected sectors that now causes such difficulty at a local level is reduced to the minimum.

[handwritten margin note: LABOUR: Devolution to British regions, Bringing Quangos into Public eye.]

In housing, this kind of participation can be expanded to a large degree without compromising other social democratic objectives. This is because households, either individually or collectively, are the best judges of their own housing situation and, given adequate supply and some collective responsibility for the repair and maintenance of the stock, the consumption of housing need have few impacts on other people. In theory, then, the state might step back from the direct provision and management of housing, only keeping control over elements (such as housing allocation or finance) that are essential for the achievement of other social democratic objectives. There are many ways in which this objective can be achieved.

One strategy would be to encourage greater tenant participation and decentralisation in the management and maintenance of public rented housing. This could include setting up tenant management co-operatives, where the local authority retains ownership of the properties but tenants are responsible collectively for management and maintenance.

Lab.
Policy

A second strategy, not inconsistent with the first, would be to encourage the diversification of public rented housing through support for a wide range of different landlords such as trusts, co-operatives, housing associations and private landlords. This would give tenants as consumers greater choice of provision. As we saw in Chapter 2, it is in fact current government policy to encourage alternatives to local authorities in the provision of rented housing. However, that approach is being carried out by deliberately structuring choices in favour of these alternatives, to the disadvantage of local authorities. For example, under the so-called 'tenant's choice' scheme, council tenants can have their homes transferred to another landlord unless the tenant votes against it. Tenants who fail to vote for whatever reason (deliberate abstention, or because they are in hospital, on holiday, etc.) will be transferred to the other landlord along with those who vote yes. Tenants living in an area designated as a Housing Action Trust could be transferred to the HAT whether they want to remain with the local authority or not (though this will be determined by a democratic voting majority). Again, financial

Lab Plcy
-get
rid of
this.

controls on local authority spending, including the utilisation of receipts from council house sales, are stringent, thus reducing the ability of housing departments to modernise and improve their stock. Thus, while there are very strong arguments in favour of greater diversification in the rented housing markets, we believe that the choices open to tenants should not be biased in favour of particular alternatives. If council tenants opt for an alternative landlord, it should be because they actively wish to, not because they have been virtually coerced or bribed into doing so.

*

A more radical social democratic strategy could be pursued by transferring ownership of all public rented housing to existing tenants to be run as a par value ownership co-operative, in which tenants would collectively own the properties, although they would have no individual equity share. One of us has argued elsewhere that this proposal would stimulate diversification and choice whilst transferring power to tenants who would be in a much stronger position to insist on high standards of management and maintenance (see Clapham, 1989).

* ACTUALLY, THIS IS DEMOCRATIC SOCIALISM
RATHER THAN SOCIAL DEMOCRACY, LABOUR
RIGHT IS TOO WIMPY FOR THIS.

Whichever approach is taken, it should be combined with a move towards the adoption of a 'strategic' role by local councils, in whose hands would be the major responsibility for the achievement of social democratic goals: through intervention in production in all tenures to ensure that an appropriate quantity and quality of housing is available; through the administration of housing subsidy and the allocation of housing to alleviate inequality; through the protection of individual (and collective) rights; and through support for democratic, flexible and decentralised structures of housing management. It is imperative that such functions should be carried out by democratically elected authorities rather than by large, centralised, unaccountable bodies such as the Housing Corporation. These issues should be important parts of local political debate, and decision-makers should be accountable to the local electorate.

The 'new' social democratic model is not, of course, without its problems. Most notably, as Turner (1986) observes, very few analysts have considered the extent to which the expansion of social rights within a national core might entail the withdrawal of such rights at the periphery. It is certainly the case, for instance, that the rights to welfare (as well as to immigration, settlement, employment and political participation) conferred on black Britons by the 1948 British Nationality Act were systematically removed during the next four decades. This is nowhere more obvious than in the example of housing (see Smith, 1988). Similar arguments might be made concerning the welfare rights of women. The stamp of democracy may mean little in a society where history testifies to the fact that 'Much talk about enfranchising minorities and empowering communities has ended with carefully structured agendas and hierarchies of representation through which vested interests can preserve their control over events' (Deakin, 1987, p. 187).

Citizenship, then, is itself a problematic 'ideal' in a racist and patriarchal society, and Mouffe's (1988) enthusiasm for the notion is extended 'on condition that it meets the challenge posed by the new movements and provides an answer to the feminist critique' (p. 30). The democratic citizenship theorists, however, are aware of these problems and they correctly contrast their vision of full participation in society with the exclusivist and intolerant imagery of 'one-nation' conservatism (a contrast explored in some detail in Smith, 1989a). For citizenship theory, 'the goal is not homogeneity; the enemy is not heterogeneity' (Harris, 1987, p. 149), but the welfare system it must embrace is nevertheless 'an institutional recognition of social solidarity' (p. 145).

There are, of course, several important practical issues to be solved if a revival of citizenship theory is not to be regarded as an over-simplistic 'solution' to a complex political problem. As Hindess (1987, p. 157) observes,

> if everything is to be understood in terms of the needs of capital, the principle of the market or of citizenship, or even in terms of some conflict between two or three such generalised explanatory principles, then there is little for social analysis to do beyond the general reduction of social facts to the alleged principle of their significance.

There is undoubtedly a problem of political naïvety in a debate between two 'ideal-type' models of welfare provision. It is, however, important to advance alternatives, naïve or otherwise, to broaden a debate which, as Deakin (1987) complains, has become unprecedentedly narrow over the last decade. There are attractive alternatives to the market model, even within the constraints of cost and efficiency. In this book we have used the example of housing policy to show why such alternatives are necessary, and we have suggested what form they might take.

References

Advisory Committee on Rent Rebates and Rent Allowances (1976) *First Report* (London: Department of the Environment).

Age Concern (1985) *Community Alarm Systems for Older People* (Edinburgh: Age Concern).

Alexander, J. R. and Eldon, A. (1979) 'Characteristics of Elderly People Admitted to Hospital; Part III: Homes and Sheltered Housing', *Journal of Epidemiology and Community Health,* 33, 1, pp. 91–5.

Al-Qaddo, H. and Rodger, R. (1987) 'The Implementation of Housing Policy: The Scottish Special Housing Association', *Public Administration,* 65, pp. 313–29.

Ashford, D. E. (1986) *The Emergence of the Welfare States* (Oxford: Basil Blackwell).

Audit Commission (1984) *The Impact on Local Authorities' Economy, Efficiency and Effectiveness of the Block Grant Distribution System* (London: HMSO).

Audit Commission (1986a) *Managing the Crisis in Council Housing* (London: HMSO).

Audit Commission (1986b) *Making a Reality of Community Care* (London: HMSO).

Austerberry, H. and Watson, S. (1983) *Women on the Margins* (London: City University Housing Research Group).

Balchin, P. N. (1981) *Housing Policy and Housing Needs* (London: Macmillan).

Balchin, P. N. (1985) *Housing Policy: An Introduction* (London: Croom Helm).

Ball, M. (1978) 'British Housing Policy and the Housebuilding Industry', *Capital and Class,* 4, pp. 78–99.

Ball, M. (1983) *Housing Policy and Economic Power. The Political Economy of Owner Occupation* (London: Methuen).

Barry, N. P. (1987) *The New Right* (London: Croom Helm).

Bayley, M. (1973) *Mental Handicap and Community Care* (London: Routledge and Kegan Paul).

Bentham, G. (1986) 'Socio-tenurial Polarization in the United Kingdom 1953–83: The Income Evidence', *Urban Studies,* vol. 23, pp. 157–62.

249

Beresford, P. and Croft S. (1984) *Whose Welfare?* (Brighton: Lewis Cohen Urban Studies Centre).

Berthoud, R. (ed.) (1985) 'Introduction' to *Challenges to Social Policy* (Aldershot: Gower), pp. 1–23.

Berthoud, R. (1989) *The Disadvantages of Inequality* (London: MacDonald and Jane).

Berthoud, R. (1989) 'Social Security and the Economics of Housing', in A. Dilnot and I. Walker (eds) *The Economics of Social-Security* (Oxford: Oxford University Press).

Berthoud, R. and Ermisch, J. (1985) *Reshaping Benefits* (London: Policy Studies Institute).

Beveridge, W. (1908) *Unemployment. A Problem of Industry* (London: Langman)

Beveridge, W. (1942) *Social Insurance and Allied Services* (London: HMSO).

Birch, E. L. (ed.) (1985) *The Unsheltered Woman* (New Jersey: Center for Urban Policy Research).

Boldy, D. (1976) 'A study of the Wardens of Grouped Dwellings for the Elderly', *Social and Economic Administration*, 10, pp. 59–67.

Bondi, L. (1985) 'Falling Rolls, Primary School Provision and Local Politics: A Manchester Case Study', paper presented to Seventeenth Annual Conference of the Regional Science Association, Manchester.

Bonnerjea, L. and Lawton, J. (1986) *Homelessness in Brent* (London: Policy Studies Institute).

Booth, P. and Crook, T. (eds) (1986) *Low Cost Home Ownership* (Aldershot: Gower).

Bowley, M. (1945) *Housing Policy and the State 1919–1944* (London: Allen and Unwin).

Brailey, M. (1986) 'Women's Access to Council Housing', *Occasional Paper 25* (Glasgow: Planning Exchange).

Brion, M. and Tinker, A. (1980) *Women in Housing* (London: Housing Centre Trust).

Brown, C. (1984) *Black and White Britain* (London: Heinemann).

Brown, M. and Madge, N. (1982) *Despite the Welfare State* (London: Heinemann Educational).

Bucknall, B. (1984) *Housing Finance* (London: Chartered Institute of Public Finance and Accountancy).

Building Societies Association (1986) 'Home Improvements', *BSA Bulletin*, 48, October, pp. 6–8.

Butler, A., Oldman, C. and Greve, J. (1983) *Sheltered Housing for the Elderly: Policy, Practice and the Consumer* (London: Allen and Unwin).

Butler, A. (1985) 'Dispersed Alarms: An Evaluative Framework', in M. McGarry (ed.) *Community Alarm Systems for Older People* (Edinburgh: Age Concern).

Byrne, D. (1974) *Problem Families: A Housing Lumpen Proletariat*, Working Paper 5 (Durham: Department of Sociology and Social Administration, University of Durham).

Byrne, D. S., Harrison, S. P., Keithley, J. and McCarthy, P. (1986) *Housing*

and Health. The Relationship between Housing Conditions and the Health of Council Tenants (Aldershot: Gower).
Carey, G. (1982) 'Community Care–Care by Whom? Mentally Handicapped Children Living at Home', *Public Health*, 96, pp. 269–78.
Carey, K. and Stein, M. (1986) *Leaving Care* (Oxford: Basil Blackwell).
Carrier, J. and Kendall, I. (1986) 'Categories, Categorizations and the Political Economy of Welfare', *Journal of Social Policy*, 15, 3, pp. 315–35.
Cawson, A. (1982) *Corporatism and Welfare* (London: Heinemann).
Cawson, A. (1986) *Corporatism and Political Theory* (Oxford: Blackwell).
Cawson, A. and Saunders, P. (1983) 'Corporatism, Competitive Politics and Class Struggle', in R. King (ed.) *Capital and Politics* (London: Routledge & Kegan Paul).
Central Statistical Office (1985) *Social Trends 15* (London: HMSO).
Central Statistical Office (1986) *Social Trends, 16* (London: HMSO).
Central Statistical Office (1988) *Social Trends 18* (London: HMSO).
CHAC (1939) *Management of Municipal Housing Estates* (London: HMSO).
CHAC (1959) *Councils and their Houses* (London: HMSO).
Chadwick, E. (1842) *Report on the Sanitary Condition of the Labouring Population of Great Britain* (reprinted 1965).
City of Bradford MDC Social Services Department (1983) 'The Future Accommodation Needs of Mentally Handicapped People Presently Living in the Community', Clearing House for Social Services Research, University of Birmingham.
Clapham, D. (1987) 'Trends in Housing Management', in Clapham, D. and English, J. (eds) *Public Housing: Current Trends and Future Developments* (London: Croom Helm).
Clapham, D. (1989) *Goodbye Council Housing?* (London: Unwin Hyman).
Clapham, D. and Kintrea, K. (1986) 'Rationing Choice and Constraint: The Allocation of Public Housing in Glasgow', *Journal of Social Policy*, 15, 1, pp. 51–67.
Clapham, D. and English, J. (eds) (1987) *Public Housing: Current Trends and Future Developments* (London: Croom Helm).
Clapham, D., Kemp, P. and Kintrea, K. (1987) 'Co-operative Ownership of Former Council Housing', *Policy and Politics*, 15, pp. 207–20.
Clapham, D., Kintrea, K. and Munro, M. (1987) 'Tenure Choice: An Empirical Investigation, *Area*, 19, 1, pp. 11–18.
Clapham, D. and Munro, M. (1988) *The Cost-effectiveness of Sheltered and Amenity Housing for Older People*, Central Research Unit paper (Edinburgh: Scottish Development Department).
Clapham, D. and Smith, S. (1988) 'Urban Social Policy', in J. English (ed.) *Social Services in Scotland* (Edinburgh: Scottish Academic Press).
CLSSAF (1987) *Disappeared: The Effect of the 1985 Board and Lodging Regulations* (London: Central London Society Security Advisor's Forum).
Cohen, S. (1985) 'Anti-semitism, Immigration Controls and the Welfare State', *Critical Social Policy*, 5, pp. 73–92.

Coleman, A. (1985) *Utopia on Trial* (London: Hilary Shipman).

Commission for Racial Equality (1984a) *Race and Council Housing in Hackney* (London: CRE).

Commission for Racial Equality (1984b) *Race and Housing in Liverpool: A Research Report* (London: CRE).

Commission for Racial Equality (1985) *Race and Mortgage Lending* (London: CRE).

Conway, J. (ed.) (1988) *Prescription For Poor Health. The Crisis for Homeless Families* (London: London Food Commission/Maternity Alliance/SHAC/Shelter).

Conway, J. and Kemp, P. (1985) *Bed and Breakfast: Slum Housing of the Eighties* (London: SHAC).

Crook, A. D. H. (1986) 'Privatisation of Housing and the Impact of the Conservative Government's Initiatives on Low-cost Home-ownership and Private Renting between 1979 and 1984 in England and Wales: 1. The Privatisation Policies', *Environment and Planning*, 18, pp. 639–59.

Crosland, C. A. R. (1956) *The Future of Socialism* (London: Cape).

Cross, M. (1982) 'The Manufacture of Marginality', in E. Cashmore and B. Troyna (eds) *Black Youth in Crisis* (London: Allen and Unwin), pp. 35–52.

Cullingworth Committee (1969) *Council Housing: Purposes, Procedures and Priorities* (London: HMSO).

Cullingworth, J. B. (1979) *Essays on Housing Policy* (London: Allen and Unwin.

Cumming, E. and Henry, W. E. (1961) *Growing Old* (New York: Basic Books).

Cunnison, S. and Page, D. (no date) *For the Rest of their Days?*, Humberside College of Education.

Curtis, S. (1989) *The Geography of Public Welfare Provision* (London and New York: Routledge).

Daunton, M. J. (1983) *House and Home in the Victorian City* (London: Arnold).

Daunton, M. (ed.) (1984) *Councillors and Tenants: Local Authority Housing in English Cities 1919–39* (Leicester: Leicester University Press).

Deacon, A. and Bradshaw, J. (1983) *Reserved for the Poor: The Means Test in British Social Policy* (Oxford: Blackwell and Martin Robertson).

Deakin, N. (1987) *The Politics of Welfare* (London: Methuen).

Deakin, N. (1988) *In Search of the Postwar Consensus*, LSE Welfare State Programme Discussion Paper 25 (London: London School of Economics).

Department of the Environment (1975) *Housing Action Areas, Priority Neighbourhoods and General Improvement Areas*, Circular 14/75 (London: HMSO).

Department of the Environment (1977) *House Policy: A Consultative Document* (London: HMSO).

Department of the Environment (1983) *Housing for Mentally Ill and Mentally Handicapped People* (London: HMSO).

Department of the Environment (1985) *Home Improvement: A New Approach* (London: HMSO).

Department of the Environment (1987) *Housing: The Government's Proposals* (London: HMSO).

Department of the Environment (1988a) *New Financial Regime For Local Authority Housing in England and Wales* (London and Cardiff: DoE/ Welsh Office).

Department of the Environment (1988b) *Quarterly Homelessness Returns: Results for Second Quarter 1987* (London: DoE).

Department of the Environment (1988c) *Large Scale Voluntary Transfer of Local Authority Housing to Private Bodies* (London: DoE).

Dexter, M. and Harbert, W. (1983) *The Home Help Service* (London: Tavistock).

DHSS (1969) *Report of the Committee of Enquiry into Allegations of Ill-Treatment and other Irregularities at Ely Hospital, Cardiff*, Cmnd 3785 (London: HMSO).

DHSS (1971a) *Report of the Farleigh Hospital Committee of Enquiry*, Cmnd 4557 (London: HMSO).

DHSS (1971b) *Better Services for the Mentally Handicapped* (London: HMSO).

DHSS (1974) *Report of the Committee of Enquiry into South Ockendor Hospital* (the Finer Report) (London: HMSO).

DHSS (1977) *Report of the Committee of Enquiry into Normansfield Hospital* Cmnd 7357 (London: HMSO).

DHSS (1978) *Social Assistance: A Review of the Supplementary Benefit Scheme in Great Britain* (London: DHSS).

DHSS (1984) *Supplementary Benefit Board and Lodging Proposals* (London: DHSS).

DHSS (1987) *Social Security Statistics 1987* (London: HMSO).

Dickens, P., Duncan, S., Goodwin, M. and Gray, F. (1985) *Housing, States and Localities* (London: Methuen).

Doling, J., Karn, V. and Stafford, B. (1986) 'The Impact of Unemployment on Home Ownership', *Housing Studies*, 1, pp. 49–60.

Donnison, D. (1982) *The Politics of Poverty* (Oxford: Martin Robertson).

Donnison, D. and Ungerson, C. (1982) *Housing Policy* (Harmondsworth: Penguin).

Duncan, S. S. (1986) 'Housebuilding Profits and Social Efficiency in Sweden and Britain', *Housing Studies*, pp. 11–33.

Duncan, S. S. and Goodwin, M. (1982) 'The Local State and Restructuring Social Relations', *International Journal of Urban and Regional Research*, 6, pp. 157–86.

Duncan, S. and Kirby, K. (1983) *Preventing Rent Arrears* (London: HMSO).

Dunleavy, P. (1981) *The Politics of Mass Housing in Britain, 1945–1975* (Oxford: Clarendon Press).

Dunleavy, P. (1984) 'The Limits to Local Government', in M. Boddy and C. Fridge (eds) *Local Socialism?* (London: Macmillan).

Dunleavy, P. and O'Leary, B. (1987) *Theories of the State* (London: Macmillan).

Edgell, S. and Duke, V. (1983) 'Gender and Social Policy: The Impact of Public Expenditure Cuts and Reactions to Them', *Journal of Social Policy*, 12, pp. 357–78.

Englander, D. (1983) *Landlord and Tenant in Urban Britain, 1838–1918* (Oxford: Oxford University Press).

Equal Opportunities Commission (1982) *Caring for the Elderly and Handicapped: Community Care Policies and Women's Lives* (Manchester: EOC).

Ermisch, J. (1984) *Housing Finance: Who Gains?* (London: Policy Studies Institute).

Estes, C. L., Swan, J. S. and Gerard, L. E. (1982) 'Dominant and Competing Paradigms in Gerontology', *Ageing and Society*, 6, 2, pp. 151–64.

Evans, A. and Duncan, S. (1988) *Responding to Homelessness: Local Authority Policy and Practice* (London: HMSO).

Ferge, Z. and Miller, S. M. (1987) 'Social Reproduction and the Dynamics of Deprivation' in Z. Ferge and S. M. Miller, *Dynamics of Deprivation* (Aldershot: Gower), pp. 296–314.

Finer Committee (1974) *Report of the Committee on One Parent Families* (London: HMSO).

Fisk, M. J. (1986) *Independence and the Elderly* (London: Croom Helm).

Fleiss, A. (1985) *Home Ownership Alternatives for the Elderly* (London: HMSO).

Forrest, R. and Murie, A. (1983) 'Residualization and Council Housing: Aspects of the Changing Social Relations of Housing Tenure', *Journal of Social Policy*, 12, pp. 453–68.

Forrest, R. and Murie, A. (1986) 'Marginalization and Subsidized Individualism: The Sale of Council Houses in the Restructuring of the British Welfare State', *International Journal of Urban and Regional Research*, 10, pp. 46–66.

Forrest, R. and Murie, A. (1987) 'The Pauperization of Council Housing', *Roof*, January–February, pp. 20–3.

Forrest, R. and Murie, A. (1988) *Selling the Welfare State: The Privatisation of Public Housing* (London: Routledge and Kegan Paul).

Foster, P. (1983) *Access to Welfare* (London: Macmillan).

Fraser, D. (1973) *The Evolution of the British Welfare State* (London: Macmillan).

Friedman, M. (1962) *Capitalism and Freedom* (Chicago: Chicago University Press).

Galbraith, J. K. (1969) *The New Industrial State* (Harmondsworth: Penguin).

Gamble, A. (1983) 'Thatcherism and Conservative Politics', in S. Hall and M. Jaques (eds) *The Politics of Thatcherism* (London: Lawrence and Wishart).

Gamble, A. (1987) 'The Weakening of Social Democracy', in M. Loney *et al.* (eds) *The State or the Market* (London: Sage).

George, V. (1980) 'Explanations of Poverty and Inequality', in V. George and R. Lawson (eds) *Poverty and Inequality in Common Market Countries* (London: Routledge and Kegan Paul), pp. 1–23.

George, V. and Wilding, P. (1976) *Ideology and Social Welfare* (London: Routledge and Kegan Paul).

George, V. and Wilding, P. (1984) *The Impact of Social Policy* (London: Routledge and Kegan Paul).

Gibson, M. S. and Langstaff, M. J. (1982) *An Introduction to Urban Renewal* (London: Hutchinson).

Gilbert, J. (1986) *Not Just a Roof* (Birmingham: Birmingham Standing Conference for the Single Homeless).

Ginsburg, N. (1979) *Class, Capital and Social Policy* (London: Macmillan).

Glennerster, H., Korman, N. and Marsten-Wilson, F. (1982) *Planning for Priority Groups* (Oxford: Martin Robertson).

Glastonbury, B. (1971) *Homelessness Near a Thousand Homes* (London: Allen and Unwin).

Goodin, R. E. (1986) *Protecting the Vulnerable: A Re-analysis of our Social Responsibilities* (Chicago: Chicago University Press).

Gordon, P. (1986) 'Racism and Social Security', *Critical Social Policy*, 6, pp. 23–40.

Goss, S. (1983) *Working the Act* (London: SHAC).

Goss, S. and Lansley, S. (1984) *What Price Housing? A Review of Housing Subsidies and Proposals for Research* (London: SHAC) (3rd edn).

Gough, I. (1979) *The Political Economy of the Welfare State* (London: Macmillan).

Grant, W. (1985) 'Introduction', in W. Grant (ed.) *The Political Economy of Corporatism* (London: Macmillan), pp. 1–31.

Greater London Council (1984) 'Black Women and Housing', unpublished report for the Director General.

Greater London Council (1985) *Relationship? Breakdown? and Local Authority Tenancies* (London: GLC).

Greater London Council (1986) *Private Tenants in London* (London: GLC).

Greve, J. (1964) *London's Homeless* (Welwyn Garden City: Codicote Press).

Greve, J., Page, D. and Greve, S. (1971) *Homeless in London* (London: Scottish Academic Press).

Greve, J. *et al.* (1986) *Homeless in London* (Bristol: School for Advanced Urban Studies).

Griffiths, R. (1988) *Community Care: Agenda for Action* (London: HMSO).

Grosskurth, A. and Stearn, J. (1986) 'They Call It Colditz', *Roof*, January/February.

Gulstad, J. (1987) *The Right to be Ordinary* (Glasgow: Glasgow Special Housing Group/Centre for Housing Research).

Hall, S. (1984) 'The Rise of the Representative/Interventionist State' in G. McLennan, D. Held and S. Hall (eds) *State and Society in Contemporary Britain* (Cambridge: Polity Press), pp. 7–49.

Hallsworth, A. G., Wood, A. and Lewington, T. (1986) 'Welfare and Retail Accessibility', *Area*, 18, 4, pp. 291–8.

Hambleton, R. (1986) *Rethinking Policy Planning* (Bristol: SAUS).

256   *References*

Harloe, M. (1982) 'Towards the Decommodification of housing? A Comment on Council House Sales', *Critical Social Policy*, 2, 1, pp. 39–42.

Harris, C. (1987) 'British Capitalism, Migration and Relative Surplus–Population: a Synopsis', *Migration*, 1, pp. 47–96.

Harris, D. (1987) *Justifying State Welfare. The New Right Versus the Old Left* (Oxford: Blackwell).

Harrison, M. L. (ed.) (1984) *Corporatism and the Welfare State* (Aldershot: Gower).

Hayek, F. A. (1960) *The Constitution of Liberty* (London: Routledge and Kegan Paul).

Henderson, J. and Karn, V. (1984) 'Race, Class and the Allocation of Public Housing in Britain', *Urban Studies*, 21, pp. 115–28.

Henderson, J. and Karn, V. (1987) *Race, Class and State Housing: Inequality in the Allocation of Public Housing in Britain* (Aldershot: Gower).

Hennock, E. P. (1973) *Fit and Proper Persons. Ideal and Reality in Nineteenth Century Urban Government* (London: Edward Arnold).

Henwood, M. (1986) 'Community Care: Policy, Practice and Prognosis', in *Yearbook of Social Policy*.

Heumann, L. and Boldy, D. (1982) *Housing for the Elderly. Planning and Policy formulation in Western Europe and North America* (London: Croom Helm).

Hill, M. (1983) *Understanding Social Policy* (Oxford: Basil Blackwell).

Hill, M. and Bramley, G. (1986) *Analysing Social Policy* (Oxford: Blackwell).

Hill, O. (1875) *Homes of the London Poor* (London: Macmillan).

Hills, J. (1987) *When is a Grant not a Grant? The Current System of Housing Association Finance*, LSE Welfare State Programme Discussion Paper (London: London School of Economics).

Hindess, B. (1987) *Freedom, Equality and the Market* (London: Tavistock).

HMSO (1988) *The Government's Expenditure Plans 1988–89 to 1990–91* (London: HMSO).

Holmans, A. E. (1987) *Housing Policy in Britain* (London: Croom Helm).

House of Commons Environment Committee (1982) *The Private Rented Sector, Volume 1: Report* (London: HMSO).

Hudson, B. (1986) 'In Pursuit of Co-ordination: Housing and the Personal Social Services', *Local Government Studies*, March/April, pp. 53–6.

Hunt, A. (1978) *The Elderly at Home* (London: HMSO).

Hunter, D. and Wistow, G. (1987) *Community Care in Britain* (London: King Edwards Hospital Fund for London).

Inquiry into British Housing (1985) *Report* (London: National Federation of Housing Associations).

Inquiry into British Housing (1986) *Supplement* (London: National Federation of Housing Associations).

Jackson, P. and Smith, S. J. (1984) *Exploring Social Geography* (London: Allen and Unwin).

Jay Report (1979) *Report of the Committee of Enquiry into Mental Handicap Nursing and Care*, Cmnd 7468 (London: HMSO).

Johnson, P. (1986) 'Some Historical Dimensions of the Welfare State "Crisis"', *Journal of Social Policy*, 15, 4, pp. 443–67.

Karn, V. (1983) 'Race and Housing in Britain: The Role of Major Institutions', in N. Glazer and K. Young (eds) *Ethnic Pluralism and Public Policy* (London: Heinemann), pp. 162–83.

Kay, J. and King, M. (1978) *The British Tax System* (Oxford: Oxford University Press).

Keane, J. (1988a) *Democracy and Civil Society* (London: Verso).

Keane, J. (ed.) (1988b) *Civil Society and the State* (London: Verso).

Keating, M. and Boyle, R. (1986) *Remaking Urban Scotland* (Edinburgh: Edinburgh University Press).

Kellett, J. R. (1969) *The Impact of Railways on Victorian Cities* (London: Routledge and Kegan Paul).

Kemp, P. (1984a) *The Cost of Chaos: A Survey of the Housing Benefit Scheme* (London: SHAC).

Kemp, P. (1984b) 'The Transformation of the Urban Housing Market in Britain c. 1885–1939', D. Phil thesis, University of Sussex.

Kemp, P. (1986) *The Housing Market in Late Nineteenth Century Britain*, Discussion Paper 11 (Glasgow: Centre for Housing Research).

Kemp, P. (1987) 'The Reform of Housing Benefit', *Social Policy and Administration*, 21, pp. 171–86.

Kemp, P. (1988) *The Future of Private Renting*, Occasional Paper in Environmental Health and Housing (Salford: University of Salford).

Kemp, P. and Williams, P. (1987) 'Housing Management: A Contested History?', paper presented to BSA Sociology and the Environment seminar, LSE, November.

King, D. S. (1987) *The New Right: Politics, Markets and Citizenship* (London: Macmillan).

King's Fund Institute (1987) *Promoting Innovation in Community Care* (London: King's Fund Institute).

Kintrea, K. (1987) *Arresting Decay in Owner Occupied Housing? The Neighbourhood Revitalisation Services Scheme: A Preliminary Analysis*, Discussion Paper 13 (Glasgow: Centre for Housing Research, University of Glasgow).

Kirby, A. (1979) *Education, Health and Housing* (Farnborough: Saxon House).

Kirwan, R. M. (1984) 'The Demise of Public Housing', in J. Le Grand and R. Robinson (eds) *Privatisation and the Welfare State* (London: Allen and Unwin).

Kleinman, M. and Whitehead, C. (1988) 'The Prospects for Private Renting in the 1990s', in P. Kemp (ed.) *The Private Provision of Rented Housing: Current Trends and Future Prospects* (Aldershot: Avebury).

Lawless, P. (1986) *The Evolution of Spatial Policy* (London: Pion).

Leather, P. and Murie, A. (1986) 'The Decline in Public Expenditure', in P. Malpass (ed.) *The Housing Crisis* (London: Croom Helm), pp. 24–56.

Leavitt, J. (1985) 'The Shelter-service Crisis and Single Parents', in E. L.

Birch (ed.) *The Unsheltered Woman* (New Jersey: Center for Urban Policy Research), pp. 153–76.

Le Grand, J. (1982) *The Strategy of Equality: Redistribution and the Social Services* (London: Allen and Unwin).

Le Grand, J. and Robinson, R. (eds) (1984) *Privatisation and the Welfare State* (London: Allen and Unwin).

Logan, F. (1987) *Homelessness and Relationship Breakdown* (London: National Council For One Parent Families).

London Housing Forum (1988) *Speaking Out. Report of the London Housing Inquiry* (London: London Housing Forum).

Loughlin, M. *et al.* (eds) (1985) *Half A Century of Municipal Decline, 1935–1985* (London: Allen and Unwin).

Lupton, C. (1985) *Moving Out: Older Teenagers Leaving Residential Care* (Portsmouth: Social Services Research and Intelligence Unit).

McDowell, L. (1979) 'Measuring Housing Deprivation in Post-war Britain', *Area,* 11, 9, pp. 264–9.

Maclennan, D. (1986) 'The Pricing of Public Housing in the United Kingdom', in Inquiry into British Housing, *Supplement* (London: National Federation of Housing Associations).

Maclennan, D. and O'Sullivan, A. (1987) 'Housing Policy in the United Kingdom: Efficient or Equitable?', in W. van Vliet (ed.) *Housing Markets and Policies under Fiscal Austerity* (Westport, Connecticut: Greenwood Press).

Maclennan, D. *et al.* (1988) *The Nature and Effectiveness of Housing Management in England* (London: HMSO).

McNicholas, A. (1986) *Going it Alone* (London: SHAC)

Malpass, P. (1982) 'Octavia Hill', *New Society,* 4 November.

Malpass, P (1984) 'Housing Benefits in Perspective', in C. Jones and J. Stevenson (eds) *The Year Book of Social Policy in Britain 1983* (London: Routledge and Kegan Paul).

Malpass, P. (1986a) 'Low Income Home Ownership and Housing Policy', *Housing Studies* 1, 4, pp. 241–5.

Malpass, P. (1986b) 'From Complacency to Crisis', in P. Malpass (ed.) *The Housing Crisis* (London: Croom Helm).

Malpass, P. and Murie, A. (1982) *Housing Policy and Practice* (London: Macmillan).

Malpass, P. and Murie, A. (1987) *Housing Policy and Practice* (London: Macmillan) (2nd edn).

Manning, N. (1985) 'Constructing Social Problems', in N. Manning (ed.) *Social Problems and Welfare Ideology* (Aldershot: Gower), pp. 1–28.

Marquand, D. (1988) 'The Lure of Tradition behind the New Right's Appeal to the Chattering Classes', *The Guardian,* 5 April, p. 19.

Marshall, T. H. (1950) *Citizenship and Social Class* (Cambridge: Cambridge University Press).

Maslow, A. (1954) *Motivation and Personality* (New York: Harper and Row).

Massey, D. (1984) *Spatial Divisions of Labour* (London: Macmillan).

Massey, D. and Meegan, R. (1982) *The Anatomy of Job Loss: The How, Why and Where of Employment Decline* (London: Methuen).

Means, R. and Hill, M. (1982) 'The Administration of Rent Rebates', *Journal of Social Welfare Law*, Summer, pp. 193–208.

Medical Campaign Project (1987) *Health Care and the Homeless* (London: Medical Campaign Project).

Mercer, G. (1984) 'Corporatist Ways in the NMS?', in M. L. Harrison (ed.) *Corporatism and the Welfare State* (Aldershot: Gower).

Merrett, S. (1979) *State Housing in Britain* (London: Routledge and Kegan Paul).

Middlemas, K. (1979) *The Politics of Industrial Society* (London: Deutsch).

Middleton, L. (1981) 'So Much for So Few: A View of Sheltered Housing', Institute of Human Ageing, University of Liverpool.

Middleton, R. (1984) 'The End of the Line: Homeless and Single Homeless People', in S. Ward (ed.) *DHSS in Crisis* (London: Child Poverty Action Group).

Miliband, R. (1973) *The State in Capitalist Society* (London: Quartet).

Miliband, R. (1977) *Marxism and Politics* (Oxford: Oxford University Press).

Milner-Holland Committee (1965) *Report of the Committee on Housing in Greater London* (London: HMSO).

Ministry of Housing and Local Government (1965) *The Housing Programme 1965 to 1970* (London: HMSO).

Ministry of Housing and Local Government (1968) *Old Houses into New Homes* (London: HMSO).

Mishra, R. (1977) *Society and Social Policy* (London: Macmillan) (2nd edn 1981).

MORI (1985) *Public Opinion in Glasgow* (London: Market and Opinion Research International).

Morris Committee (1975) *Housing and Social Work: A Joint Approach* (Edinburgh: HMSO).

Mouffe, C. (1988) 'The Civics Lesson', *New Statesman and Society*, 1, pp. 28–31.

Munro, M. and Smith, S. J. (1989) 'Gender and Housing: Broadening the Debate', *Housing Studies*, 4, pp. 3–17.

Murie, A. (1983) *Housing Inequality and Deprivation* (London: Heinemann).

Murie, A. and Leather, P. (1986) 'The Decline of Public Expenditure', in P. Malpass, (ed.) *The Housing Crisis* (London: Croom Helm).

Needleman, L. (1965) *The Economics of Housing* (London: Staples Press).

Niner, P. (1989) *Housing Needs in the 1990s* (London: National Housing Forum).

O'Connor, J. (1973) *The Fiscal Crisis of the State* (New York: St Martin's Press).

Offe, C. (1982) 'Some Contradictions of the Modern Welfare State', *Critical Social Policy*, 2, 2, pp. 7–16.

Offe, C. (1984) *Contradictions of the Welfare State* (London: Hutchinson).

260   *References*

Office of Population Censuses and Surveys (1982) *General Household Survey 1980* (London: HMSO).
Office of Population Censuses and Surveys (1989) *General Household Survey 1986* (London: HMSO).
O'Higgins, M. (1985) 'Inequality, Redistribution and Recession: The British Experience 1976–82', *Journal of Social Policy,* July, pp. 279–307.
Omarshah, S. (n.d.) *Asian Women and Housing* (London: ASHA Asian Women's Research Centre).
O'Sullivan, A. (1984) 'Misconceptions in the Current Housing Subsidy Debate', *Policy and Politics,* 12.
Pahl, R. E. (1975) *Whose City?* (Harmondsworth: Penguin).
Parker, G. (1985) *With Due Care and Attention. A Review of Research on Informal Care* (London: Family Policy Studies Centre).
Patten, J. (1987) 'Housing–Room for a New View', *The Guardian,* 30 January, p. 23.
Peach, C. (1968) *West Indian Migration to Britain: A Social Geography* (London: Oxford University Press for IRR).
Phillips, D. (1986) *What Price Equality?,* Policy Report 9 (London: GLC).
Piachaud, D. (1987) 'Problems in the Definition and Measurement of Poverty', *Journal of Social Policy,* 16, 2, pp. 147–64.
Plant, R. (1984) *Equality, Markets and the State* (London: Fabian Society).
Power, A. (1984) *Local Housing Management* (London: Department of the Environment).
Power, A. (1987) *Property Before People* (London: Allen and Unwin).
Purkis, A. and Hodson, P. (1982) *Housing and Community Care* (London: Bedford Square Press/NCVO).
Randall, G. *et al.* (1982) *A Place For The Family* (London: SHAC).
Raynsford, N. (1986) 'The 1977 Housing (Homeless Persons) Act', in N. Deakin (ed.) *Policy Change in Government* (London: Royal Institution of Public Administration), pp. 37–62.
Richards, J. (1981) The Making of the Housing (Homeless Persons) Act 1977 (Bristol: University of Bristol School for Advanced Urban Studies).
Ridley, N. (1987) *Conservative Proposals for Housing* (London: Conservative Central Office).
Robinson, R. (1979) *Housing Economics and Public Policy* (London: Macmillan).
Robinson, R. (1986) 'Restructuring the Welfare State: An Analysis of Public Expenditure, 1979/80–1984/85', *Journal of Social Policy,* 15, 1, pp. 1–21.
Ryder, R. (1984) 'Council House Building in County Durham, 1900–1939', in M. J. Daunton (ed.) *Councillors and Tenants: Local Authority Housing in English Cities 1919–39* (Leicester University Press) pp. 39–100.
Sargeant, T. (1979) 'Joint Care Planning in the Health and Personal Social Services', in T. Booth (ed.) *Planning For Welfare* (Oxford: Blackwell and Robertson).
Saunders, P. (1984) 'Beyond Housing Classes: The Sociological Significance of Private Property Rights in Means of Consumption', *International Journal of Urban and Regional Research,* 8, pp. 202–7.
Saunders, P. (1986a) 'Reflections on the Dual Politics Thesis: The Argu-

ment, Its Origins and Its Critics', in M. Goldsmith and S. Villadsen (eds) *Urban Political Theory and the Management of Fiscal Stress* (Aldershot: Gower).

Saunders, P. (1986b) *Social Theory and the Urban Question* (London: Hutchinson) (2nd edn).

Schafer, R. and Ladd, H. (1981) *Discrimination in Mortgage Lending* (Cambridge, Mass.: MIT Press).

Schmitter, P. C. (1974) 'Still the Century of Corporatism?', *Review of Politics*, 36, pp. 85–131.

Seebohm Committee (1968) *Report of the Committee on Local Authority and Allied Personal Social Services* (London: HMSO).

Sharpe, J. (1984) 'Functional allocation in the welfare state', *Local Government Studies*, 10, pp. 27–45.

SHIL Health Sub-Group (1987) *Primary Health Care for Homeless Single People in London* (London: Single Homeless in London).

Sim, D. (1984) 'Urban Deprivation: Not Just the Inner City', *Area*, 16, pp. 299–306.

Smith, D. (1976) *The Facts of Racial Disadvantage* (London: PEP).

Smith, S. J. (1987) 'Residential Segregation: A Geography of English racism?', in P. Jackson (ed.) *Race and Racism*, (London: Allen and Unwin) pp. 25–49.

Smith, S. J. (1988) 'Political Interpretations of Racial Segregation in Britain', *Environment and Planning D: Society and Space*, 6, pp. 426–44.

Smith, S. J. (1989a) *The Politics of 'Race' and Residence* (Cambridge: Polity Press).

Smith, S. J. (1989b) 'Social Relations, Neighbourhood Structure and Fear of Crime in Britain', in D. Evans and D. T. Herbert (eds) *The Geography of Crime* (London: Routledge and Kegan Paul).

Smith, S. J. (1989c) 'Confronting the Challenge of Urban Crime', in D. Herbert and D. M. Smith (eds) *Social Problems in Cities* (Oxford: Oxford University Press) (2nd edn) pp. 193–227.

Smith, S. J. (1990) 'Income, Housing Wealth and Gender Inequality', *Urban Studies* (In press).

Smith, S. J. and Mercer, J. (eds) (1987) *New Perspectives on Race and Housing in Britain* (Glasgow: Centre for Housing Research).

SSAC (1987) *Fifth Report of the Social Security Advisory Committee* (London: HMSO).

Stafford, B., Ford, J. and Doling, J. (eds) (1988) *The Property Owning Democracy* (Aldershot: Gower).

Supplementary Benefits Commission (1978) *Annual Report 1977* (London: HMSO).

Swenarton, M. (1981) *Homes Fit For Heroes* (London: Heinemann).

Tarn, J. N. (1973) *Five Per Cent Philanthropy* (Cambridge: Cambridge University Press).

Taylor-Gooby, P. (1985) *Public Opinion, Ideology and State Welfare* (London: Routledge and Kegan Paul).

Taylor-Gooby, P. and Dale, J. (1981) *Social Theory and Social Welfare* (London: Edward Arnold).

262 *References*

Thomas, A. D. (1986) *Housing and Urban Renewal* (London: Allen and Unwin).

Tinker, A. (1984) *Staying at Home: Helping Elderly People* (London: HMSO).

Titmuss, R. M. (1955) 'The Social Division of Welfare', the 6th Eleanor Rathbone Memorial Lecture, reprinted in Abel-Smith, B. and Titmuss, K. (eds) (1987) *The Philosophy of Welfare* (London: Allen and Unwin), pp. 39–59.

Titmuss, R. M. (1968) *Commitment to Welfare* (London: Allen and Unwin).

Titmuss, R. M. (1974) *Social Policy: An Introduction* (London: Allen and Unwin).

Townsend, P. (1962) *The Last Refuge* (London: Routledge and Kegan Paul).

Townsend, P. (1984) *Why are the Many Poor?*, Fabian Trust 500 (London: Fabian Society).

Townsend, P. (1987a) 'Conceptualising Poverty', in Z. Ferge and S. Miller (eds) *Dynamics of Deprivation* (Aldershot: Gower), pp. 31–44.

Townsend, P. (1987b) 'Deprivation', *Journal of Social Policy*, 16, 2, pp. 125–46.

Tunley, P., Travers, T. and Pratt, J. (1979) *Depriving the Deprived* (London: Kogan Page).

Turner, B. S. (1986) *Citizenship and Capitalism* (London: Allen and Unwin).

Twine, F. and Williams, N. J. (1983) 'Social Segregation and Public Sector Housing: A Case Study', *Transactions of the Institute of British Geographers*, new series, 8, 3, pp. 253–66.

Tyne, A. (1978) *Looking At Life–in Hospitals, Hostels, Homes and 'Units' for Adults who are Mentally Handicapped*, Enquiry Paper No. 7 (London: Campaign for the Mentally Handicapped).

Tyne, A. (1982) 'Community Care and Mentally Handicapped People', in A. Walker (ed.) *Community Care* (Oxford: Basil Blackwell and Martin Robertson).

Underwood, J. and Carver, R. (1979) 'Sheltered Housing: How Have Things Gone Wrong–What's Coming Next?', *Housing*, 15, nos. 3, 4, 6 (March, April, June).

Veit-Wilson, J. (1986) 'Paradigms of Poverty: A Reply to Peter Townsend and Hugh McLachlan', *Journal of Social Policy*, 15, 4, pp. 503–8.

Venn, S. (1985) *Singled Out* (London: CHAR).

Victor, C. R. (1987) *Old Age in Modern Society* (London: Croom Helm).

Wagner, G. (1988) *Residential Care. A Positive Choice* (London: National Institute for Social Work/HMSO).

Waldegrave, W. (1987) 'Some Reflections on Housing Policy' (London: Conservative Party News Service).

Walker, A. (ed.) (1982a) *Public Expenditure and Social Policy: An Examination of Social Spending and Social Priorities* (London: Heinemann).

Walker, A. (ed.) (1982b) *Community Care* (Oxford: Basil Blackwell and Martin Robertson).

Walker, A. (1984) 'The Political Economy of Privatisation', in J. Le Grand, and R. Robinson (eds) *Privatisation and the Welfare State* (London: Allen and Unwin), pp. 19–44.

References 263

Walker, B. (1987) 'Public Sector Costs of Board and Lodging Accommodation for Homeless Households in London', *Housing Studies*, 2, pp. 261–77.

Walker, R. (1985) *Housing Benefit: The Experience of Implementation* (London: Housing Centre Trust).

Walker, R. (1986) 'Aspects of Administration', in P. Kemp (ed.) *The Future of Housing Benefits*, Studies in Housing 1 (Glasgow: Centre for Housing Research).

Watchman, P. and Robson, P. (1983) *Homelessness and the Law* (Glasgow: The Planning Exchange).

Watson, S. (1986a) 'Women and Housing or Feminist Housing Analysis', *Housing Studies*, pp. 1–10.

Watson, S. (1986b) 'Housing and the Family–the Marginalisation of Non-family Households in Britain', *International Journal of Urban and Regional Research*, 10, pp. 8–28.

Watson, S. (1987) 'Ideas of the Family in the Development of Housing Form', in M. Loney (ed.) *The State or the Market* (London: Sage), pp. 130–40.

Watson, S. and Helliwell, C. (1985) 'Home Ownership–Are Women Excluded?', *Australian Quarterly*, 57, pp. 21–31.

Watson, S. with Austerberry, H. (1986) *Housing and Homelessness: A Feminist Perspective* (London: Routledge and Kegan Paul).

Weale, A. (1983) *Political Theory and Social Policy* (London: Macmillan).

Welsh Office (1983) *All Wales Strategy for the Development of Services for Mentally Handicapped People* (Cardiff: Welsh Office).

Wheeler, R. (1985) *Don't Move: We're Got You Covered* (London: Institute of Housing).

Whitehead, C. M. E. (1984) 'Privatisation and Housing', in J. Le Grand and R. Robinson (eds) *Privatisation and the Welfare State* (London: Allen and Unwin), pp. 116–32.

Widdowson, B. (1987) 'Homelessness in the International Year of Shelter for the Homeless', in M. Brenton and C. Ungerson (eds) *The Year Book of Social Policy 1986–7* (London: Longman).

Wilensky, H. and Lebeaux, C. (1965) *Industrial Society and Social Welfare* (New York: Free Press).

Wilkin, D. (1979) *Caring for the Mentally Handicapped Child* (London: Croom Helm).

Williams, F. (1987) 'Racism and the Discipline of Social Policy: A Critique of Welfare Theory', *Critical Social Policy*, 1, pp. 4–29.

Williams, N. J., Sewel, J. and Twine, F. (1986) 'Council House Allocation and Tenant Incomes', *Area*, 18, 2, pp. 131–40.

Williams, P. (1976) 'The Role of Institutions in the Inner London Housing Market', *Transactions of the Institute of British Geographers*, vol. 1.

Willmott, P. (1986) *Social Networks, Informal Care and Public Policy*, Research Report 655 (London: Policy Studies Institute).

Wirz, H. (1981) *Sheltered Housing in Scotland–A Report* (Edinburgh: Department of Social Administration, University of Edinburgh).

Witherspoon, S. (1986) *A Woman's Place* (London: SHAC).

Wohl, A. (1977) *The Eternal Slum: Housing and Social Policy in Victorian London* (London: Edward Arnold).

Working Group on Joint Planning (1985) *Progress in Partnership* (London: DHSS).

Yelling, J. A. (1986) *Slums and Slum Clearance in Victorian London* (London: Allen and Unwin).

Young, M. and Willmott, P. (1957) *Family and Kinship in East London* (London: Routledge and Kegan Paul).

Index

274   *Index*